6.25

Prairie Perspectives 2

Selected Papers of the Western Canadian
Studies Conferences, 1970, 1971

Prepared by the Department of History
University of Calgary
Calgary, Alberta

Edited with an Introduction by
A. W. Rasporich
H. C. Klassen

Holt, Rinehart and Winston of Canada
Limited

Toronto   Montreal

Distributed in the United States of America by Winston Press,
Minneapolis

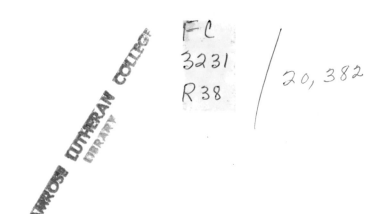

Acknowledgements

The editors would like to extend their thanks to a number of people who have made this volume possible. We are especially indebted to our departmental chairmen, J. B. Toews and J. B. Owen, for the sustained interest they have shown in the Conferences as well as in the publication of the papers. The department has been most fortunate in having the assistance of Mrs. L. von Wolzogen both for organizing the conferences and for supervising the preparation of the manuscripts. A particular debt is owing to Mrs. Beverley Murphy and Mrs. Mae Ko for their prompt and efficient typing of the papers. And finally, we are grateful to the editorial staff of Holt, Rinehart and Winston for their generous help and enthusiastic support of this project.

The volume would not exist of course were it not for the individual contributors who have been most co-operative in submitting their well-prepared manuscripts to us, and most patient in awaiting the final result.

Contents

Contributors

W. L. Morton:
Department of History, Trent University, Peterborough, Ontario

J. M. S. Careless:
Department of History, University of Toronto, Toronto, Ontario

Paul Phillips:
Department of Economics, University of Manitoba, Winnipeg, Manitoba

J. G. Nelson:
Department of Geography, University of Western Ontario, London, Ontario

G. S. Dunbar:
Department of Geography, University of California, Los Angeles, U.S.A.

John Warkentin:
Department of Geography, York University, Toronto, Ontario

Grant MacEwan:
Lieutenant Governor of Alberta

Bruce Proudfoot:
Department of Geography, The University of Alberta, Calgary, Alberta

James Seldon:
Department of Economics, University of Manitoba, Winnipeg, Manitoba

Hugh A. Dempsey:
Director, Glenbow-Alberta Library and Archives, Calgary, Alberta

Lewis H. Thomas:
Department of History, The University of Alberta, Calgary, Alberta

Eli Mandel:
Department of English, York University, Toronto, Ontario

Introduction

Until recently, Western Canada's cultural heritage has been the dearly bought harvest of a few determined scholars and writers. A handful of them have ploughed furrows across the prairie West, sometimes singly as with G. F. G. Stanley, Edward McCourt, and Grant MacEwan and sometimes in matched teams with identical surnames, like the Mortons, the Thomases and the Grays. Without their persistent efforts against a highly resistant and unliterary landscape, as W. L. Morton has put it elsewhere, the intellectual traditions of western Canada would still be as dark as Sinclair Ross's bleak tale of the thirties - "The Lamp at Noon." Sometimes the direct victims of the "dirty thirties" or its lesser victims in the poorer universities of the West, these men established a sense of the West where there was little or none. And by the nineteen fifties they had succeeded in producing a durable strain of western culture as tough as its northern wheat, calculated to grow and mature in a few short summer months, with a minimum of watering from granting agencies.

By comparison to their efforts, the founding conference of Western Canadian Studies in February of 1969 was the apparent child of luxury. Generously underwritten by the University of Calgary, it was seasonally adjusted by its founder, David Gagan, to take advantage of the spring mid-term break and the providential chinooks of late February. Perhaps it lacked only the perfect locale of its spiritual forbear, the Centennial Conference on the History of the Canadian West, held at Banff in the summer of 1967. But the Western Canadian Studies Conference differed from that first in another more fundamental aspect. It operated on the premise that scholars would be prepared to give and to listen to papers of a cross-disciplinary character from both academics and well-known authors of Western Canada. The papers delivered at this first conference were subsequently published in 1970, opening the way and setting high standards for subsequent investigations of western culture and society. Whatever their special interests, those who attended the first conference were generally enthusiastic in their response to this inter-disciplinary conference and the first volume of *Prairie Perspectives*.

This common interest in western studies led to the decision to perpetuate the conference as a regular medium of debate and discussion. And fortunately, through the interest displayed by the Department of History at the University of Calgary and by the Canada Council, the conference found sustaining support in 1970 and 1971. Again it appeared that the high standard of papers given warranted a further publication of the conference papers. While some of the papers have appeared elsewhere, the great majority of the collected essays from the 1970 and 1971 conferences are collected together for the first time in this volume. It is difficult, given the diverse interests of the authors, to link their addresses thematically, but there are common clusters of subject matter and approach which appear to fall naturally together. A principal theme linking the first three papers is that of region and nation, and some of the special constitutional, economic and social interrelationships between the two. Following these, the Prairie landscape emerges in geographical relief. The tangible changes in the physical landscape are matched in this section by the intangible perceptions of the prairies and how these have influenced Western development. The next group of papers is then devoted to economic themes in western development - from wheat to settlement and migration patterns of population. The last section, somewhat arbitrarily perhaps, links three themes in western literature - British travellers' accounts of the West, the writing of local history, and a breathtaking excursus of modern fiction in Western Canada.

In the opening paper W. L. Morton looks back over a century of change in the Canadian West, and reveals how deeply pragmatic the national authorities have been until recently in their attempts to fashion western society. The establishment of French- and English-Canadian institutions in the Manitoba and the Northwest of the 1870's, he demonstrates, represented the federal government's acceptance of the demographic realities of the West, not its recognition of the principle of duality. Ottawa's multi-cultural immigration and settlement policy for the West before 1890 - a policy also based upon practical considerations - made possible a basic alteration in the complexion of the population which forced dualism to yield to pluralism. Having thrown off the traditional duality of an Anglo-French Canada, the pluralistic society of the twentieth-century West embraced a new and broader conception of Canadian nationality, and was naturally disturbed by the federal government's unprecedented action of extending dualism in principle across the nation through the Official Languages Act of 1969. Morton, however, favours this latest form of duality because he is hopeful that it will give, without threatening the natural pluralism of the western community, the same advantage to the French outside Quebec as the English have in that province.

A sense of what Winnipeg, Edmonton, Calgary and Vancouver were like in the period before the First World War is captured in the paper by J. M. S. Careless. These four cities, all owing their rise to railway technology, and holding a substantial portion of the western population, swiftly became great centres of economic and social power, and left their own profound mark upon the development of the West. Yet, for the western urban dwellers the big railways themselves, symbolizing not only local prosperity but also eastern business domination, were as much objects of hostility as they were sources of happiness. Scarcely touched by frontier democracy, the western city governments, like their eastern counterparts, were soon controlled by elite in-groups. Whatever distinctiveness the lifestyle of the western cities possessed by 1914 came to some degree from civic pride in their individual achievements and identification with their particular surroundings. At the same time, the urban West in such aspects as its central business sections and its socially stratified residential districts bore a close resemblance to the urban East.

The connection between the national policy and the character of western Canadian labour is explored in P. A. Phillips' paper. He argues that the structure given to the western economy by regional resources and especially by the national policy contributed to the emergence of a labour movement which developed its own distinctive features. The economic instability created by the unprotected primary industries of the West certainly hurt the western workers, and their distress, besides widening the gulf between them and the conservative eastern workers who were better off as a result of the security which they derived from the sheltered eastern Canadian manufacturing enterprises, led to the rise of a militant western labour class which preferred radical industrial unionism to the orthodox craft unions of the East as a means of organization.

The paper by J. G. Nelson appraises the ways in which such agents as the bison, beaver, Prairie dogs, locust, and fire helped to alter the landscape of the northwestern plains of North America in the years before extensive settlement by Europeans. Among the many agents that shaped this landscape, the bison occupied a prominent place. Until the 1850's the contribution by the heavy grazing of this animal to the development of a short-grass region in the southern Canadian Prairies was spectacular. In some measure, the appearance of longer and more luxurious grasses by the 1870's arose from the lighter grazing of the rapidly dwindling herds. Man's changing conception of the West, it is further suggested, owed something to the waning impact of the bison upon Prairie vegetation. Hence, an examination of the bison landscape partly explains why John Palliser in the fifties regarded much of the southern region as a desert and why John Macoun a generation later saw in the same area the makings of a great wheat country.

Lorin Blodget, an American climatologist, entered the debate over the agricultural potentialities of the Prairie lands in the late 1850's when he published his work on the climatology of North America. His role in revising the image of the Northwest and in fostering western settlement is assessed in G. S. Dunbar's paper. Challenging the idea that adverse climatic conditions often lay at the root of the difficulties of the Red River farmers, Blodget produced isothermal maps which showed that the Red River and Saskatchewan region had strikingly warm summer temperatures. The whole area, he argued, had enough warmth and rainfall to support the cultivation of wheat and other cereals. Blodget's bold assertion heightened the enthusiasm of Canadian newspaper editors and politicians for western colonization, and they were quick to popularize his favourable interpretation of the weather scene in the West.

The dominant images of the western interior of Canada in the eighteenth and nineteenth centuries, as John Warkentin's paper makes clear, had an enormous bearing upon economic activity and empire-building on the Prairies. For the fur traders the barren grounds of the southern Prairies were not a desert wasteland but a rich source of buffalo meat, and their conception of the West as a fur empire, with its command of abundant provisions, prevailed well into the nineteenth century. The publication of the impressive Palliser map in the 1860's at once reinforced and undermined the British and Canadian dream of an agricultural empire in the West by giving both good and bad land images to the western interior: the northern and southern regions were respectively called the Fertile Belt and the Great American Desert. Although the optimism of John Macoun, the coming of the railway and the spread of settlement in the southern Prairies did much to modify the desert image, it could never be completely snuffed out and became a part of the complex resource picture that grew out of the accumulation of more precise knowledge of the quality of the interior lands.

Stressing the continuing importance of western wheat in the Canadian economy, Grant MacEwan's paper describes the pains and pleasures of growing wheat on the Prairies from the days of the Selkirk settlers to the present. Damage to their fields of grain by frosts, grasshoppers, rust, and drought, worries because of depressed prices and uncertain markets, and delight with the golden stands of wheat and the saleable bumper crops - all these experiences became entwined in the collective history of the Prairie farmers.

The paper by Bruce Proudfoot is a discussion of the changing picture of settlement in the agricultural region of northern Alberta during the last sixty-five years. These years witnessed many fascinating changes. Social and economic integration occurred among the various ethnic groups with the imposition of a uniform lifestyle upon the settlers by the bush environment, the township system, the English-language schools, the advance of roads and railways, and the common farming activities. Log cabins soon gave way to prairie farm homes, and today many farmers enjoy the comforts of modern dwelling houses. Finally, the demographic pattern of both the rural areas and urban centres was altered particularly by mechanization and the gradual retreat of the quarter-section family farm in favour of larger farms.

In his paper James Seldon analyzes the problem of migration and the Canadian West after World War II. He develops a model to examine Canadian population movements, at the interprovincial and international levels, and looks at ways in which the western provinces have benefitted or suffered from the inflows and outflows of people. By their substantial contributions to the increasing populations and consequently to the development and wealth of Alberta and British Columbia, the provinces of Manitoba and Saskatchewan have become poorer, and, as Seldon suggests, will probably continue to do so unless they themselves provide job opportunities that will effectively check the migrations outwards.

Professional historians engaged in research on the Canadian West, Hugh A. Dempsey suggests in his paper, should stop ignoring local histories by amateurs and begin utilizing the valuable information found in them. Without denying the fundamental shortcomings - factual errors, tedious repetition and indiscriminate use of materials - of these works, he argues that they frequently contain data on immigration, settlement problems, the growth of social institutions and, most important, they include reminiscences, letters and diaries of the first and second generation pioneers of the western farm communities. The timely appearance of numerous local histories during the past decade has therefore considerably increased the sources available to the student of the West.

Illuminating descriptions of the Canadian West in the three decades before 1914, as the paper by L. H. Thomas shows, flowed from the pens of middle class British travellers. They wrote about the monotony and beauty of the Prairies, as well as the grandeur of the Rockies. They commented upon the belief each of the large cities had in its own superiority, the English character of Victoria and Calgary and the lack-lustre appearance of the small towns. Their travel accounts revealed the habits and practices of homesteaders, wheat and mixed farmers, ranchers, fruit growers, and market gardeners. In the eyes of the British visitors western Canadian society was generally confident and industrious, wasteful in using its natural resources, materialistic in outlook, tolerant in religion and relatively free from class-prejudice in the rural communities.

In the closing paper, Eli Mandel ranges freely and widely in his examination of western Canadian fiction. The basic unity of the fiction of western Canada, he argues, lies in its own forms rather than in its relationship to the historical and social landscape of the West. While some western fiction can be read as social realism, the works of many contemporary writers belong to a world of romance that is not primarily concerned with mirroring the actualities of the western social experience. What we have in novels like Sheila Watson's *The Double Hook* and Robert Kroetsch's *The Studhorse Man* are attempts to define our identity in terms of a developing literary tradition which can be traced back far beyond the chronological and geographical limits of the settled West. In *The Double Hook*, for example, Mrs. Watson employs such conventional forms of the western Canadian imagination as the regional novel, the ethnic story, and the western tale, and through parody knits them together with the patterns of a much wider literary world that includes Shakespeare and the Bible. From a consideration of these and other writings, Mandel concludes that the fictional Canadian West, though relatively uninformative about social and political life, has an identity derived from and enriched by the forms and visions of writers not only of Canada but also of the cosmopolitan culture of America and Europe.

Here, then, are twelve papers about the Canadian West by writers who have themselves lived in this section of the country for longer or shorter periods. As the reader reflects upon their writings, he should feel some interesting aspects of the West coming alive in his consciousness. In W. L. Morton's analysis, one can see the West, fully aware of its pluralistic character since the turn of the century, once again agonizing about the ancient problem of cultural dualism. To J. M. S. Careless the urban West in its formative years appears as a proud and ambitious society, a society whose government provided little scope for democracy and whose riches were concentrated in the hands of an economic elite. The national policy, P. A. Phillips points out, was a definite factor in the radicalization of the western working classes. J. G. Nelson, G. S. Dunbar, and John Warkentin draw our attention to the ways in which a variety of images of the West - short-grass country, warm summers, barren lands, desert, garden - have affected people's conceptions of the Prairies. From the papers by Grant MacEwan and Bruce Proudfoot we learn something about the significance of the wheat economy on the Prairies and agricultural activity in northern Alberta. James Seldon's discussion reveals how the development of the four western provinces after the Second World War has been influenced by out- and in-migrations. That local histories and travel accounts are useful source materials for western studies is amply demonstrated by Hugh A. Dempsey and Lewis H. Thomas. Lastly, in Eli Mandel's analysis, we see a complex and mature fictional West that is rooted in Canadian, American, and European literary traditions.

What then is the true Canadian West? Does it merely exist in the eyes of the beholder? Or is it the objective reality of staple production - a land of tractors, barbed wire, and grain elevators? The answer that emerges from these papers is clearly both. In a sense the dichotomy is as old as civilization itself, of idealism versus realism, of the world of form versus function, of the spiritual versus the material world. The West of the historian and the writer is essentially a progressive extension of civilized forms - of metropolitan culture, laws, art, myth, the city, the traveller - all in tension with western reality of space, environment, primitiveness, and materialism. The West of the geographer and of the economist represents in varying degrees of scientific exactness the environment and human experience as it was, is, and will be. In this view civilization is occasionally a villain, altering Prairie ecology or distorting the true environment to the purposes of economic exploitation. Particularly in the view of the western economist, metropolitan forces of technology whether from the east or south perpetually condemn a regional economy to resource exploitation and to a steady drain of population and capital to central Canada. This is not to say however that the proponents of civilization and metropolitanism are any less sympathetic to western environment and aspirations, or that the geographers and economists do not see the value of metropolitan development and western culture. They merely see western development differently, and this collection of essays is a testimony to their mutual agreement to differ in their perceptions.

A. W. Rasporich
H. C. Klassen
May 2, 1972

The West and the Nation, 1870-1970

W. L. Morton

I

What happened in the Northwest in 1870 was a consequence of what
had happened in Confederation. To see the former in full perspective, it
is necessary so to see the latter.

Confederation was threefold: first, a general union; second, the
separation of the Canadas; third, the expansion of the new union, to include the unorganized territories of the Northwest and the colony of
British Columbia.

The main factors in Confederation which led to that multiple act of
union, separation and expansion were also threefold. The first was a
new statement of the relations of French and English in Canada, more
precisely, in the province of Quebec. Second was the imperative need to
set going and keep in balance a reciprocating process of expansion east
as well as west, west as well as east. Third was the haste to assert the
independence of Canada in North America, in face of a United States re-
united and the sole major power in the continent.

The last two made urgent as well as necessary the acquisition of the
Northwest. Without it Ontario would resent the building of the Intercolonial Railway without which there would have been no union with
the Maritimes, and would have been baulked of the Northwest as its
special interest in return for the Intercolonial.[1] Without the Northwest
therefore the new union would have dissolved, probably to be absorbed
into the United States following the withdrawal of British troops from
the St. Lawrence in 1871.[2]

To acquire the Northwest, however, would be to take over a vast
territory with no organized government except in Red River. It would
also be to impose a frontier of land settlement on an Indian and fur
trade wilderness. The latter old Canada had really never had.[3] In short,
the Northwest was an unclaimed empire, and Canada had little in the
way of traditions or institutions of government for the administration
of an unorganized and largely unpeopled territory. The tasks it would
face would be the old imperial ones, first of how to administer a territory without law or police, and second of how to provide traditional
Canadian government as population warranted. Because Canada had no
imperial experience to guide it, it was to solve the problems of empire

as they arose pragmatically and without explicit guiding principles; certainly none drawn from Confederation itself.

In light of the current discussion of the original character of Confederation and of the significance for Canadian history of the political settlement of the Northwest in 1870, it is of first importance to remark to what a degree both Confederation and the organization of the Northwest were improvised, and decided pragmatically, by political expedience rather than accepted principle.[4]

In slight elaboration of that observation, it is worthwhile to note how Confederation itself was contrived. In spite of the efforts of those who wished a legislative union, Lord Monck and John A. Macdonald in particular, it is clear that the cornerstone of the settlement was provincial self-government, especially in Quebec.[5] What is even more pertinent for this discussion was the fact that in the province of Quebec the actual duality of the people of that province, French and English, was given constitutional recognition in the B.N.A. Act itself.[6]

This institutionalized duality of people and language in the province of Quebec, and in the federal Parliament and Courts, is of course the full and only recognition of duality in Confederation. The claim that Confederation was in any way a treaty or compact, political or cultural, is the purest mythology without a shred of historical evidence to support it. It is simply of first importance to emphasize that the definition of English and French relations was a pragmatic recognition and constitutional embodiment of what the facts, French and English, were in the province of Quebec in 1867. It was nothing more. That a similar duality might exist in the other provinces, or in the Northwest, was not mentioned, much less discussed, or recognized, in 1864-67.[7]

In other words, local self-government was used in 1867 to express the recognized duality of Quebec. To do so was in fact to apply the basic tradition of Canadian government, that it be responsible to actual local circumstances. In the Northwest, however, such a tradition could not be applied except perhaps in Red River. The rest of the expanse of the Territories, until peopled, called for territorial, or Crown colony, government. If self-government were to be applied in Red River, it might have to be organized, as in Quebec, in terms of the actual composition of that settlement, roughly half French, half English, if largely also of mixed blood.

II

The recognition of duality, moreover, was not present alone in the province of Quebec; it also characterized the mission sent to complete the negotiation for the transfer of the Northwest to Canada. The two inevitable delegates were William McDougall of Ontario, a long-time advocate of expansion, and George-Etienne Cartier, now expansionist but also the most effective defender of Quebec's interests in his day. A third and English delegate was sought but not found.[8] The interest of Quebec in the Northwest and its effect on the equilibrium of Confederation was clearly recognized.

The wisdom of acknowledging French interest in the Northwest is perhaps well illustrated by the error, which had been avoided in the exploring expeditions of 1857 and 1858, of not having any French Canadians in two parties sent to Red River in 1868 and 1869. The first was the party of axemen sent under John Snow to work on the Dawson route from St. Boniface to the Lake of the Woods. It was meant to put some money in circulation and give some work in Red River, severely tried by famine in the winter of 1868. The party attracted few of the *métis*, however; it bought its supplies largely from the leader of the Canadian party, John Schultz. One of its members was Thomas Scott, who became known as a hot-tempered man, particularly when he was fined in the Quarterly Court of Assiniboia for assaulting Snow.[9] The chief result of its work in the colony was to create the impression that it was English Ontario alone that would take over the Northwest.

The presence and work in 1869 of a wholly English survey party confirmed that impression, although the party behaved well, and with the utmost discretion.[10] The transfer, it seemed in Red River and especially to the *métis* and their priests, was being prepared for the exclusive benefit of English Canada.

The impression was no doubt mistaken; there is little reason to think that the Canadian government had any purpose except to prepare for an orderly transfer. All the people of Red River could learn, however, was what they observed from the character and behaviour of the two Canadian parties. They were too sensitive, it may be, about the rough language of the axemen and the militia uniforms some surveyors had brought with them. But the tactics of the "Canadian party" led by Schultz, and the staking of land claims by Canadians, gave grounds for suspicion. There was then some reason for their fear that they, their lands and their institutions would be overrun by land-seekers from Ontario before they had legal protection.

The essential issue was becoming clear; would the new regime established by Canada allow them to preserve their position as it had been in Red River, or would it provide for a transfer of power to a majority of English and Protestant incomers? The latter seemed all too likely and the first provision of the Canadian government for the government of the Northwest would probably have had that result. The Act for the Temporary Government of Rupert's Land, passed in the session of 1869, for one year, authorized the appointment of a Lieutenant-Governor and an appointed council, some members of which were to be residents of the Territories, to govern and advise Ottawa on a future form of government. In itself this was well calculated to meet the circumstances. But it is significant that it was just what Schultz wanted.[11] It would hold the gate open for an English majority, and it might afford opportunity for quick and easy occupation of Northwest lands. An immigrant majority from Ontario would probably confirm what they had done.

III

The basic question in 1869 was, it is evident, who would control the immediate future of the new Canadian territory when the transfer took place? Would the future be settled by the votes of new-comers, or would the rights of old settlers be protected? The Canadian government on the spot would have little effective means to enforce the law: no troops, few police, principally only a governor and his small suite. That the Temporary Act provided that existing officers should continue in office meant little; they had had little authority for a decade and the chief of these, Judge John Black, in fact left in the spring of 1870 for Ottawa and England. The provision made in the Act would be quite insufficient to keep order. Red River had seen repeated acts of lawlessness since the withdrawal of the last troops in 1861, often involving members of the Canadian party. It was certain the transfer would increase the daring of the rougher elements among the Canadian party and the Canadian incomers.

As if to confirm the impression that the transfer was for English Canada, the new governor was Hon. William McDougall, representative of English Canadian expansion, and unfavourably known to the French missionaries for his part in the negotiation of the Manitoulin Island Treaty of 1862.[12]

For these reasons, it was urgent to ensure that the government of Red River on the immediate morrow of the transfer should guarantee that the lands and rights of the old settlers would be safeguarded. The best assurance of this would be a government in which they were represented according to their numbers before the immigration set in, and in which the circumstances of 1870 were enshrined in constitutional law. That was Louis Riel's purpose, no more, no less, when he began the Red River Resistance by stopping the survey party on October 11, 1869. It was resistance, not to the transfer, but to an English Canadian takeover. To put it dramatically, Riel set out to thwart Schultz, and he did so.[13]

In doing so Riel had the staunch support of nearly all *métis*, and gained the reserved co-operation of the majority of English half-breeds. He was able to discredit, expel, or confine the members of the Canadian party, except their supporters at Portage la Prairie. The Americans in Red River supported him with embarrassing enthusiasm. Except for the Canadians, Riel was able to obtain to an impressive degree the support, if often doubtful and reluctant in the English parishes, of the whole of Red River for a policy of obtaining from Canada local self-government of the Northwest as it was.

These terms were expressed in no less than four Bills of Rights, two considered, the second approved by public meetings representative of the whole Settlement, two revised and added to by the Executive Council of the Provisional Government. All claimed for Red River everything any frontier community might be expected to ask, from self-government to a railway.[14] They also sought protection for local rights peculiar to Red River. The chief of these, which appeared in all four, was the official equality of the French and English languages. That equality had been the working rule in Red River since 1854.[15] The principal change in the third was the addition of the demand, refused in the preparation of the second by representatives of all Red River, for provincial status for the Northwest, with a provincial senate to safeguard minorities. Riel added that provision in defiance of that body. The chief modification in the fourth was the addition, perhaps made at the suggestion of Bishop Taché,[16] that a denominational school system be granted. The Settlement had had denominational schools for almost half a century. These did not make up a public system, but they had received some grants from the Council of Assiniboia. Thus the actual duality of Red River, slowly elaborated in discussion prolonged over four months, was embodied in the terms prepared for negotiation with Canada.

The preparation of the Bills must, however, be criticized adversely, except that of the second. The first Bill was debated, on the whole approved but not ratified by a public meeting of delegates of the Red River parishes. The second was drawn up in a session of delegates of the parishes elected at the call of a mass meeting arranged by Donald A. Smith, representative of the Canadian government. That session was the free and authentic voice of the Red River Settlement, and the second Bill, which Macdonald and Cartier sought to make the basis of negotiation, must be taken to include the terms on which all elements of the settlement could agree. The addition of provincial status and a denominational school system by Riel's Council, not publicly known until 1889-1890, was beyond question in the case of the former a defiance of the popular will of Red River, and of the latter a matter which had never been discussed.

Nevertheless provincehood had been rejected in the second Bill by a narrow vote, and the matter of schools was a manifest oversight. Nothing was asked for with respect to schools which did not already exist in Red River, except the sanction of constitutional law. In short, the Bills did not until the fourth version fully express the character of Red River, especially its historic duality, and provide all possible safeguards for the preservation of that duality.

The practice of duality in fact constantly asserted itself. The first two representatives of the Canadian government, Rev. J. B. Thibeault and Charles de Salaberry were French with experience of the Northwest; the third had been Donald A. Smith of the Hudson's Bay Company with friends and relatives in the Northwest. The delegates he invited to take the second Bill to Ottawa were elected by the session of the Provisional Government which drew up the Bill. One was Rev. N. J. Ritchot, one of Riel's most active clerical supporters; the second was Judge John Black; the third was Alfred Scott, an Englishman naturalized in the United States and a representative of the American party. He was not active in the negotiations and the part he played in the events, if any, remains obscure. A Canadian delegate was both unnecessary and impossible. The delegation thus reflected both the duality of the Settlement and its actual circumstances in February of 1870.

The Canadian participants in the secret negotiations held in Ottawa in April inevitably reflected the dual nature of Canadian political life. They were Macdonald and Cartier, the elected political leaders of Ontario and Quebec.

The course of the negotiation, so far as it has been traced, reveals that the fundamental issue was how to safeguard the French element in the Northwest. The active negotiators were Ritchot, Cartier and Macdonald, and Ritchot forcibly pushed the particular French objects, the official status of the French language, a system of denominational schools, a provincial constitution with a senate to safeguard minorities, the land claims of the *métis*, an amnesty for the leaders of the Resistance.[17] All but the amnesty he obtained, but for a province of Manitoba, not for the whole Northwest. The result may be viewed as either Red River in the guise of a Canadian province, or as a little Quebec except for the Civil Law. Either way it recognized Red River as it was.

The Manitoba Act of 1870 was thus a victory for the duality of Red River, but it was a defensive victory. It was a means to buttress the French element in Red River. Moreover, it was a rearguard action fought to gain time until the French element might be strengthened after the transfer by aid from Quebec, and so perhaps preserve itself in the Northwest. The Act would prevent the immediate overrunning of the *métis* by English land-seekers and the consequent establishment of a western Ontario which might not think it desirable to protect a minority language or to preserve a system of denominational schools.

The Red River Resistance was in fact caused at bottom by two things. One was the "nationalisme" of the *métis*, which was Indian as well as French. They had imposed their will in the Resistance because they were the only armed body of men accustomed to disciplined action in the Northwest. The second was the concern of the French Catholic missionaries for their charges. Neither *métis* nor most missionaries had many or close ties with Quebec.[18] Quebec, itself, was in fact not too deeply concerned with the fate of the French element in the Northwest. Not until the duality of Manitoba was institutionalized as was that of Quebec, did the fate of duality in the Northwest become of interest in the original home of duality. Nor was Ontario either greatly concerned. In so far as it had an attitude it was one of confidence that numbers - "squatter sovereignty" - would decide the political and cultural future of the Northwest. To most the Act was viewed, it would seem, as a necessary concession to the French of Red River, perhaps as a good-natured gesture to the French of Quebec. But Ontario could have no doubt whose emigrants would dominate the Northwest. The English therefore bowed to political expediency, and waited for the actual pioneers to make the final decision. That is, they did not accept duality as a principle, but waited for the actual circumstances to change. They did not accept Taché's hope that the Manitoba Act might be the Quebec Act of the Northwest.

IV

If, however, the Manitoba Act is to be seen as simply a concession made to the actual circumstances of Red River in 1870 by a reluctant and doubtful Canadian government, and not a clear adoption of the principle of duality in the Northwest, it would follow that the policy of the Government of Rupert's Land Act, discarded in Manitoba, would prevail in the remainder, almost the whole, of the North-West Territories. What in fact happened between 1870 and 1885 suggests that at least the Canadian government would not exert itself to reject duality. It was bound both by the provisions of Section 133 as to the use of French in Federal Courts and by the political necessity of not risking the loss of French votes, whether the party in power was Conservative or Liberal. Nothing explicit was done until the passage of the North-West Territories Act of 1875 by the Mackenzie administration. The Bill was amended at the last moment on the suggestion of Edward Blake to provide for separate schools in the territories, and the amendment passed.

The motives of Blake, not at the time a member of the administration, are unknown. But the government, if it had not proposed the measure, accepted it. In doing so it was mindful both of the English-French accord, worked out during the Union of the Canadians and on which Confederation rested, mindful also of the still unsettled New Brunswick School Question which was agitating Quebec. In 1877 another amendment to a Bill for the Territories, moved by Senator M. A. Girard of Manitoba, made French an official language in the Territories, and the second of the main pillars of duality was set up. There was some resistance by members of the House to the measure when the amended Bill returned to the Commons. The government again accepted a measure it had not proposed but of the origins and implications of which it was well aware. The philosophy of some of its members no doubt was that of John A. Macdonald, expressed in the debate of 1875: "At the right time they could pass an Act introducing the popular element into the North-West."[19] But as the government of a Confederation in which the constitution of a principal member, Quebec, rested on duality, it had to agree to the Girard amendment.

The two episodes have not yet been completely explored. It is therefore possible to argue that the seemingly casual and haphazard manner in which these two measures, essential to duality in the Northwest, were dealt with reveals how little weight the federal government attached to the matter. The argument has some weight. It is also possible, however, that the argument to the contrary may cut closer to the bone. The basic question was, who should decide the future institutions of the Northwest, local voters or federal parliament? Until there were local voters, clearly Parliament, with the need of support from Quebec for any administration, a Quebec commited to duality within Quebec and not wholly indifferent to the fate of the French element in the Northwest, might be forced, however reluctant some of its members, to legislate for duality in the Territories. This was clearly so, and the fact meant that the amendments designed to establish duality, once made, could not be rejected until there was opposition in the Northwest. Any exercise of squatter sovereignty had to wait on an increase of settlement.

In short, the recognition of duality in the Northwest where it actually existed was a recognition that it also existed in Quebec, a pragmatic, if not a principled recognition. Both French and English Canadians believed that there would be a French minority and an English majority in the Northwest. The English accepted a pragmatic settlement, confident that time and a local majority would really settle the question. The French used the actual position of French equality in Red River in 1870 to attempt to get a settlement in principle which would protect the eventual French minority. The same situation existed in the Territories until the end of the 1870's. Parliament, based in significant part on Quebec, had both to decide, and to decide for duality.

Did the same pragmatic acceptance of duality exist, however, in the other federal institutions created for the government of the new empire of 1870? Except in the Manitoba Act and the North-West Territories Act, and of course, any federal court, it did not. There was no legal requirement, and apparently no intention to carry duality into the federal service on principle; the services were simply open to all, provided they had a working knowledge of English. In the most fundamental of federal acts, the land survey, it is at once apparent that duality had no place and it is therefore of some importance to recall that the beginning of the land survey was one of the chief and immediate causes - indeed the symbolic cause - of the Resistance. In the Dominion Land Survey and its concomitant, the Homestead Act, the English drive to make the Northwest English Canadian was carried on without check. And nothing could have been more alien to the land survey and communal convention of the old Northwest, than, in the abstract, the square survey and the individual homestead. The river lot survey, of Red River, similar to, perhaps adopted from that of Quebec, was a basic part of the *métis'* way of life. It gave access to water, access to the plains behind, and shelter and fuel in the winter. It was a response at once to the climate and the customary life of the community. The new survey introduced the American pattern of geometric indifference to natural features or social customs. Its sole virtues were economic; it was cheap to make and reduced litigation. It was itself an economic concept; it treated land as a commodity to be cut and sold like broadcloth on a counter. It was emphatically not an expression of social community, much less the cradle of a race. The square survey was rather the sieve through which people would be shaken into mixed and diverse settlement. It was to a degree hostile to ethnic grouping, and in general a preparation for an individualistic and assimilative society.[20]

The survey did not, of course, prevent group settlement. The Mennonites of Manitoba were able to practise their village life on the square survey; the survey itself could be adapted to the needs of *métis* settlement at Batoche. It was in fact the introduction of ethnic groups such as the Mennonites and Icelanders which began the movement away from demographic and political duality to demographic plurality and political unitarianism. The survey, however, operated to dissolve slowly all but the most coherent groups, such as the Hutterites, and make the individual farm, and with the homestead an individualistic and plural society come into being. The survey, then, was uncongenial to, if not immediately prohibitive, of group settlement. It could admit of duality, as the French settlements of the Northwest were long to demonstrate, but it exposed even those to the strains of plurality.

The second institution for the government of the Northwest, the North-West Mounted Police, was of course a particular expression of federal authority. The force recruited openly and French Canadians served in it.[21] It had, however, like the Canadian Militia, English as the language of command and administration and, unlike the militia, no French-Canadian formations. The North-West Mounted Police were, as their title inferred, a special regional and not a popular or territorially based force. The modelling of the force on the Royal Irish Constabulary and the British Army, indeed made it a force designed to preserve a remote and impartial order among a mixed and essentially alien population. Like the survey, the Police neither contradicted nor affirmed the principle or practice of duality. It was simply an assertion of federal authority and in itself implied no more than the equality of all men, without distinction, before the law.

Much the same in character was the third institution created to govern the Northwest, the Department of the Interior. In it, despite its political function, the assertion of federal authority and indifference to duality seems perhaps more evident than elsewhere. No French Canadian held office either as minister or deputy-minister during the period of settlement, 1870-1914. As the ministry which directed the survey and land settlement, the North-West governor and Council, and the Mounted Police, the department was the federal government in the Northwest. Like them, but more so, it was the expression of federal purpose and authority; even more than them, it seems to have been the tool of the English Canadian purpose to settle the West and mold it in its own image. Yet it had also, because it was a department of the federal government, to accept and uphold the practice of duality in the Northwest.

V

That brief survey suggests that on balance the federal government in the Northwest neither affirmed nor denied duality, but accepted it as a practice, not as a principle. Clearly duality had no legal place in the federal service outside the courts as it is now given. Duality was practised where the existence of French population made it necessary; elsewhere it was ignored. This was in accord with the pragmatism with which duality had been recognized in the B.N.A. and Manitoba Acts. But the federal government by general policy, especially in land settlement and immigration, prepared the way from the simple pattern of duality and ethnic settlement of the old Northwest. It opened, consciously or unconsciously, the way from duality to plurality.

The determining element in the growth of the Northwest in fact and of course as everyone, Riel as well as Schultz, knew it would be, was immigration, the numbers and speed with which people settled there, and the kind of people. The events of 1869-1870 themselves had been touched off by the anticipation of immigration. How the political settlement of 1870 would develop would depend on the volume and character, French, English and other, of immigration into Manitoba. Duality did not require that the inflow of French and English be equal, but it did require at least a French effort to increase the French element. In fact the immigration during the first decade was largely English from Ontario and the British Isles. Very few French came from Quebec, nor did the French of Quebec show much interest in the Northwest, despite Bishop Taché's efforts.[22] Only the great depression of the mid-1870's gave him a considerable number of immigrants from the mills of Massachussetts.

Did duality, moreover, also assume that immigration be always French and English? It certainly assumed assimilation to one group or the other. Yet "group" settlement was held out as an inducement to much needed immigrants and implied something less than assimilation. In fact, some such groups were to reveal considerable coherence and integrity of language, religion and settlement. The group immigrants therefore also opened the way to the replacement of duality by plurality and doomed duality in fact, if not in principle.

The changes in the composition of the population between 1870 and 1890, with all their implications, were then the true cause of the ending of duality in the Northwest. The actual events which registered the ending, however, had to be in the idiom of Canadian politics, and that was the idiom of duality. Both political parties competed for the support of French-Canadian voters. Thus it was that the change from duality to plurality was recorded in 1890 by the abolition of the official use of French and of the school system of 1870 in Manitoba, although not of the latter, thanks to the federal power, in the Territories. The causes and course of the Manitoba School Question are classic ground in Canadian history, and need not be gone over here. Suffice to note that the abolition was on the surface of party politics a response to the reappearance of duality in the Saskatchewan Rebellion and the racial overtones of the agitation produced by the hanging of Riel. Manitoba, which had responded to the facts of population, was little moved by, and took little part in, the controversy which followed 1890. It had without fanfare repudiated duality and replaced it with plurality.

But what was plurality? Manitoba had of course asserted the provincial right to control education and in so doing proved to have ended the effective force of Section 22 of the Manitoba Act and Section 93 of the B.N.A. Act, 1867. In doing so it secularized the public schools and created a school system in which the schools would be the agents of social policy, a policy of assimilation. Manitoba had done what Ontario had partly failed to do, and had rejected the duality of the B.N.A. Act and of Quebec. Here was the ground work, partly followed in the Territories, for a Northwest different in popular coherence and political outlook from central Canada.

To put the matter so simply is, of course, to give it a clarity which in fact it lacked. Manitoba was actually to modify the stand of 1890 in the Laurier-Greenway Compromise of 1897. The Compromise, however, did not restore duality; the clause that teaching was to be in "French or such other language and English on the bilingual principle" - as though French had no special status in Canada - recognized the fact of plurality. Other languages than French could be used with English to teach "on the bilingual system."

In this was not only the adoption of the principle of assimilation, but also as it proved, the principle of the mosaic. In it was also the repulse of the federal power in the Northwest, used under the influence of Quebec to maintain duality. The Compromise of 1897 and the Autonomy Bills of 1905 indicated, however, more the diminution of federal power in the Northwest than it did its continuation. It was this rejection of duality that made impossible any acceptance of Henri Bourassa's concept of a Canada which should be equally French and equally English. Moreover, the support extended Laurier in the election of 1896 indicated that general opinion in Quebec had lost interest in the Northwest. Duality had withdrawn almost wholly within the boundaries of Quebec and the limits of Section 133. The process of once more identifying French Canada with Quebec, as had been done in 1867, had begun again. Now, however, it was the first step to *separatisme*.

The making of history, be it said in apology for statements so sweeping, is like the making of wine. The juice of events must ferment before it clarifies. So it was with the ending of duality in the Northwest; so it was with the beginning of plurality. Neither had been accepted on any clear ground of principle, each was a position determined by pragmatic action. If the schools had been made the agents of assimilation, what, for example, was to be the product of assimilation? English Canadians perhaps? The abolition of the Laurier-Greenway Compromise in Manitoba in 1916 certainly suggested as much. Said the Minister of Education on the legislation:

We are building for the Canada of to-morrow, and our common

school is one of the most important factors in the work. In this Dominion we are building up, under the British flag, a new nationality. We come from many lands and cast in our lot, and these various factors these must evolve a new nationality which shall be simply Canadian and British.[23]

The new nationality, that is, was to be English-speaking, but its constituent elements would be much more diverse than just French and British.

Two facts were to affect that process of nation-building. One was the assumption that the Northwest French-Canadians were immigrants to be assimilated like others. That assumption flew in the face both of history and the federal constitution, and the French of the Northwest have resented it with patient moderation ever since it formed. The second was that assimilation was to an established standard, the historic English Canada of Ontario or the Maritimes. It was not to work out that simply. For one thing, the wake of duality left behind it the feeling that Canada was not a land of assimilation. Group settlement, the Laurier-Greenway Compromise, the cultivation of the "immigrant vote," perhaps a certain moderation of temper in the old Canadians, all added to the feeling that mere assimilation to an existing standard was not the answer. Neither was the inadequate metaphor of a "mosaic" with its suggestion of unchanging elements. What is now perhaps emerging is the concept of a pride of heritage in each group of the population and the acceptance of a common future and undefined goal which will be Canadian unhyphenated, neither English nor French, Ukrainian nor Mennonite.

It was in some such way that the West, to use the current term, was committed to plurality. That commitment means that socially the West is developing its own version of Canadian nationality as it has perhaps developed its own version of Canadian political institutions - positive, populist and provisionally a-political.[24] If that is true, it follows that the west today from Ontario to the Rockies has its own peculiar character, social and political. The West is at once a federal creation and also an emancipated colony of old Canada with its own kind of government and life. It may be that it is in a very real sense the most authentic expression of federal, or Canadian, nationality.

The West, in other words, during the past century, has been Canadianized, but in a new plurality, not in the old duality of Quebec, or of French and English Canada. That is to say that in part it was Ontarioized; John Schultz has finally prevailed over Louis Riel. Yet because Ontario in its time has become one pillar of the duality of central Canada, English Ontario with French Quebec, the West has become a third element in the political nationality of Canada. The West has its own integrity; it is to a degree a-political in politics and wholly pluralistic in society.

In the light of such a development the concern, and even hostility, which the Official Languages Act of 1969 has aroused in the West is understandable. That Act is not only an assertion of the duality that the West rejected; it is also an extension in principle of duality across Canada. As such, it is a contradiction of the experience of the West since 1870.

VI

Is one to conclude, then, that the recognition of duality in 1870 was a mistake? I venture to think not, in spite of the outcome down to 1969. The conclusion one comes to depends on how one judges Riel's actions in the Resistance and the Rebellion, and the errors and actions of the Canadian government on the eve of both. If there was a mistake in 1870, it was in Riel's policy of negotiating from armed force, a force which led to the shooting of Thomas Scott. That mistake, however, might have been lived down peaceably had it not been for a counter-mistake in 1885. That was Macdonald's refusal of clemency to convicted Riel. So the double irony arose, that Riel defeated Schultz, but Schultz prevailed; Macdonald hanged Riel, but Riel by his death touched off events that destroyed Confederation as Macdonald had made it. The West began to develop its own form of nationality; Quebec began to withdraw into itself. Because duality failed in the West it has come in our own day to be threatened in Quebec where it is entrenched under the B.N.A. Act.[25]

To that threat, not to any hasty interpretation of Canadian history, the official Languages Act was a response. It too was a pragmatic reaction to an actual situation. But it is more. It is not only an attempt to meet the demands of actual circumstances; it is also an attempt to assert a principle in federal law in terms which may have a permanency that the language and schools provisions of the Manitoba and North-West Territories Act did not have. The Act will apply only where it makes sense to apply it, but in intent it opens all the doors of Canada to all Canadians, French-speaking as well as English-speaking.

After a century of pragmatism, it seems to the writer a wiser thing to season pragmatism with principle, and recognize Canada for what it is, a country of dual origins, French and English, however diverse we have become in our history and whatever the course of our future development. Clearly, if there are no guarantees for the French outside Quebec, there can be scant ground in morality for guarantees for the English in Quebec. As always, what happens in the rest of Canada conditions and reverberates to what happens within Quebec. Equally important, with such a duality generalized throughout Canada, it is possible to reconcile the principle of duality with the plurality of Western society. Equality in citizenship is as possible under duality as under plurality. There is no reason in statesmanship why English Canadians anywhere should suffer from such a duality. The French outside Quebec have and do suffer from plurality, and the English of Quebec benefit from duality. As it was in the beginning, so it is now, the operation of Confederation is reciprocating; what happens in the duality of Quebec must affect what happens in the plurality of the West, what takes place in the West that which occurs in Quebec. Seen in this light, the official Languages Act of 1969 actually is a return to the nationality, the "political nationality" of Cartier, embodied in the B.N.A. Act of 1867.

Footnotes

1
A. S. Morton, *History of the Canadian West 1870-1871* (Toronto, 1939), pp. 825-937.

2
W. L. Morton, *The Critical Years* (Toronto, 1964), pp. 250-256.

3
That is, in the sense of fighting caused by friction between the Indian economy and that of an agricultural frontier.

4
D. G. Creighton, "John A. Macdonald, Confederation and the Canadian West," *Transactions, Historical and Scientific Society of Manitoba, 1967, 111* (23), pp. 5-14.

5
P. B. Waite, "The Quebec Resolutions and *Le Courrier du Canada,*" *Canadian Historical Review*, XL, 4 (December, 1959).

6
F. R. Scott, "Political Nationalism and Confederation," *Canadian Journal of Economics and Political Science*, VIII, 3 (August, 1942), p. 397.

7
Language as a means of instruction was surely always implied in Section 93. Thomas D'Arcy McGee seems to have been alone in recognizing the extension of French Canada beyond Quebec. *Speeches and Addresses* (London, 1865), pp. 288, 290, 301-2 in J. M. Bumsted, *Documentary Problems in Canadian History, 1* (Georgetown, 1969), pp. 279-280.

8
D. G. Creighton, *Macdonald: The Old Chieftain* (Toronto, 1955), p. 25.

9

W. L. Morton (ed.), *Journal of Alexander Begg* (Champlain Society, 1957), p. 25; PAM, Record of the Quarterly Court of Assiniboia.

10

Morton, *Begg's Journal*, p. 38.

11

G. F. G. Stanley, *Louis Riel* (Toronto, 1963), p. 55.

12

Morton, *Critical Years*, p. 242.

13

That Schultz was the opponent of Riel does not imply that he was the villain of the drama about to unfold. He represented the aggressive frontier of squatter sovereignty, Riel the preservation of minority rights in a majoritarian democracy.

14

Morton, *Begg's Journal*, pp. 447-449.

15

It had been demanded in the Sayer insurrection of 1849, and in effect granted by the appointment of F. G. Johnston, lawyer of Montreal, as Recorder of Assiniboia in 1854.

16

Morton, *Begg's Journal*, p. 121.

17

W. L. Morton (ed.), *Manitoba: The Birth of a Province* (Altona, 1965), pp. 140-154.

18

This was limited in Quebec to *La Minerve*, the "clerical" newspaper of Hector Langevin, a few of the clergy and to L. F. R. Masson. The chief support in money, and some of the missionaries, came from France.

19

L. H. Thomas, *The Struggle for Responsible Government in the North-West Territories, 1870-1897* (Toronto, 1956), pp. 77-78. Creighton, "Macdonald, Confederation and the Canadian West," pp. 11-12. The text of the preceding page and the two following has been altered since delivery in response to the deeper analysis of the debate by Ralph Heintzman in his, "The Spirit of Confederation: Professor Creighton, Biculturalism, and the Use of History," *Canadian Historical Review*, L11, 3 (September, 1971), 261-267.
It is of interest to note that what emerges from this discussion is that the legislation by the federal Parliament to provide for schools and the French language in the Northwest was not only a political necessity, but also in the minds of many members of Parliament at best a transitional thing until local institutions could make local decisions, at least on the provincial subjects of education and the language of instruction. I suggest that this element of the provisional and the constitutional is the gist of Professor Creighton's case.

20

The square survey, approved if not planned by Thomas Jefferson, was of course a perfect expression of the bland but abstract rationalism of the eighteenth century.

21
J. P. Turner, *The North-West Mounted Police, 1* (Ottawa, 1950), p. 99, "There was a good quota of French Canadians" (in the original force.)

22
The matter of French interest in the North-West has for the first time been illuminated by A. I. Silver, "French Canada and the Prairie Frontier, 1870-1890," *Canadian Historical Review*, L (March, 1969), 11-36.

23
W. L. Morton, *Manitoba: A History* (Toronto, 2nd ed., 1967), pp. 352-353.

24
In the sense which I set out in my paper, "A Century of Plain and Parkland," *Alberta Historical Review*, (Spring, 1969.)

25
It is of course curious that Riel should be a hero in the West today, as the West refused what Riel demanded, equal rights of French and English. It is as a hero of the Resistance, of protest and the assertion of Western "rights" against a remote and uninformed Ottawa, of course, that he is now remembered.

Aspects of Urban Life in the West, 1870-1914

J. M. S. Careless

I

This is a tale of four cities - Winnipeg, Edmonton, Calgary and Vancouver - or rather, a comparative treatment of some features in their
life and growth down to the First World War. It is obviously a pretty
selective treatment, in leaving out major centres like Regina and Victoria, not to mention a host of emergent urban places in the West from
Brandon to Nanaimo. The limit of space in a paper is one good reason
for thus restricting the selection. Another, even better, is that the
author has a good deal more yet to learn. But the choice does take in the
two largest western cities, along with two rising smaller ones in the
period, and represents a broad regional distribution. Hence it should
still be possible to say something in general about the life of the urban
West, in its initial, formative era.

It bears affirming at the outset that the urban West was decidedly a
fact of life before 1914, however much more fully it was to develop in
later periods. The settlement of the plains agricultural frontier, the rise
of mining frontiers in the western mountains or lumber frontiers in
river valleys and on the coast, must not obscure the basic fact that with
them, integrally related to them, went continued and important urban
growth. By 1901, half the population of British Columbia was urban
(50.48 percent). Although the relative lack of farming land in the Pacific
province, and the concentrating tendency of mines and sawmills, can of
course explain this comparatively high degree of urbanization, it is
notable that even on the prairies over a quarter of Manitoba's population then was urban (26.89 percent), and well over a third (37.88 percent) of the future Alberta. Moreover, by 1911 the urban segment of
the population had risen to 51.9 percent in British Columbia, 38.07 percent in Alberta and 43.43 percent in Manitoba, suggesting that during
the great western boom urbanization in these provinces was actually
proceeding a bit faster than rural settlement - and markedly so in the
older community of Manitoba, which exhibited an urban increase of
over 16 percent, double the national average for the decade.

In short, in these large jurisdictions the town grew more than the
country in the classic era of the rise of the West, although the rate of urban growth naturally was tied to the ups and downs of the general process of land settlement. In particular, Winnipeg, Edmonton, Calgary

and Vancouver rose to become economically affluent, technologically advanced, and socially fast-maturing urban units. Calgary and Edmonton, especially, might not yet compare in size to leading eastern Canadian cities; but then neither did the latter to giant American or European centres: what was more meaningful in every case was the relation of each place to its own surrounding community. Here again the four western cities stood out significantly. Vancouver in 1911 had a population of 121,000 to 392,000 for British Columbia, Winnipeg 136,000 to Manitoba's 461,000, and Calgary and Edmonton 43,000 and 31,000 respectively to 374,000 in Alberta (giving Edmonton, incidentally, a far higher proportion of its province's total population than Toronto had had in reference to Ontario at the time of Confederation). But simple demographic quantities give only part of the story. Qualitatively speaking, the four cities also displayed much power over communications, trade patterns and development processes in their regions, exercised growing social and cultural influence, and two of them of course also enjoyed political dominance as provincial capitals.

Clearly, then, the urban factor strongly represented by western cities should enter into any broad assessment of western development before 1914; and their origins and characteristics should be traced back further than just the era of manifestly rapid urban growth in the early twentieth century. That effort might well extend, in any full analysis of western urban history, to the very beginnings of town-style life in fur trade posts or mining camps. But for our purpose here it should at least go back to the 1870's for Winnipeg's emergence as a city, to the 1880's for the others. This I propose to attempt by picking out certain aspects of western urban life in the period that seem particularly to invite comment, though many others might certainly be chosen also. On any of them I can do little more than offer generalizations or reflections. Yet this paper can only be a "probe" (to use Marshall McLuhan's favorite expression for a fast way out) into a field that needs a great deal of investigation: investigation that is under way in graduate theses, but has not issued in much scholarly publication so far.

II

The first aspect for consideration derives from the pre-eminent importance of nineteenth-century industrial technology in the rise of the western Canadian cities. Though they emerged on far-spread frontiers, virtually from the start they were involved in the steam-and-steel technology of transport, which alone, then, could overcome continental distance and swiftly end frontier isolation. In this experience they were indeed like similarly evolving American western cities of the railway age;

but our concern here is with their evolution in Canada. And if it be a truism to assert the vital importance of the technology of transport to their growth, then this, like many truisms, is still worth examining.

All four cities were to a critical degree creations of the railway, a fact that marks them off in a significant way from the older main urban communities of eastern Canada. It goes without saying that Halifax and Saint John, Quebec and Montreal, had emerged in an age of basic water transport as nodes on oceanic or riverine traffic systems. So did Victoria at the other side of the continental land-mass, while Toronto was already a well-established urban entity and wholesale entrepot before the coming of the railway, whatever consequences the new means of transport would have for the lake city. Similarly, Montreal industry took off in the day of canals and water power, before the impact of steam in factories and on rails - great as that was to be. In general, in the eastern cities, the patterns set by water continued to have great weight, even as the railway age developed, whereas in the West their role by comparison was minor, indeed.

True, Vancouver was an ocean port and grew with the waterborn commerce that came to its spacious harbour on Burrard Inlet. Yet spacious harbours alone have seldom made great cities, without good access inland to valuable hinterland trades or without good reason to break bulk and tranship cargos for distribution into other areas. And Fraser River navigation offered only difficult and limited access to the interior, while coastal shipping could carry on only a restricted kind of exchange along the rugged British Columbian shorelines. It was the railway, of course, which made Vancouver. The new technology of land transport - though it assuredly needed the Fraser Valley for access - joined the interior to the little sawmill community on Burrard Inlet and made it the terminus of a continental traffic system. Land lines gave value to sea lanes for Vancouver. That fact was clearly evidenced by its rapid urban development after the C.P.R had reached to its waterfront in 1886-7, as compared with the relative stagnation of New Westminster, the river port, and Victoria, the older island centre of maritime trade.

Within four years a modern city of brick and stone emerged from slash and forest at Vancouver. Through rates on the C. P. R. awarded it regional dominance as a distributing point. Though development slowed drastically in the depressed nineties, mining in the West Kootenays and the Klondike rush brought new stimulus, and in the prosperous new century growth shot up in a fast ascending spiral. More stimulus was added as the Great Northern, Canadian Northern, and Grand Trunk Pacific all made plans for entry into the city. Real estate values exploded in the trade and population boom. By 1911 land office business showed a gain of 4100 percent over 1891. No wonder the advice then given on how to get rich in Vancouver was, "Take a map of the Lower Peninsula, shut your eyes, stick your finger anywhere and sit tight."[1] And though deflation might come by 1914, nothing changed the fundamental fact that railways had brought a new Pacific metropolis into being.

As for Winnipeg, while York boats and waterways had first shaped the transport pattern for the little settlement on the Red northward and later, cart brigades and river steamboats did southward, its urban development was commanded by the railway. R. C. Bellan puts it effectively in a discussion of Winnipeg's contest with Selkirk for the Canadian Pacific's "Rails across the Red." He notes that as far as geographic site was concerned, Winnipeg should have been located twenty miles further north: its riverside location might have mattered in the days of fur trading and pioneer settlement, but for its growth as a major distributing centre for a commercial agricultural community, location on the railway main line was crucial. It was the bending of the C. P. R. southward to the town that enabled it to grow as a wholesale entrepot, leaving Selkirk, not Winnipeg as the hamlet of unrequited hopes.[2]

Actually, the railway had already set its mark on Winnipeg's development before this great victory (by negotiation) in 1881. Steamboats on the Red in the 1860's had been ancillaries to Minnesota rail connections, and they in turn were supplemented in 1878 by the Pembina Branch line south to American tracks at the border. The emergence of Winnipeg as a city in the seventies was thus greatly stimulated by railway contact and railway expectations, climaxing in the frantic land boom of the early eighties, well before the line from the East was complete. But then, it has been well recognized that the effects of railways on cities lie not only in their construction or operation but in their projection as well. Certainly Winnipeg was powerfully affected by the image and prospect of rail transport. And whether its offers of bonuses for bridges and branch lines were well considered, or its bargain with the C. P. R. in lands and tax exemptions, the city did become the focus of a rail network that ties an expanding farm hinterland into the transcontinental traffic route. Thus it grew with the prairie West as its foremost gathering and distributing point - thanks to the technology of railways.

Again, Calgary's and Edmonton's locations on the long Saskatchewan River system had small consequence for their rise as urban places. If early Edmonton did see steamboats like the dauntless *Sir Stafford Northcote*, the difficulties of the waterway, with its shallows, currents and shifting sand bars, made overland trails fully necessary in the pre-railway era, as more than supplements to water traffic. The coming of the railway, indeed, profoundly altered the traffic potentials of both places. In Calgary's case, the C. P. R.'s choice of the Kicking Horse Pass route and its arrival at the Elbow River in 1883, so clearly and so quickly changed a Mounted Police post into a flourishing cattle, freighting and lumber-milling town that no elaboration is required here. In the case of Edmonton, the impact was less immediate and direct - precisely because that village did not find itself on the Pacific railway as had been expected from the Sandford Fleming survey before the change to the southern route. But the opening of the Calgary and Edmonton Railway in 1891 undoubtedly facilitated development in the Edmonton area, leading to the incorporation of the town of Edmonton the following year, despite the fact that the C. P. R. track, which stopped on the south side of the river at what became Strathcona, was both a hindrance and a sore point - thus the acclaim for the grandly named Edmonton, Yukon and Pacific (all four thousand yards of it), which by 1902 crossed the Low Level Bridge to the north side of the Saskatchewan, bringing rail connections with the south. The whole situation was much improved when in 1913 the C. P. R. itself at last came directly into town over the new High Level Bridge.

But meanwhile the Canadian Northern had arrived by the north bank in 1905, providing through service to Winnipeg. And the Grand Trunk Pacific was on its way, to give Edmonton access to still another transcontinental, as well as having the link south to the C. P. R. One evident result was the rise of the well-served city's wholesale trade. There were two wholesale firms in 1906; by 1911 the number had risen to nearly fifty. "Edmonton's future is absolutely assured as the great metropolis of Western Canada,"[3] it was proclaimed, as railways and expectations from railways sparked a roaring boom through 1912-14. The amalgamation of Strathcona with Edmonton in 1914 was virtual recognition of the fact that they had been bound by steel into one urban entity, with fresh ambitions of its own to dominate still more hinterland by branch lines north and west.

As for Calgary, it had risen to commercial dominance in southern Alberta through its position on the Canadian Pacific main line and as the rail gateway to Edmonton and the north after 1890. The opening of the Canadian Northern route to Edmonton might lessen the latter role at a time, too, when Calgary was deeply rankling over the northern town becoming capital of the new province of Alberta. Yet meanwhile the building of the Crows Nest Pass line had linked Kootenay mining development to Calgary's supply trade. Indeed, a promotional supplement to the *Herald* in 1910 could grandly declare, "For 150 miles to the north, south, east and west of us lies a large section of land all of which is absolutely tributary to us, rich in agriculture, in minerals, forests and natural resources, and probably without parallel in the Dominion in the possibilities of growth and development."[4] Rosily promotional indeed; but anticipations of such possibilities brought on the great Calgary boom of 1910-12. And while much of it was the mass hysteria of real estate speculation in paper fortunes, underlying the concurrent growth in urban concentration was also the focusing, dominating potential of rail transport - Calgary's prime cause for existence.

One consequence of the strategic importance of transport technology to western urban life was a celebrated love-hate relationship with railways. City-dwellers as well as farmers wanted the railway, then deplored its pervasive power. City journalists extolled the wealth and progress it would bring to their community, then attacked its unjust rate structure, its selfish, greedy, heartless tyranny. In Winnipeg in the eighties the Board of Trade took a vigorous lead in protesting the Canadian Pacific's monopoly privileges and "suicidal" rates policy to Ottawa.[5] An Edmontonian, commenting in print on Calgary in the early 1900's, found it "C. P. R. everything; the coffee you got was C. P. R. and the very hens laid C. P. R. eggs," although, in his own town, the same line had now "reluctantly loosed the shackles, snarling at every encroachment on the vindictive privileges granted this blood-sucking corporation."[6]

In Vancouver, a writer in the *British Columbia Magazine* of 1911 began his discussion of Vancouver and the Railways with, "once upon a time a city gave itself away in order that a great railway might be induced to establish its terminus there" - a somewhat fast epitomizing of the complex real estate deals that had accompanied the extension of the C. P. R.[7] However, he concluded happily, while once Vancouver was on its knees to railways, now they could not stay away! But it was Bob Edwards in the *Calgary Eye Opener* who duly had a last, best western word. In his enjoyable feud with that rising politician and C. P. R. solicitor, R. B. Bennett, Edwards climaxed the photographs of the various accidents on the railway which he had been running with one of Bennett himself, under the simple caption, "Another C. P. R. Wreck."[8]

Now it is true that easterners had their own discontents with railways, from the temporary frustration in mid-century Montreal with the Grand Trunk's indifference to the city's interests to the vehement attacks of George Brown, the Toronto *Globe* and the Clear Grits on that railway "octopus." But for sheer enduring care and concern, one would have to give the decision to the westerners. Whereas the East had had, and to some extent still had, alternatives by water or American through routes to keep railway power in check, the West was far more exposed to transport monopoly enhanced by distance, tariffs, and its narrower economic base - and what is more it could readily see its dependence and subordination.

Still further, main-line railways were obvious embodiments of outside metropolitan forces; something Montreal had once felt regarding the London-based Grand Trunk, or Toronto had sensed in respect to the same line, seeing it instead as enhancing Montreal's domination of Upper Canadian traffic. As for western cities, they might view local lines that served their own regional metropolitan interests as "good" (as Winnipeg did MacKenzie and Mann's complex in Manitoba). But the main lines were all too often "bad" exemplifications of outside control. Here was, in fact, a characteristic response to the metropolitanism inherent in the industrial technology of transport that was both shaping and mastering the development of the West. Hence the broad significance of the reaction in the young western cities to railways, which had made them yet continually threatened to unmake them again.

III

Much more could be said of attitudinal responses in the rising urban West to questions of transport, beyond the specific material concerns of economic interest groups. But it is necessary to turn to another area, this time to the kind of institutional pattern in which urban life was organized in western communities. The primary institutional pattern was obviously that of municipal government. Here one might expect a political structure not too different from the mayors and councils of the older eastern cities. Yet one might also expect a different spirit to inform it: a greater manifestation of popular democracy in towns so recently sprung from the frontier, unlike the established elitist ways of older eastern centres. If so, one might be rather quickly disappointed.

It is true that a kind of open camaraderie persisted in western cities that had grown so quickly from pioneer villages, and where - for years after 1914 - there were many who well remembered the original huddle of houses and shanties on the open prairie or among the stump fields. Nevertheless, the sense of common achievement in city-building often displayed at civic celebrations and community social occasions, did not go far enough to sustain a lively common interest or participation in municipal political affairs. In general, government in the cities was soon left in the hands of an elite in-group. This municipal elite had links with wealthy business interests, and often contained prominent mercantile figures; but it was more widely drawn from lawyers and lesser entrepreneurs who made a fairly regular profession (or business livelihood) out of directing government for a citizenry that normally preferred to be left alone. On occasion, however, there might be challenges from the latter body, often stimulated by the business community seeking to lower costs and taxes, as when in Winnipeg, in 1884, the Board of Trade successfully pushed a "citizens' ticket," which was elected to expel interests that had presumably fostered extravagance and speculation in the late-lamented Winnipeg land boom.

At times, too, there were more clamorous scandals; for instance, the Calgary "land grab" of 1904, when city fathers had apparently arranged a quiet sale of real estate for friends, until irate taxpayers forced the sale to be revoked and several heads to roll at City Hall. On the whole, however, elitist urban government seemed broadly acceptable and sufficiently effective. And in particular, it did make the municipal regime a satisfactory vehicle for community sentiment and aspirations, guarding city interests against outside forces, embodying civic pride and encouraging local development. This point is aptly made, again regarding Calgary, in a recent study by Mr. M. L. Foran, but it seems to me broadly true of municipal authority in the other cities under consideration.[9]

As for the relative failure of a western frontier environment to produce more than a brief initial democratic activity in town government, W. L. Morton has observed that the frontier scarcely existed as a conditioning process to instill democracy or individualism in the American West after 1870.[10] Railway technology (once more) had brought frontiers within a few days' reach of older regions: democracy and Americanization in the West would thenceforth be the product of a total American environment, not of a separate frontier world. Hence in the Canadian West - where, indeed, the railway instrument of eastern metropolitanism and industrialism often preceded the settlement of land frontiers - society would be especially likely to exhibit not only the forms but also much of the content of eastern institutions, including the municipal. Of course there were differences. But they were less the result of frontier influences *per se* (however these are to be read) than of the fact that this assuredly was a different region: with different terrain, climate and resource patterns, and with distinctive problems of distance, development and population needs.

One might add that, when strong democratic surges did subsequently manifest themselves in Western urban life, they were as likely to stem from Winnipeg's North End or the Vancouver docks as from the frontier; but that largely takes us past our period. Returning to it, the western urban elites generally continued to maintain themselves throughout with little difficulty, despite some efforts to reform civic administration towards the end of that time.

In Vancouver at the start, the election of Mayor MacLean in the first civic contest in 1886 in some degree marked the defeat of the original pioneer "aristocracy" of sawmill operators by an energetic new-comer group of real estate entrepreneurs, contractors and wholesalers, heavily involved in developing their extensive Vancouver properties. Thereafter, leadership largely remained in a relatively small, develop-ment-oriented circle; though at times this produced notable figures like David Oppenheimer, mayor from 1888 to 1892. One of the city's first and most powerful wholesale merchants, Oppenheimer held land all over Vancouver, along with electric light and street railway interests and drainage and improvement companies. Under him the city acquired municipal waterworks and sewerage facilities - together with Stanley Park - and at his death in 1897 he was eulogized by the Vancouver *World* as "one of the Fathers of Vancouver."[11] In any case, Vancouver grew so fast that it was hard to integrate new elements into social leadership, as H. C. Klassen's study has indicated, so that its class structure perhaps remained more rigid than that of other large Canadian cities.[12]

The civic elite in Winnipeg also had its outstanding figures; for in-stance, J. H. Ashdown, reputed the largest hardware dealer in the West, who was alderman on the first council after the Town's incor-poration in 1873 and mayor of the city in 1907-8. A pioneer inhabitant of Winnipeg since the early sixties, Ashdown had led in seeking incorpora-tion, in negotiations to bring the railway there in the seventies; and, in the eighties, as President of the Board of Trade, carrying Winnipeg's protests against the railway monopoly to Ottawa. Other typical repre-sentatives of the city's political leadership were its first mayor, F. E. Cornish (a London, Ontario, lawyer), later successors Mayors Waugh and Evans (insurance and real estate) and John Arbuthnot (a lumber dealer) who had three terms of office in the early twentieth century.

It was also typical when the Winnipeg *Commercial* observed, in 1893, that the city council of that year consisted of five lawyers, three real estate and insurance agents, two wholesale merchants, one con-tractor, and one member "with no particular profession" - an un-fortunate situation when "Winnipeg is almost solely a commercial city . . . whose existence depends so completely on its distributing trade."[13]

Generally, Winnipeg's principal businessmen seemed to prefer par-ticipation in the Board of Trade to activity in civic government, as an in-stitution better calculated to promote the city's basic economic in-terests. Certainly the Board of Trade, established in 1879, was re-markably effective in asserting Winnipeg's growing impulses to regional metropolitan dominance. Not only did it energetically take on Ottawa and the C. P. R., but also won a significant victory by getting the right to set western wheat grades transferred from eastern cities to western boards of trade; and it gained control itself of Manitoba wheat-grading. Then, as a concomitant of Winnipeg's advancing control of the grain trade, it fostered the establishment of the Grain Exchange in 1887. Boards of Trade similarly emerged in Vancouver, Edmonton and Calgary as another institutional expression of western urban life. Yet the Winnipeg Board was clearly the most powerfully developed: perhaps an indication of the greater maturity of that city's business interests. The Calgary Board, on the other hand, began and died three times in the town's early years, before it finally took hold.

Calgary, as Foran has pointed out, had its own in-group of continuing municipal politicians; men like the hard-working Wesley Orr, journalist and real estate dealer, councillor from 1888 to 1893 and mayor in 1894-5; a man whose very life became civic politics. But major businessmen like A. E. Cross, the brewer and ranch owner, Pat Burns, the meat-packer, and the leading lawyer (Senator) J. A. Lougheed, left municipal affairs to a lesser entrepreneurial circle, while they took the decisions outside that might do much more to shape the growth of Calgary. And so the "Big Four" cattlemen, Cross, Burns, George Lane and A. J. McLean, themselves put up $100,000 to launch the first Stampede in 1912; it was hardly a municipal product.

Edmonton, similarly, although the smallest and closest to the frontier of the four cities, also showed elitist tendencies. Indeed, it was its Board of Trade, founded in 1889 as the first west of Winnipeg, which decided to seek the town's incorporation. The civic regime begun in 1892 again took on the characteristic pattern of government by an in-group of community leaders, such as the pioneer settler, Matt McCauley, chairman of the first regular school board, mayor from 1892 to 1894, legislative member and later warden of the federal penitentiary; or John McDougall, the wealthy general merchant and financier, and mayor in 1897 and 1908. Yet in any case, provincial politicans could often do more for Edmonton than municipal worthies, such as confirming it as capital in 1906 or giving it the provincial university in 1907. And then there was Frank Oliver of the *Edmonton Bulletin*, the city's federal member. As Laurier's Minister of the Interior, he was a highly influential figure - but none of this really redounded to strengthen an Edmonton municipal democracy.

In sum, the constructive, assertive vigour in early western urban life was not necessarily displayed in the somewhat conservative, civic political institutions. It lay far more in individual entrepreneurs and the advancing business community. Municipal government might be a useful public sounding board, and was certainly necessary to provide police and fire protection, street improvements, water and light or even street railways. But the citizenry usually remained content to leave such matters to a relative few, and rely on their sense of public service. The new western cities did not produce an upsurge of democracy. In their elitism they were remarkably like the older eastern ones. But there still was a significant degree of difference here, just because they were new. There was thus both a greater cost of development and greater pride in it, greater confidence instilled when it succeeded. The city had to grow, by popular will; and every individual citizen - in his private capacity - could and must share in making it grow. In this there was a special strain of democracy and individualism in the western city - perhaps derived, after all, from the newness and potential of a frontier West.

IV

Once more, much could be added about other institutional forms of life in the cities: the courts and law enforcement, schools and beginnings of higher education, religious, cultural and recreational associations, class and ethnic structure and mobility within it. But once more it is time to move on to a final aspect, which I can only call "urban ambiance," an immaterial quality of atmosphere encompassing a city, which can be felt, if not measured, and certainly is real enough. This urban "feel," to coin another useful, if awkward phrase, is a composite of many things arising from the physical and human environment: actual physical layout and construction, in streets, parks, buildings and architectural practices; occupational and residential patterning; social amenities and social awareness; life style, cultural interests and climate of opinion. As usual, in the scope of this paper, I can only touch on just a few of these in passing - but sufficiently, I hope, to express the ambiance or "feel" of the young western cities.

First, their physical appearance was full of contrasts, chiefly the result of rapid and virtually uncontrolled growth. Humble little frame structures of village years stood by the heavy, brick and ornamental stone elegance of the 1890's; simpler workaday brick stores and warehouses of the 1880's beside the new secular, classical temples of banking that went up in the 1900's. Nevertheless out of rawness and internal contrasts each of the four cities had soon produced a definite central business district, while well before 1914 one could identify a graded pattern of residential districts whereby occupational and income groups increasingly lived separate from their place of employment. This separation, so typical of the modern industrial urban community, developed with remarkable speed in these all-but-instant cities. But then they were the product of the over-night process of city-building made possible by steam and steel technology.

Furthermore, they had space to build on, and from the nineties on-ward, the electric street railway. Urban sprawl was already inherent in the western city before the further technology of the automobile made its full impact, to produce a wider urban expansion, or explosion, across the surrounding landscape. And it was significant that the automobile did arrive in the first decade of the twentieth century in all four cities; perhaps significant as well that Vancouver could lay claim to Canada's first gas station, established in 1908.[14] In any event, given the confident hopes of city greatness and the major industry of real estate promotion, one might expect excessive spread into grandly-named mud pastures; exhibited, for instance, in the conquering annexations that more than tripled Edmonton's area between 1904 and 1914.

Winnipeg, indeed, in 1903 was looking to "swiftly whirling trolleys" to tie the outlying areas into the city's heart.[15] That year its paper, *Town Topics*, commented on the "almost magical transformation" that had occurred in this Chicago of the North. "Where lately we waded in mud, today we walk on stone pavement. Where a short time ago un-sightly wooden business blocks reminded us of pioneer days, today stately buildings and modern conveniences fill the eye."[16] Certainly all four cities had come a long way by 1914 in achieving an urban co-ordina-tion out of the seeming confusion of old, new, and the welter of con-struction; of streets half paved and half dug-up in Edmonton and Cal-gary, of skyscrapers rising in Winnipeg and Vancouver.

Civic amenities were growing. Vancouver had its Stanley Park, opened in 1888, happily transformed from a military reserve. Winnipeg already had six parks by 1903, and the public library founded by its Historic and Scientific Society in 1881 became the nucleus of the fine new Carnegie Library opened in 1906. Libraries, rinks, sports grounds, opera houses (a generic name that covered very little opera), were there for recreation, along with older rooted amusements like taverns, race tracks and bawdy houses. Even urban planning raised a tentative eye by 1914, as in Vancouver's negotiations for the False Creek harbour area development, or the abortive Mawson report of 1914 in Calgary for rendering it the city beautiful.

In each case, by 1914, the city had acquired a structured physical character, identifiable despite its own internal contrasts. No doubt much of the identity simply derived from setting: Vancouver's sea and mountains, Calgary's back-drop of the Rockies, the soaring river-bank front view of Edmonton, and even Winnipeg's waterside location at the forks of the Red and Assiniboine. No doubt, too, Vancouverites were willing to claim civic credit for their mountains, and Winnipeg to take a perverse hometown pride in its winter rigours. The fact remained that the inhabitants of the western cities did identify ardently and proudly with their communities, as visitors often remarked. And they even had their own local building characteristics, as in Calgary's grey sandstone public and commercial structures, or bungalow residences of a Pacific coast variety - which its local press in 1910 lauded as "elegant and cosy."[17]

Western urban pride easily became boosterism, as a testament of civic faith. Thus, for example, Vancouver's slogan of the boom years after 1905, chanted out to a drum beat by parties of boosters touring the city: "In 1910, Vancouver then, will have one hundred thousand men."[18] Or thus the admission by *Town Topics* in 1902 that "Winnipeg in fact has been rather given to the practice of announcing from the roof tops that she considers herself some potatoes."[19] Or thus even the inter-city rivalry that brought the Vancouver *Province* to note unkindly in February, 1913, "Winnipegers are congratulating themselves on the fine winter and are looking forward with great expectations to an early spring in the next five or six months."[20] The reference might be light-hearted; but the belief of the western urban dweller in the innately superior blessings of his own city could be much more fully documented, and was a basic attribute of the early urban West.

The belief in manifestly destined progress that could only be thwarted by malign forces like the C. P. R. or the undue political influence of rival capital cities (Victoria to Vancouver, Edmonton to Calgary) informed the climate of opinion in western urban centres and even added a distinctive ingredient to their lifestyle. Otherwise that lifestyle was none too different from the urban East. Though the noted actress Lilly Langtry might make the prejudiced and prejudicial comment in Calgary in 1913 that, "Everyone in Edmonton is either an Indian or a squaw,"[21] the busy bowler-hatted inhabitants of the northern city bustling about their new concrete-and-steel McLeod or Tegler Buildings, looked and acted much the same as those who thronged King and Yonge Streets in Toronto. The mansions of Vancouver's West End set similar standards of material achievement and conspicuous consumption as those of Sherbrooke Street in Montreal.

Winnipeg's slogan of 1913, "Do it out of rush hours,"[22] showed that the urban traffic problem had arrived in the West no less than the East. And social pretensions in Calgary were all too similar to those in older, more ritualized eastern cities - a fact Bob Edwards was particularly adept at satirizing. Of course there were the signs and survivals of a pioneer past - as well as of a changing future, in the greater freedom and larger role which women were achieving - but lifestyle in the western cities had very soon become largely a counterpart of eastern.

This simply indicated the common conditions of modern urban living, for the urban West had virtually become contemporaneous with the urban East by 1914. What were basic differences lay in the expansion of space and the compression of time. The western centres felt they had all God's room to grow in - although this, on the other side of the ledger, was the liability of distance and the nagging problem of transport. At the same time, they had in a few short decades compressed a century or so of eastern urban growth from which came their pride, expectations and frustrations, their rawness and internal contrasts.

They had also been able to achieve this sudden growth through the application of industrial technology, chiefly exemplified in the railway - which takes us back almost to where we began. It has been held that the general historic process of urbanization may be expressed in terms of four great factors: the environment, the population that occupies it, the technology and organization that mediate the relations of the first two. In this frame of reference, the western natural environment had been occupied at certain nodal points on traffic routes by considerable concentrations of population homogenous to the degree of still being largely English-speaking in language and culture. The young western cities generally did not have influential non-Anglo-Saxon components much before 1914, even though immigrant elements had certainly made their urban presence known - Asians in Vancouver; Icelandic, Mennonite or Jewish groups in Winnipeg. The original predominantly homogenous society, whether derived from eastern Canada, Britain or the United States, had readily transferred urban institutions and municipal organizations from the older East to the West - so that the organizational factor was not of much innovative importance in the latter case. Much more important, naturally, was the technology of transport which had also been transferred.

This was the prime mediating factor between environment and population in the ecology of the urban West, the most vital urbanizing force there. Sprung from and tied to eastern metropolitanism, railway technology essentially integrated the new western cities into a continent-wide metropolitan pattern. They would build their own regional metropolitan domains within this pattern. They would contend against its overriding controls. But most of all, they would require a great deal more examination than I have been able to give them here.

Footnotes

1
R. J. McDougall, "Vancouver Real Estate for Twenty Five Years," *British Columbia Magazine* (June, 1911), p. 607.

2
R. C. Bellan, "Rails across the Red - Selkirk or Winnipeg," *Transactions of the Historical and Scientific Society of Manitoba*, Series III, No. 18, 1964.

3
Edmonton *Journal*, March 18, 1911.

4
Calgary *Daily Herald, Magazine Supplement*, August, 1910.

5
Ninth Annual Report of the Winnipeg Board of Trade for 1887 (Winnipeg, 1888), p. 17.

6
Malcolm Melville (J. W. Dickson), *Edmonton's Progression* (Edmonton, 1908), p. 3, 15.

7
W. Playfair, "Vancouver and the Railways," *British Columbia Magazine* (June, 1911), p. 498.

8
Grant MacEwan, *Eye Opener Bob* (Calgary, 1957), p. 171.

9
M. L. Foran, "The Calgary Town Council, 1884-1895: a Study of Local Government on a Frontier Environment," unpublished M. A. thesis for the University of Calgary, 1969.

10
W. L. Morton, "The Significance of Site in the Settlement of the American and Canadian Wests," *Agricultural History*, 1951.

11
Vancouver *World*, January 1, 1898.

12
H. C. Klassen, "An Intellectual History of Early Vancouver," unpublished paper, University of British Columbia, 1955, at Provincial Archives of British Columbia, p. 11.

13
Winnipeg *Commercial*, December 25, 1893.

14
J. S. Matthews et al., "Early Vancouver," typescript, Archives of British Columbia, p. 307.

15
Winnipeg *Town Topics*, May 30, 1903.

16
Ibid.

17
Calgary *Herald, Magazine Supplement*, August, 1910.

18
J. P. Nicholls, "Real Estate Values in Vancouver," typescript, Archives of British Columbia, p. 22.

19
Town Topics, December 13, 1902.

20
Quoted in *Town Topics*, February 1, 1913.

21
Ibid., January 11, 1913.

22
Ibid., December 13, 1913.

The National Policy and the Development of the Western Canadian Labour Movement*

Paul A. Phillips

Regionalism, economic and political, has been a most pervasive aspect of the Canadian nation throughout its history. Canadian governments have struggled with the problems created by the regional nature of the country with but limited success, hampered as they have been by the history of judicial interpretation, political provincialism and changing trade patterns, all of which have tended to balkanize the country. And this has been exacerbated by an increasing unwillingness of federal governments to maintain an economically integrated nation state against the pull of continentalism emanating from the industrial and institutional structure of North America and the demand for raw materials and captive markets by industry in the United States.[1] The development of the labour movement in Canada reflects in bold relief this pattern of regional development, paralleling prominent surges of agricultural revolt; and the West has been conspicuous in the role that it has played. Canada's general strikes have been concentrated in the west. The main surge of radical unionism began organizationally in Calgary in 1919 and the major continuing vehicles of labour-socialist political activity became most successful in the western provinces. The predominantly western character of these mass social movements can hardly be considered coincidental. Rather, it will be argued that the economic nature of the western region(s) moulded the western labour movement in a pattern distinct from that of central Canada, just as the western farmers' movement bears the imprint of the character and organization of the wheat economy. Western workers protested against their position in the price system as it was shaped by the national policy, and the character of the labour movement in the region reflected this stance.

First, however, can British Columbia and the Prairie Provinces be legitimately treated as a single economic unit? Despite obvious structural differences between the two areas, the West may be considered a unified region in terms of its economic role within the Canadian

*I am indebted to Professor H. C. Pentland for his helpful suggestions and comments on this paper.

economy. The national policy was based on a two region model, the primary-export goods west and the secondary-manufacturing east. To some extent this model no longer accords with reality, and labour institutions have modified accordingly, but even today, the regional structure created by both natural resources and government policy in the period of nation-building exerts a pervasive influence upon the history of the labour movement.

The National Policy and Western Economic Development

The story of the national policy, ". . . collectively that groups of policies and instruments which were designed to transform the British North American territories of the mid-nineteenth century into a political and economic unit," has already been outlined in considerable detail elsewhere.[2] Nevertheless, it is desirable to remind the reader of the main foundations of the policy and its effects on western economic structure. In order to weld the diverse economic regions of British North America into one economic system in defense against the continental aspirations of the United States, the new federal government had to defend and extend the east-west orientation of the northern part of the continent by the ". . . establishment of a new frontier, an area where commercial and financial activity could readily expand and where labour and capital might find profitable employment."[3] The three pillars of the policy are well known, the agricultural settlement of the West with the supporting immigration policies, the creation of an all-Canadian east-west transportation link, and the development of a protective tariff system to ensure an east-west trade pattern and thereby to force traffic onto the railroad.

To capture the commerce of western staple development has always been the elusive dream of eastern Canadian business.[4] The national policy was a further manifestation of these eastern interests' commercial aspirations. In fact, the national policy represents the triumph of commercial interests (as opposed to agricultural or industrial interests) in the struggle for control of the destiny of Canada, an alternative to continentalism which, with the nonrenewal of the reciprocity treaty, had ceased to be a viable policy.

The domination of commercial values (which may be described as Canadian mercantilism) over agriculture, labour, industry and government, bears the stamp of the formative period of the Canadian nation. The effects for the West in terms of industrial structure and relative price levels have been summarized by V. C. Fowke:

The tariff, then has provided no scope for western industrial expansion and has had the unmitigated effect of curtailing the expansion of export activity because of the pronounced increase in the costs to which it gives rise . . . The lack of industrialization in the west today is due in part to the impossibility of achieving competitive competence as against eastern industries long since firmly established with the aid of protection.[5]

In British Columbia the mineral and forest industries as export staples faced a similar situation.[6] Maurice Dobb has observed more generally that,

> . . . this type of policy had the significance, not only of excluding the competition of foreign industries from the home market, but of tending to raise the internal level of industrial prices while maintaining agricultural prices at the world level, thereby turning the terms of trade inside the national boundaries to the advantage of industry; just as within a system of metropolis and colonies the Mercantile System had previously done.[7]

The national policy, therefore, fostered western Canada as an economic colonial hinterland subjected to the mercantile aspirations of the politically dominant eastern Canada. The economic effects may be summed up as: (a) turning the internal terms of trade against primary production in favour of eastern industry (that is, in relation to what would have been the case in the absence of the national policy, raising the price of goods imported into the West relative to exports from the West), (b) raising the costs of primary production by tariffs on inputs, (c) encouraging investment in commercial, transportation and, only where necessary, primary processing industries, and (d) providing little or no scope for industrial expansion in the West through raised input costs and the competition of eastern industry already established behind the wall of protection.[8]

Space limits us to a broad review of the course of industrial and occupational structure and growth which is the operative framework in which trade unionism developed.[9] The completion of the Canadian Pacific Railway in the mid-eighties provided the potential for the opening of the agricultural West, but it was not realized until the late years of the nineteenth century. The sharp depression after World War I marked the end of the rapid growth phase of the Western economy associated with the establishment of the wheat economy on the prairies and of the lumber and mining staples of British Columbia. The interwar years, by comparison, are unimpressive, a decade of at best slow growth, at worst relative stagnation, followed by that international debacle, the great depression. Economic performance after 1939 is indeed impressive despite the problems of inflation and, more recently, unemployment, but what is significant for this study is the change in trading patterns, the distribution of labour force and output, and the relative decline of agriculture in the Western economy. These changes and their effects will be discussed later.

On the prairies, the establishment of the wheat economy produced a particular pattern of population and labour force distribution that was not conducive to wide scale unionism. The urban centres in the Prairies which developed in response to the agricultural development, that is, distribution and transportation centres, were normally small and, as Innis has pointed out, dispersed in response to the demands of the transportation technology.[10] Winnipeg was the only centre of major size with a more diversified economy.

An exception to this dispersed pattern of labour force distribution in the early period of prairie development resulted from the opening of coal mining in the Lethbridge area during the 1880's. This development was closely related to the wheat economy and, in particular, to the spread of the railways.

> Production in Alberta started with railway construction by the Canadian Pacific Railway Company. Development of other coal fields followed railway construction by the Grand Trunk Pacific in 1911 and 1912, and by the Canadian Northern Railway in 1913. The railways provided a market in themselves and afforded transportation to other markets. The development of Alberta production from practically nothing in 1880 to over 5,250,000 tons in 1913 is tied directly to railroad expansion. In the case of the Crowsnest Pass area, development of the metallurgical plants in British Columbia and the United States was an added factor.[11]

Before the Second World War, then, the prairie economic structure was characterized by independent wheat farming, relatively low urbanization, and a lack of significant large scale industry outside of the railways and coal mines. As a result, in 1931 over four fifths of prairie employment in manufacturing was in industries serving local or regional markets, mainly in small scale operations providing little or no scope for union organization.[12] It was not until after the war that the gradual process of urbanization and industrialization with the emergence of new resource industries created significant organizable concentrations of workers in the service and manufacturing industries.

The economic development pattern of British Columbia was basically dissimilar. Agriculture played a relatively minor role. The province was founded on the short-lived gold staple but permanent growth was based on the forest, mining and smelting, and fishing industries. As early as 1881, three quarters of employment in the top ten manufacturing industries was in food preserving (mainly fish canning) and processing lumber products. Nor did this dependence on natural resource processing decline over time. Fish, forest and mineral processing represented 86 percent of employment in the ten major manufacturing industries in 1911, and 82 percent in 1951.[13] Particular growth surges in British Columbia history can be associated with the opening of mining in the interior of the province in the 1890's and 1900's, railway construction before the First World War and the secular but unsteady growth of the forest industries, including pulp and paper, in recent years.

Despite these dissimilarities in the resource bases of the two western regions, there is a common orientation fostered by the national policy and continued by natural advantage. The first and obvious similarity is the dependence of the two regions on a natural resource base. Because agricultural products, in particular grain, do not require considerable processing, the manufacturing industries in the Prairies developed less than in British Columbia. Except where such processing was required, manufacturing in the West was concentrated in those industries where proximity to the market was required, generally small service-oriented industries with a locational distribution similar to that of total population. They have little in common with specialist and durable manufacturing or with resource processing both because of their small average size and because of their integration into and dependence on the local community.

Secondly, except where urban areas were centres of a resource processing industry, the urban function has been primarily one of commercial and governmental service to the resource hinterland. The dependence on commercial rather than industrial pursuits promoted, as Professor Pentland has suggested, a short term rather than a long-term view toward labour issues. The result is to minimize employer concern with developing a permanent and peaceful relation with the labour force.[14]

Thirdly, the frontiers associated with the staple developments in the West necessitated a large construction sector, particularly during periods of railway construction. While the slowing of extensive development in the Prairies after the first war temporarily depressed construction, the trend to urbanization in recent years has reactivated demand. In British Columbia almost continuous population growth, investment in resources and in transportation facilities, as well as rising urban demands have placed considerable, if somewhat unstable, pressures on the construction industry.[15]

A knowledge of economic structure is important to the discussion of the development of trade unionism for two reasons. In the first place the development of Canadian unionism took place in a period when the law was either hostile, or at best neutral, to labour organization and employers, virtually without exception, were opposed. In order to organize, employees had to be in a strategic position in the production process so that their collective action could bring maximum pressure to bear on the employer but where they could not be easily replaced by nonunionized workers. Also in this category were highly skilled workers, large groups of workers geographically isolated or protected by a tight labour market, employees in noncompetitive markets where price competition is not shoved back onto labour costs. Or, it might occur as well in industries with heavy fixed capital where a shutdown might involve large fixed expenditure losses which cannot be recouped.

Conversely, one can expect trade unionism to meet maximum obstacles in unskilled markets with readily alternative labour supplies facing competitive markets and with a high labour input relative to fixed investment. Also, employers with a short-run, commercial outlook tend to place a higher premium on quick returns (thereby leading to attempts to minimize labour costs) than those with a longer-run, industrial outlook who are willing to forego immediate gain in favour of stability and growth and thus may be more willing to develop a stable working relationship with union organizations. To some extent the former would tend to be those employers with low fixed-to-variable capital ratios while the latter with high fixed-to-variable capital ratios.

Given these influences on the ability of labour to organize, it should be expected that the structure and state of the regional economy would have a pervasive effect on the course and timing of the development of organized labour movement in western Canada. Secondly, it will be argued that the economic differences between east and west were a major cause of division in labour union structure and policy.

The Early Development of Western Trade Unionism

In his well-quoted statement, Professor Logan said "the West seems to have taken to the trade union idea from the beginning."[16] But such a statement does less than justice to the complex relationship between economic development and union growth. During the British Columbia gold boom in the late 1850's and early 1860's, the earliest labour organizations are recorded, three craft unions in Victoria, at that time the commercial and service centre for the gold rush. The potential for unionism also existed in the Nanaimo coal fields which served residential and marine markets in Victoria and San Franciso. But it was not until 1877 that any organization developed out of a bitter and largely unsuccessful battle with the Dunsmuir coal empire. In 1883 the issue of oriental labour emerged among the miners and subsequently throughout British Columbia labour. The threat, as seen by the workers, to employment and safety standards posed by the orientals, both weakened and strengthened the labour movement - weakened it in that it divided labour in those relatively large scale industries such as mining and fishing where the men, unprotected by skills, were forced to rely on worker, or class, solidarity in the face of hostile employers; but strengthened it in its resolve to unite for political purposes to gain legislative limitation of oriental immigration.[17]

In the prairie region during the same period, labour history by contrast was a blank page. The progression of the region from fur trade to rudimentary agricultural production provided no scope for unionization. Agriculture of the proprietary type did not in itself provide an organizable labour force and, until the railway came, there was no significant investment frontier and, hence, little of an industrial or even commercial labour force.

The construction of the CPR, completed to Vancouver by 1887, changed the entire economic milieu in the Western region and created conditions conducive to several types of union development. Railway building created a large but unorganizable wage labour group and a pool of labour for subsequent economic development. However, the most direct role the railway played was as a direct employer of labour. The heavy fixed capital structure, the need for skilled occupations in the running trades, and the prior existence of trade union organization in the same trades in the United States and Eastern Canada created very favourable conditions for organization.

Nevertheless the Knights of Labour were the first to benefit, in industries stimulated by the new transportation developments. While the first western local appeared in the early 1880's, the main phase of expansion followed CPR construction when locals began appearing on the British Columbia mainland and interior. The Knights introduced a new element to the west (although already established in the east), the continental union concentrated in the United States but with branches in Canada. In British Columbia it was truly an all inclusive union with craft, industry and general or mixed assemblies and with activities that extended to co-operative and political action, the latter mainly related to oriental exclusion. In fact it was possibly the inclusiveness, the broad goals and the political bias of the Knights that provided the broad appeal that the union undoubtedly had.

Nevertheless, the Knights declined for a number of reasons. These were the slow down in economic expansion after the railway boom, the failure of political action to halt the influx of orientals, and the emergence after 1886 of international craft unionism which was more conducive to collective bargaining in industries where unionism proved most feasible. Locals of printers, moulders, shipwrights, and building trades predominated at the time and while many were originally purely local organizations, most eventually affiliated with the international organizations. By 1889 the urban craft unions were numerous enough to form city Trades and Labour Councils in Victoria and Vancouver. The third union concentration at Nanaimo centred on the miners and Coast Seamen's Union. Union expansion also took place along the railway in the form of the railroad brotherhoods after 1886, but their association with the rest of organized labour was minimal. As a consequence, they did not take any part in the first provincial labour federation, the short-lived, politically-oriented Federated Labour Congress organized in 1890.

On a somewhat smaller scale, the same general pattern prevailed on the Prairies. The first few craft unions appeared in Winnipeg in 1881, all with international connections.[18] Then, as in British Columbia, the injection of railway investment coincided with the entry of the Knights of Labour. The first assemblies were formed in Winnipeg in 1884 providing general coverage, including the CPR shops. They also were involved in co-operative activities and in establishing a short-lived Winnipeg labour council before they declined in the later years of the decade. Winnipeg's second labour council, comparable to the Vancouver and Victoria bodies, was organized in 1894. Again, the decline of the Knights was hastened by the rise of the craft unions. However, in the Prairies there was but one urban union concentration, in Winnipeg, based on the skilled crafts, and no resource-based unions comparable to the Nanaimo miners. What was far more important in the Prairies was the spread of the railway brotherhoods.

Thus, with the decline of the Knights of Labour, the labour movement, such as it was, was composed of three major groups: the urban crafts dominated by the building trades who were fairly easily organized in the construction boom associated with the opening of the West and who played an important role in the organization of the city labour councils; the resource-based miners and associated trades around Nanaimo; and the widely dispersed railway unions largely isolated from other labour organizational centres.

Basically, throughout the Prairie regions this pattern remained for some time except in the south west of Alberta. As the *Labour Gazette* reported in 1903, "the most noteworthy feature [in Manitoba] is the extent to which the movement has been confined to the city of Winnipeg, thirty-six of the forty-six unions reported in the province being located in that city alone."[19] Outside of the railway unions, most of the thirty-six were skilled craft unions in the metal and printing building trades. In the rest of the province, there is no record of any unions except railway unions. In the Northwest Territories a similar preponderance of transportation unions existed at the turn of the century.

The major industrial development that prompted the emergence of two new union concentrations in the West was the opening of the hard-rock mining frontier in the Kootenay Valley of British Columbia and the development of coal mining centred on the Crowsnest Pass and stretching into south west Alberta. Both these developments came around the last decade of the nineteenth century coinciding with the opening of the western agricultural frontier to extensive development.

The first miners' union in the interior area, a local of the Western Federation of Miners, was formed in 1895 and by 1899 District 6 of the WFM followed with thirteen locals in British Columbia and one in Alberta, mostly embracing the metal miners but also some coal miners. In 1903 the United Mine Workers of America (UMWA) had taken over jurisdiction in the coal industry and its district organization spread rapidly through British Columbia and Alberta in the ensuing years.

The decade or so that encompassed the rise of these mining unions in western Canada was a period of crucial importance in both the growth and character of the labour movement in the West and in the legislative framework of collective bargaining. The growth manifested itself in terms of both increasing numbers of unions, and of their membership and in increased consolidation of inter-union connections, particularly of the western unions with the Trades and Labour Congress of Canada. The changing character encompassed both the rise of socialist-labour politics in the West and the growing demand for industrial unionism. The changing legislative framework was a response, not primarily to the growth of political action in labour, although this certainly played a part, but rather to a cycle of strikes that occurred in the boom conditions engendered by the rapid growth of the Western economy.

Statistics on Canadian unionism are scarce before 1911. Nevertheless, on the basis of *Labour Gazette* surveys as reported by Logan, the growth was substantial. The number of locals formed in the 1880's and which lasted until the end of the century was ten in British Columbia and eight in Manitoba and the territories.[20] The two Victoria unions formed in the sixties and still in existence forty years later brings to twenty the number of known locals by the end of the 1880's which continued on in the West. By 1902, Logan reports 161 locals in British Columbia, 81 in the Prairies, or a total of 242 in the West.[21] This, of course, cannot be interpreted as a twelve-fold increase in locals over the decade since a number of unions formed in the 1880's, in particular the Knights of Labour, did not last until 1902. A five-fold increase may be a more reasonable estimate but in any case the growth was rapid. By the end of 1906 the *Labour Gazette* figures are 154 for

British Columbia and 186 for the Prairies, a total of 340.[22] In 1902 the western locals represented 22.5 percent of the Canadian total, by the end of 1906, 26.7 percent.

The second aspect of growth after the turn of the century was the spread of inter-union organization including a spate of city labour councils in virtually all of the major urban centres of Saskatchewan and Alberta. There were also eight labour councils in British Columbia. More significant perhaps was the development of connections with the TLC. Previously the West had had little identification with the supposedly national organization.

> Geographically, the Congress [TLC] was, until 1889 when it held its convention in Montreal, for all practical purposes an Ontario organization, and down to the end of the century its meetings were composed largely of delegates from the two provinces, Quebec and Ontario . . . distance proved a barrier to direct contact, and the affairs of the west were dealt with by the Congress on the basis of correspondence between it and the trades councils of Victoria and Vancouver . . . Manitoba and the Northwest took little part before the holding of the convention in Winnipeg in 1898.[23]

It is interesting to note that Ralph Smith of the Nanaimo Miners, TLC president from 1898 to 1902, was soon expressing reservations about the Americanization of the craft union movement.[24] However, in 1902 the AF of L achieved control over the TLC thus contributing to the alienation of the West from the central body, a trend that culminated in the One Big Union movement after the First World War.

The changing political character of the Western movement in the period was noticeable in the rise of socialist and labourist politics within labour. Several results of this "political explosion" in the West should be noted. First was the electoral (and legislative success in British Columbia) of Labour and Socialist candidates. Second, the growing socialist influence observable in British Columbia and in Manitoba was closely allied with industrial unionism, both in fact and in sentiment. It is most observable in the frenetic union and strike behaviour in the West. The unskilled railway workers and supporting trades were most significant, but the conservative running trade brotherhoods gave little or no support to these strikes and in fact were usually charged with actively opposing them.

The culmination of the strike movement which had the effect of welding the West together was the United Brotherhood of Railway Employees (UBRE) strike in 1903. While support for the strike was considerable among many labour bodies in the West, craft unions and labour councils included, opposition came from the headquarters of the established craft unions and railway brotherhoods who apparently feared the socialist and industrial union sentiment that backed the strike. Hence they helped defeat the strike. They were aided by a federal royal commission (whose secretary was Mackenzie King) which, contrary to the bulk of the evidence presented, declared the strike a great American-socialist conspiracy "to sweep all employees of the Canadian Pacific Railway into the United Brotherhood, and all coal miners into the Western Federation."[25] Another labour dispute of major proportions was the coal strike in District 18 in 1907 which threatened the winter fuel supply for the Prairies.

These strikes deserve special notice, not only because they reflect the spiral of aggressive unionism in the West in the boom period of the western frontier, but also because they initiated much of the Canadian labour legislation that was passed at the time and which subsequently governed industrial relations in the country for almost half a century. Among these were the Conciliation Act of 1900, the British Columbia Trade Union Act of 1902, the Railway Labour Disputes Act of 1903 and the Industrial Disputes and Investigation Act of 1907. The strikes also prompted the 1903 Royal Commission whose recommendations influenced Mackenzie King's industrial relations policies which were to prevail until the Second World War. The fact that the West set the tone of industrial relations legislation and government intervention policies speaks eloquently of a qualitative difference between the west and the east reflecting the importance to the West of large and critical industries, railways and mines in particular.

Western economic growth after the initial boom, although somewhat unstable, was accompanied by continued union growth. From 1903 to 1911 the number of union locals in the west rose by almost 70 percent, outstripping the east. Railway locals continued to lead in numbers but increasingly urban trades and miners' organizations led in growth. Also, strong inter-union organization, in particular the British Columbia and Alberta federations were created. At the same time the gulf between the western and eastern movements widened perceptibly as patience in the West with conservative craft unionism grew short. At the 1911 TLC convention in Calgary with western delegates predominating, the Congress endorsed industrial over craft unionism and elected a young British Columbia socialist as president. But the following year the Congress met in the east with the west underrepresented and the industrial union policy was emasculated. From that point on, the issue became increasingly divisive, an important cause of western dissatisfaction with existing union institutions.

The exuberance of western unionism was somewhat dampened by the prewar depression that followed the end of railway construction.

The slowdown affected all of western labour as indicated by the following table.

Table 1 - MEMBERSHIP AND UNION LOCALS IN WESTERN CANADA*

	1911		1914		1915	
	B.C.	Prairies	B.C.	Prairies	B.C.	Prairies
Union locals	231	353	235	427	216	400
Union locals reporting membership	162	233	122	249	120	239
Membership reported	22,599	19,974	13,017	22,006	10,757	18,912

*Source: Labour Organization in Canada, 1912, 1914, 1915.

It was two years after the outbreak of war that economic conditions improved to the point that unions once more began to expand. By 1918 membership had almost doubled. At first east-west union relations were more harmonious (despite some dissension between the anti-war minority and the pro-war majority) given the western strength in the TLC executive and the common stand taken against conscription. The rupture of this tenuous harmony came at the 1917 and 1918 conventions, first with the reversal of policy on conscription in 1917. Then in 1918 at Quebec came the repudiation by the Congress of industrial unionism, the defeat, by fair means or foul of the more radical western candidates for the executive, and the refusal to support western wartime political demands. These changes provided the immediate background to western revolt.

Why was the eastern leadership so anxious to obliterate the radical position which was concentrated in the West, and why was it able to do so? H. C. Pentland has suggested a plausible explanation for the first. Given the economic conditions during the war, with high employment, rising inflation and war profiteering, there was a growing desire and ability to organize, particularly in the east where economic conditions improved earlier than in the west. The appeal of militant industrial organization associated with western leadership was increasing among newly organized and unorganized eastern workers who had only a limited place in traditional conservative craft unionism. To maintain the dominance of the existing orthodox unionism it was felt necessary to eliminate the radical challenge. As Pentland states:

> It had a relationship, though one impossible to specify exactly, with the unionization of previously unorganized eastern workers for whom industrial unionism was very suitable. There was a considerable possibility, therefore, that the radical western unionists could carry a substantial number of eastern unionists with them into a new organization.[26]

The traditional union hierarchy was able to turn back the challenge within the Congress, not only because the conventions were held in the east with the west under-represented, but also as a result of the resurgence of unionism in central Canada with the wartime conditions, and the control that the international union "roadmen" or full-time union representatives had over the delegates from these unions.

The failure of the TLC to deal with western grievances led to the calling of the western caucus and ultimately to the formation of the One Big Union movement. Many of these grievances, as the Robson Commission found, were directly related to the Winnipeg General Strike and the host of other strikes in the West at the time, including

> ... the high cost of living, long hours, low wages, poor working conditions, profiteering, the growing 'intelligence' of the working class concerning the inequalities of modern society, and the refusal of the employers to recognize labour's right to bargain collectively ...[27]

While the suppression of the Winnipeg strike may have indeed, as Pentland has suggested, "[sapped] the strength and drawing power of the local consumer market, and [dissuaded] employers from making the effort to improve efficiency and to innovate, ..."[28] it was felt necessary to prevent the emergence of an independent radical industrial unionism in western Canada. Government and employers were not the only forces ranged against the strikers. The international unions, fearing the western movement's influence in challenging the conservative craft hegemony over the Canadian labour movement, played a significant part. As Professor Masters has said of the Winnipeg General Strike trails, "One cannot escape the conviction that the real prisoner in the dock was the OBU ..."[29] Despite the defeat of the strike and the persecution of its leaders, the OBU retained a measure of vitality until it was defeated by the combined influence of the sharp postwar depression and the concerted opposition of the international unions.

Union membership declined in the wake of the depression but, even when recovery took place, the western labour movement was spent and unable to throw up new waves of mass organization. It is difficult to escape the conclusion that the combined forces of economic depression and international business unionism had delivered to employers a docile craft unionism, uninterested in organizing the mass of nonskilled industrial workers and largely incapable even of retaining its own market power because in destroying the industrial unions spawned in the West, it had removed the main inducement of the employers to seek accommodation with the craft unions.

New manifestations of discontent with the dominant union institutions in the form, first of the All Canadian Congress of Labour and later the Workers' Unity League, appeared in the late 1920's as membership in the four western provinces rose in the decade 1920-31 by 50 percent, slightly exceeding the rate of nonagricultural labour force growth. More unexpected growth occurred during the 1930's when western membership rose by almost 10 percent. Almost all of this growth occurred in the primary industries through the agency of a new union structure that finally broke through the constraints of the orthodox craft union hegemony which had prevailed since the defeat of the western movement after World War I. Certainly the Workers' Unity League played an important initiating role but it was the rise of the Congress of Industrial Organizations unions which ultimately encompassed the majority of WUL affiliates and leaders. They provided the locus and mechanism for organizing the primary industries of the west, in particular in British Columbia, and the mass production industries of the east which had resisted organization under craft divisions. This also supports the argument that the surge of unionism after 1935 was not primarily related to legislative changes, such as the Wagner Act in the United States, as is often assumed, but rather to a more pervasive and widespread influence.

Thus, it can be argued that the movement of social and industrial unionism that had been spawned in the west of Canada against the control of orthodox business unionism with its connections and compromises with the dominant business elite of the east, gave way to a more powerful wave of militant unionism based not just in dependent regions but also in those very industries that the conservative leadership had feared would rally to the western cause in the earlier period.

The spread of federal authority during World War II, particularly after P.C. 1003 in 1944 which granted compulsory union recognition, encouraged already burgeoning union membership. Regional divisions were, however, limited by the existence of two labour congresses covering industrial and craft workers, low unemployment and rising prices, and the existence of a viable labour-oriented party with roots in the West. At the same time, internal conflicts between congresses and with communist unions and leadership (in part a manifestation of the cold war) directed attention inward.

Table II - WESTERN CANADIAN UNIONISM*

	End 1939	End 1946	Beginning 1951	Beginning 1955
Union locals	1022	1475	1757	1963
Locals reporting Membership	950	1261	1588	1742
Membership	85,481	193,565	257,100	300,150
Percentage of Canadian Membership	23	23	25	29

*Source: *Labour Organization in Canada, 1939, 1946, 1950 and 1955.*

By 1956 when the two congresses merged much had changed. These changes included uncertain economic conditions, rapid technological change, the challenge of growing white collar employment, and most important, a decline in the national integration of the Canadian economy. It is difficult to escape the conclusion that the existing union structure is at least partially unsuited to the western economy if not, in fact, to the Canadian economy. The western region is no longer the hinterland for eastern Canadian interest but rather for the multinational corporation centred in the United States.

Western Labour and the National Policy - An Interpretation

A central theme of this paper is that the economic structure of the West fostered by the national policy has had a pervasive effect on the structure and course of western labour organization. Regional isolation no doubt played a part in dividing the Canadian Labour movement but it was the difference in economic interests which appears more significant. The unprotected nature of western output meant greater fluctuations in demand and price which created greater insecurities of employment and wages and much of the union organization can be explained as reaction to these insecurities, to frontier conditions, and to the commercial attitudes of the frontier employers who wanted to shift as much of the entrepreneurial risk onto the employees as possible. Because these pressures were different in unprotected natural resource industries and because the possible solutions varied considerably from those that could be applied to the east, the modes, methods and policies of western labour could be expected to vary from its eastern counterpart. This is most apparent in eastern labour's support of tariff protection and resulting community of interest with employers.[30] No such accommodation was possible in the West.

Thus, western union sentiment favoured industrial, radical (socialist) class unionism, naturally considered more threatening by employers than the conservative, craft-oriented business unionism dominant in the east. Western sentiment, therefore, was also a threat to the established union structure, nurtured in the protected eastern regions of the United States and Canada. Significantly, radical industrial unionism was a feature of western North America, not just of Canada. The West took to unionism from the beginning because of the great insecurity that prevailed on the resource frontier - but it also took to a very much more militant and class-conscious type of union. Thus when contact was established between west and east after a quarter century of western unionism, peaceful relations were not to be expected.

The particular pattern of western union growth must be interpreted in terms of the perceived benefits and costs of forming and maintaining unions by the workers involved. A change in either benefits or costs will affect the growth and behaviour of labour organizations. Benefits are best conceived of in terms of broadly defined worker security including economic, social and personal "prestige" security. Thus, unemployment, accidents, illness, discriminatory discharge, automation, wage decreases, short-time and inflation are obvious threats. Less apparent but nonetheless real are changes in relative wages, or hours of a particular group or a decline in the workers' control of the work environment. As Hobsbawm has argued, a general expansion of labour organization may be expected to occur when a significant group of workers becomes less well off.[31] This will hold whether the decline is relative or absolute.

Increased insecurity is not a sufficient cause of union expansion. The costs must also be appraised - costs in terms not only of barriers to organization raised by economic conditions and by employers and government but also of the political and co-operative alternatives. Costs will tend to vary with such variables as the level of employment, the degree of skill protection, employer and government attitudes, worker solidarity and technology.

Significantly, unionism in the West appeared first among small numbers of skilled workers, not easily replaced, during rapid economic development and without particular opposition from employers or government. The successful spread of the railway brotherhoods likewise reflects low barriers to organization. In this context, the high capital/labour ratio of the railways is probably an important cause. In contrast, the Nanaimo miners, faced with notorious working conditions and wage insecurities, were largely unsuccessful in organizing given the fanatic opposition of Dunsmuir and the large minority of oriental workers. Immobile, unacculturized and docile under threats of deportation, they constantly undermined worker solidarity.

The importance of these barriers is accentuated by comparison with the successful unionism of the interior miners. During the boom period of 1896-1910 both skilled and unskilled labourers were scarce and much of the labour force was drawn from the United States copper region and from Britain, both areas where a strong tradition of union solidarity already existed. Of particular importance, however, was the fact that unlike the coast area, the threat of replacement by oriental workers was minimal or nonexistent. Nor were the employers as determined to resist unionism while local legislators gave considerable support to labour.

The ascendancy of the Knights of Labour in the boom of the 1880's is particularly interesting. The railway-induced expansion produced a shortage of labour, particularly among unskilled labour[32] and the fact that the Knights operated as an industrial or general labour union made it a popular form of organization. At the same time, its structure and goals were amenable to political action and hence became a vehicle for the battle to limit oriental immigration. Its decline coincided with the end of boom conditions and the strengthening of the craft unions.

The labour movement in the West as an important and significant economic institution should probably be dated from the 1890's. Almost immediately a process of disaffection with the eastern movement became apparent as economic interests diverged. Despite conflicts of interest, however, bonds were not stretched to the breaking point until the strains of war exacerbated these conflicts. The trend, however, can be seen in certain turning points, the first being the "takeover" of the Canadian congress by the AFL in 1902,[33] which not only constrained unionism to a narrow craft path but extended the eastern hegemony over union development and policy in the West. The fruits were harvested in 1903 with the defeat of the UBRE strike.

Certain gains were made for the western interest at the 1911 Calgary convention of the TLC with the endorsement of industrial unionism and many western demands, but these positions were never accepted by the eastern hierarchy. The crisis came in the war period. Insecurity, bred by the prewar depression and the fear of postwar unemployment and by the failure of the craft unions to organize effectively in the primary industries at a time of growing employer power and hostility, sowed the seeds of discontent. Western labour looked to several possible solutions: a restructured labour movement (the OBU); political action (the various political-labour parties); and concerted strike action to force collective bargaining (the Winnipeg General Strike and the many other western strikes). For political and economic reasons these solutions engendered little support, and sometimes active opposition, from the eastern international establishment.

The postwar depression and hostility of government, international union and employer thwarted these attempts, and stagnation resulted for most of the following decade despite relatively improved economic conditions. Professor Pentland offers a plausible explanation:

> The craft unions' strategy . . . was to win employer acceptance (or toleration) of themselves by demonstrating their devotion to the established structure and, particularly, their value to the employer by their vigilant opposition to every manifestation of industrial or radical unionism - if the two did not appear together they were forced together. The price sought for this loyalty was recognition of craft unionism as a junior partner of management - a pay-off frustrated in the 1920's because employers found the existing unionism so weak that it was not worth bothering with. That is the prevalence of radical unionism had led craft unionism, in following its traditional policies to overplay its hand in 1919. But the strategy does provide part of the explanation for a phenomenon that has been held to be curious - the stagnation of unionism throughout the 1920's despite the high level of employment after 1923. [34]

It is less clear why the political organizations of western dissent, the labour parties and the Progressives also stagnated, since it has often been argued that political action is the alternative to industrial action when the costs of the latter become prohibitive because of market conditions. Professor Robin has argued a converse case, ". . . Spurts of political action can be correlated with and related to sudden leaps in the size and strength of union organization and activity whether or not the qualitative leaps in union activity are directly related to the business cycle." [35] Internal division, growing antipathy by other sectors of the community, a sense of defeat, and possibly rising real wages appear to have undermined both union and political party.

It is interesting to speculate what might have happened if the prosperity of 1928-29 had continued for several more years since new alternative institutions had begun to emerge and attract support in the West. But, of course, the depression intervened. Nevertheless, the resilience and aggressiveness of the labour movement during the thirties is somewhat surprising. Its strength was reflected not in the orthodox craft unions who reacted in traditional manner by isolation and the monopolizing of available jobs for their members, but primarily in the industrial type unions largely organized by political unionists. The high proportion of extractive industries in the West - mining in both the Prairie and British Columbia regions, lumbering, fishing and longshoring in British Columbia - were most susceptible to the new appeal.

The greatest union growth occurred among the unemployed and the West suffered disproportionately from unemployment. The importance of the unemployed movement lies not so much in its effect at the time, but rather in the attitudes of radical militance that specially young workers brought into organized labour as employment improved. Worker discontent, therefore, was channeled into the politically-motivated industrial unions and into the related unemployed organizations or into the socialist-leaning farmer - labour political party that emerged as the CCF. It is significant that the CCF was born in the West with the western unions and labour political parties acting as both parent and midwife.

The Second World War marks a major watershed both in the growth of organized labour in Canada and in the relations between east and west. Across the country unionism took a dramatic upturn in the face of improved employment conditions and a new conciliatory attitude by the federal government, which had just assumed control of national industrial relations. Yet management, particularly in the primary sector, was less willing to alter its traditional opposition to collective bargaining and it took almost four years of conflict before the federal government was forced, reluctantly it would appear, to step in to enforce collective bargaining across the country through PC 1003. Because of uninterrupted maintenance of full employment accompanied by almost continuous inflation, the spread of compulsory collective bargaining legislation to the provinces, and the continued influence of depression-bred insecurity, the West participated fully in promoting increased unionization, at least to the mid-fifties. Under such conditions, regional differences did not loom large. At the same time, the shift in the orientation of Canadian trade to American markets significantly reduced the eastern domination over the western economy. The subservience of the western frontier economy to eastern capital and industry, central to the first national policy, was largely replaced by the hegemony of the multi-national corporation over the unionized sector of the Canadian economy.

The focus of western labour discontent is therefore shifting. The West in the early part of the century rebelled against a form of unionism which was incapable of dealing with the problems raised by the economic structure of the West but was oriented to meeting the needs of a small minority of skilled workers in crafts protected by the national policy. Recent discontent, still at minimal levels, appears to be with the structure and aversion to change exhibited by the existing international, American-dominated labour movement and its failure to deal with the problems raised by the economic structure of Canada within the larger continental economy. These problems are again most noticeable in the export-oriented West where, additionally, the relative sparseness of population and the lack of large secondary industries have left some unions too small to service their locals adequately or organize the small firms. All this may suggest that, where once the West generated waves of vibrant unionism opposed to its subservience to the east, as fostered by the national policy, the same labour movement may contribute to a wave of nationalist unionism opposed to Canada's dependence on the American empire, as fostered by the lack of any national policy and the resultant continental drift.

Footnotes

1
For a fuller discussion of these problems see Kari Levitt, *Silent Surrender* (Toronto: Macmillan, 1970).

2
V. C. Fowke, *The National Policy and the Wheat Economy* (Toronto: University of Toronto Press, 1957), p. 8. See also Fowke, "National Policy - Old and New," *CJEPS*, XVIII, No. 3 (August, 1952).

3
V. C. Fowke, *Ibid.*, p. 58.

4
D. G. Creighton, *The Commercial Empire of the St. Lawrence* (Toronto: Ryerson Press, 1937).

5
V. C. Fowke, *op. cit.*, p. 67.

6
See, for example, V. C. Fowke, *An Historical Analysis of the Crows Nest Pass Agreement and Grain Rates: A Study in National Transportation Policy*, Government of Saskatchewan, 1960, p. 33.

7
Maurice Dobb, *Studies in the Development of Capitalism* (London: Routledge, Kegan and Paul, 1947), p. 194.

8

This does not imply that the national policy was not important, if not necessary, to the formation of the Canadian nation. The distribution of the costs and benefits and the failure to adapt policy to changed circumstances is, however, another matter.

9

For a more detailed discussion see R. Caves and R. Holton, *The Canadian Economy* (Cambridge: Harvard University Press, 1961), Ch. 6.

10

H. A. Innis as quoted in G. E. Britnell, *The Wheat Economy* (Toronto: University of Toronto Press, 1939), p. 23.

11

Report of the Royal Commission on Coal (Ottawa: Queen's Printer, 1946), p. 67.

12

P. A. Phillips, *Structural Change and Population Distribution in the Prairie Economy, 1911-1961*, unpublished M.A. thesis, Saskatchewan, 1963, p. 34.

13

Caves and Holton, *op cit.*, pp. 220-221.

14

H. C. Pentland, *A Study of the Changing Social, Economic and Political Background of the Canadian System of Industrial Relations*, unpublished M.S., 1968, pp. 24-26.

15

S. M. Jamieson, "Economic Instability and Industrial Conflict - The Construction Industry in British Columbia," *Industrial Relations Research Association Papers*, 1963, p. 15.

16

H. A. Logan, *Trade Unions in Canada* (Toronto: Macmillan, 1948), p. 48.

17

A brief discussion of the early labour political action can be found in T. R. Loosemore, *The British Columbia Labour Movement and Political Action, 1879-1906*, unpublished M.A. thesis, University of British Columbia, 1954, and in P. A. Phillips, *No Power Greater* (Vancouver: B. C. Federation of Labour and the Boag Foundation, 1967), p. 9. Much of the following story of B.C. Labour is based on the latter source.

18

M. Robin, *Radical Politics and Canadian Labour* (Kingston: Industrial Relations Centre, Queen's University, 1968), p. 21.

19

Labour Gazette, Vol. II, May, 1903, p. 591.

20

Logan, *op. cit.*, p. 48.

21

Ibid., p. 54

22

Pentland, *op. cit.*, p. 111. In B. C. this was a decline from a high of 216 in July of 1903.

23

Logan, *op. cit.*, p. 59. A few delegates from the West did take part in the TLC in the early 1890's. B. C. first sent three delegates in 1890.

24

See Logan, *op. cit.*, pp. 71-2.

25

Canada, *Royal Commission on Industrial Disputes in the Province of British Columbia*, 1903, p. 67.

26

Pentland, *op. cit.*, pp. 115-116.

27

K. McNaught, *Prophet in Politics* (Toronto: University of Toronto, 1959), p. 129.

28

H. C. Pentland, "Fifty Years After," *Canadian Dimension*, VI, No. 2 (July, 1969), p. 17.

29

D. C. Masters, *The Winnipeg General Strike* (Toronto: University of Toronto, 1950), p. 133.

30

See Pentland, *A Study of the Changing Social, Economic and Political Background of the Canadian System of Industrial Relations*, pp. 90-91.

31

E. J. Hobsbawm, "Economic Fluctuations and Some Social Movements Since 1800," *Economic History Review*, Second Series, Vol. 5, No. 1.

32

Pentland, A *Study of the Changing Social, Economic and Political Background of the Canadian System of Industrial Relations*, pp. 90-91.

33

Ibid., pp. 134-137.

34

Ibid., p. 107. It can also be argued that, at least in some parts of the West, unemployment did not fall to a level that significantly lowered the costs of organizing until very late in the decade.

35

Robin, *op. cit.*, p. 292.

Animals, Fire and Landscape in the Northwestern Plains of North America in Pre and Early European Days*

J. G. Nelson

Few North Americans have an accurate image of what the land was like before the arrival of the white man. This study aims to help fill this gap by providing information on: 1) the diversity and quantity of animal life in the northwestern plains area in pre and early European days; 2) the effects of these animals and of fire on the landscape; and, 3) the significance of these effects for certain problems of long-standing interest to students of the Canadian West, an example being the differing perceptions of plains aridity exhibited by Palliser, Macoun and other nineteenth century visitors.

The study is based on a review of historical records and secondary sources as well as on some field work. It is part of a larger investigation of landscape change in the Cypress Hills area of southern Alberta, southern Saskatchewan and northern Montana (Figure 1).[1] In this larger study the Cypress Hills area is examined not so much for its own sake as because its isolated position between the Missouri and South Saskatchewan resulted in its being an end point for the waves of change that proceeded up these rivers with the advance of the white man. The Cypress Hills is a mirror of the recent landscape history of much of the northern plains and a measure of the profound environmental impact of the white man in the short span of about two hundred years.

The journals and reports of fur traders and travellers such as Anthony Hendry, David Thompson, Peter Fidler, Lewis and Clark and John Palliser strongly reflect the abundance and variety of animal life in the Cypress Hills area in the eighteenth and nineteenth centuries. Buffalo, elk, antelope, wolves, big horn sheep, cougars and other cats, beaver and other fur-bearers, the grizzly bear, ground squirrels — all were common in their thousands and millions. Birds also were multitudinous - plovers, pigeons, hawks, eagles, ducks, geese innumerable. One is reminded of photographs of parts of Africa, of plains swarming with animal life of all kinds.

---

*This essay constitutes Chapter XI of *The Last Refuge* by J. G. Nelson to be published by Harvest House in 1972.

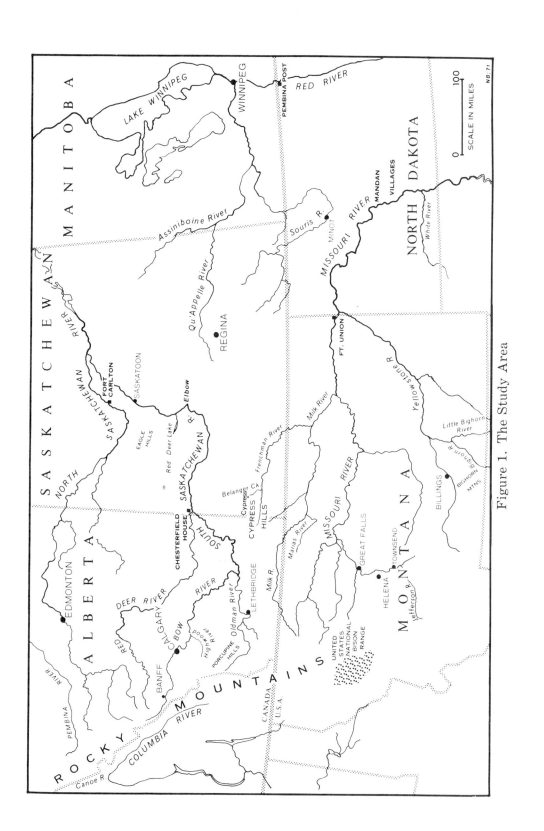

Figure 1. The Study Area

Animal Variety and Numbers

Many early descriptions of animal variety and numbers are found in the journals of the Americans, Lewis and Clark.[2] On April 26, 1805, while travelling west along the Missouri toward the Rockies, they reached the country around the mouth of the Yellowstone River, where the plains spread themselves before the eye "animated by vast herds of buffalo, deer, elk and antelope." By early May Lewis and Clark had advanced to the junction of the Missouri and the Milk River which drains the southern side of the Cypress Hills. Here wildlife was so plentiful that it became "a mere amusement to supply the party with provisions." The bison were numerous enough to be a definite hindrance to travel and so gentle that the men were "obliged to drive them out of the way with sticks and stones." The ravages of the beaver were very apparent; the woods in one place were reported as being "entirely prostrated for a distance of three acres in front of the river, and one in depth, and a great part of it removed, although the trees were in large quantities and some of them as thick as the body of a man."

Peter Fidler's Chesterfield House journals (Figure 1) show that the northern side of the Cypress Hills also was incredibly rich in wildlife.[3] During his trip up the South Saskatchewan in early fall, 1800, this Hudson's Bay Company trader encountered many bison and other animals. One creek reportedly was "entirely full of beaver." Dams were located every twenty to forty yards along the stream bed. Near the Elbow of the South Saskatchewan, elk could be observed all along the river wherever there were "small woods" of any kind. In this vicinity Fidler also witnessed a grizzly attack on some bison. The bear chased the animals into the river and swam after them, "cutting the sinews of both hind legs of a young bull." By the time Fidler and his men reached the bear, over a distance of about a tenth of a mile, it had skinned much of the buffalo and was enjoying a hearty meal. At least eight bears were seen by Fidler's party in the next few days and the animals continued to be numerous throughout the remainder of the journey to the site of Chesterfield House, near the junction of the Red Deer and the South Saskatchewan.

During his months at Chesterfield House, Fidler made numerous references to wildlife, notably the bison — the staff of life for the trader. The wanderings of this animal sometimes brought it near the post and sometimes took it far away. For example, in December, 1800, very few could be found nearby. By early January, however, the bison were very plentiful, and immense numbers were seen on January 11, 1802 when, as Fidler said, "the ground literally was black with them for a great distance."

Buffalo, deer, antelope, wolves and other animals were sometimes observed in large associated groups, one reason being that predators such as the wolf fed on the young, infirm and old animals. Palliser described his encounter with such groups when presenting some details on a hunt north of Calgary on July 31, 1858:

> Having ascended the slightly elevated ridge we then beheld our game, four or five thousand buffalo, some lying down, some grazing with old bulls on the outskirts. At our appearance the wolves who almost invariably accompany bands of buffalo sneaked out and around, eagerly watching our movements, and perfectly aware that the events about to come off were to terminate in an abundant meal after the field was left to themselves. A few antelope were gracefully moving near the buffalo, and over the heads of all noisily soared some crows and ravens, and appeared quite aware that something was in the wind . . .[4]

While in the Highwood Valley area in 1787, David Thompson saw a similar association of animals. The herds of bull bison came first, followed by the cows and then by "small herds of doe and red deer," wolves and foxes. Such masses of wildlife placed heavy pressures on the grass and forage; the animals observed by Thompson were said to have come north from the Missouri country after eating "the ground bare of grass" in that quarter.[5]

The Bison Landscape: Grazing, Walking, Wallowing and Other Effects

Similar observations of heavy grazing, notably by bison, have been made elsewhere in the northern plains. For example, on August 2, 1805, the Canadian trader, François Larocque, noted that the grass along a stream near the Big Horn Mountains of present-day Montana had "been completely eaten by buffalo and deer."[6] On October 3, 1857, the Palliser expedition camped near the Red Deer Lakes, south of Fort Carlton and the North Saskatchewan River where the buffalo were very numerous and had "eaten the grass down considerably." On June 23, 1858, while near the Eagles Hills, not far from Carlton, the members of the expedition camped by a swamp "containing miserable herbage which had been cropped bare by the buffaloes . . ."

Aside from heavy grazing, the bison and associated animals affected the landscape in other ways. The ground was frequently marked with deep trails or paths, especially near streams and river valleys. Such paths often were referred to by travellers; for example, while near the forks of the North and South Saskatchewan in 1808, Alexander Henry (the Younger) described "deep beaten paths, where the buffalo ford the river."[7]

The bison also disturbed the ground by wallowing, that is by rolling in the dust or mud, apparently for a variety of reasons, including the desire to escape insect attacks when the winter coat was lost in spring. The resulting depressions were not uncommonly about forty feet long, fifteen feet wide and a foot deep and extended over a large area. When Matthew Cocking was somewhere in the triangle between the North and South Saskatchewan rivers in 1772 he stated that: "All over the Country where buffalo resort were many hollow places in the ground . . ." He attributed these to the agitation of the bulls in the rutting season.[8]

The bison also deposited large quantities of dung, other organic debris and bones upon the landscape. The dung was laid down in sufficient quantities to serve as fuel for the campfires of generations of Indians as well as many fur traders and settlers. The bones were copious enough to provide employment for thousands of natives, Métis and early white settlers who sold them for manufacture into fertilizer and other purposes in the 1880's. An impression of the organic productivity of the bison can be gleaned from the writings of the Hudson's Bay Company man, Isaac Cowie, who fell in with a large number of the animals north of the Qu'Appelle River, in present-day Saskatchewan, in 1869. As he described it:

> Our route took us into the midst of the herd, which opened in front and closed behind the train of carts like water round a ship, . . . the earth trembled day and night, . . . as they moved . . . over the inclinations of the plains. Every drop of water on our way was foul and yellow with their wallowings and excretions.[9]

Other travellers' accounts remind us that the Prairies rang with different sounds in the buffalo days. One of the best descriptions of the noise of the buffalo has been given by the naturalist, J. J. Audubon. While on a barge running down the Missouri near Fort Union on August 20, 1843, he ran into large numbers of bison whose sound made a deep impression on him. "Thousands and thousands of Buffalo," he wrote, "the roaring of these animals resembles the grunting of hogs, with a rolling sound from the throat." The next day the buffalo could be seen all along the river banks and bars, "with many swimming; the roaring could be heard for miles."[10]

Observations on Present Wildlife Reserves

Some further appreciation of the impact of the bison on landscape can be gained by studying present national parks and wildlife reserves. The

United States National Bison Range in Montana, and Wood Buffalo National Park in northern Alberta, contain hundreds and thousands of bison respectively. However, the effects of these animals on landscape undoubtedly are different than on the plains in the past. Grazing of the bison on the Montana reserve is controlled by fencing and other means. Nevertheless, numerous well-developed wallows can be observed in various parts of the range.[11] The bison of Wood Buffalo Park roam freely over thousands of square miles, with much less control over their activities. But their numbers are occasionally reduced by shooting in attempts to control anthrax and other diseases. It is doubtful, therefore, if observations in Wood Buffalo or other present-day reserves provide an accurate replica of the effects of the bison in the Cypress Hills country and other parts of the northwestern plains in the past.

Nevertheless, observations in wildlife refuges do confirm and elaborate on certain of the effects described in the historical sources. Some of the most interesting information has been provided by J. Dewey Soper, a biologist, who worked in Wood Buffalo National Park in the 1930's.[12] According to Soper, multitudes of dry wallows are among the outstanding signs of bison occupation:

> Most of these are created during the height of the fly season when the animals roll furiously every day to dislodge swarms of mosquitoes and "bulldogs." In doing this, round or elliptically shallow depressions are eroded in the ground, stripped of all vegetation, and in the majority of cases, the top soil is also completely removed.

> These hollows are normally rather superficial, saucer-like and from six to fifteen feet in diameter; depth varies from mere impression when new, to a foot or more when old ... While usually on level ground, some are located on gentle hillsides; in such cases the inner portion may be cut down a full three feet so as to be levelled off to the lower rim. The great majority of the wallows are seen on sandy ridges among the pines, or on similar ground of broader uplands. A few are met with in harder clay.

In referring to a particularly magnificent compound wallow Soper says:

> In this and similar fly-fighting bivouacs, the wallows are thickly situated in glades and among the trees. Their edges often meet, or overlap, and in some cases become so completely merged that the ground over a wide space appears as one large cantonment. In semi-open forest the wallows are necessarily hedged about by trees which from the violent actions of the animals have the bark deeply scored, frayed, or entirely removed ...

Soper found that the bison trails in Wood Buffalo Park formed a great network covering hundreds of square miles. Many of the trails were small and not particularly impressive. However, as

> they necessarily converge upon the better secondary trails ... they become increasingly worn until the climax of wear and tear is reached on the trunk highways ... From these the innumerable routes spread fan-like in all directions to local or more distant pastures. Trails which lead to superior wallowing and feeding areas are always conspicuous ... Trail depth varies widely depending on the nature of the ground and the amount of the traffic. On hard, semi-baked prairie, for example, only a moderate impression is made, though the general run of ordinary trails is from three to six inches deep. Where major trails occur on acute slopes, rains often tend to deepen the cuts. In some situations erosion may be so great, together with boulder outwash, as to cause abandonment in favour of new, parallel routes.

Soper also comments on the effects of bison on vegetation. According to him the clearest visible mark of the animal on plants is shown on rubbing trees or rubbing posts:

> Trees habitually used are rubbed smooth, the bark completely removed and the wood polished to a glossy amber or mahogany colour. Examples are commonly noted with the rind thus entirely ripped off from near the ground to a height of six or seven feet ...

> The great majority of larger trees used (and these chiefly pines) though completely girdled, still remain alive ... Many young pines and spruces are overridden, ... broken, torn up by the roots, and destroyed. Willow thickets are sometimes so thoroughly slashed, ... as to be literally beaten to death. In such scenes, depicting almost cyclonic violence, the ponderous, swashbuckling power of the bison becomes very real indeed.

Soper also saw the bison as a possibly very important source of fertilizer. In his opinion the buffalo "chips" from many thousands of animals must have had a positive effect on soils and vegetation. "Anyone who has seen the great quantities of this material, distributed in a single season, over plain and meadow, is impressed with the possibilities."

Overall, however, Soper thought that the bison of Wood Buffalo National Park had little lasting effect on the landscape. Their impressions notably in the form of trails and wallows, were "of a more or less ephemeral nature." Owing to the vast extent and perennial growth of the forest, their effects on vegetation were considered as quite insignificant, "fleeting losses," of no "measurable or lasting effect." The principal areas of denudation were located around waterholes or the approaches to stream fords; "at sink hole ponds in semi-wooded, or open prairie land, the habitual campaigning of herds utterly destroys the turf, to be replaced by wastes of naked earth."

How applicable are Soper's conclusions to the present study? In the first place his ideas must be questioned on conceptual grounds. At times, at least, he thinks of the bison as somewhat distinct from other elements of the landscape or ecosystem. For example, in discussing the wallows and trails made by the bison in Wood Buffalo National Park, he says that "were these outgrowths not periodically renewed, they would soon be obliterated by the normal forces of nature." This suggests that the bison was not a "normal" part of the landscape, something with which many observers would disagree. Certainly the animal can be thought of as exotic, as many plains buffalo were introduced into Wood Buffalo Park from reserves on the plains in the 1920's. However, that type of buffalo known as the wood bison has lived in the area for many centuries. Furthermore, the bison is very much a part of the landscape today, persistently living in and working through large parts of the park year after year. It is true that some of its effects are clearly uneven, apparent in one place for a time and then in another. On the other hand these effects are repeated over a period of years and many trails, wallows and other features are maintained in one location for long periods of time.

This brings us to a second major point, that the effects of the bison were undoubtedly more intense and widespread in the Cypress Hills country in the past than they are in Wood Buffalo National Park today. In their heyday, tens of thousands of bison lived in and worked through the country around the Cypress Hills. Their numbers and the extent of their wanderings may well have varied over the years. Fires, hard winters and other influences might have kept many of them out of much of the area for a year or so. But in the long run the great herds were an integral part of the landscape. Under such circumstances heavy grazing must have been a frequent or normal effect in the Cypress Hills country. Indeed, at least one biologist has suggested that the grazing of the bison helped to maintain short grass vegetation over large parts of the northern plains.[13]

Other bison effects, such as wallowing and trail networks, must also have been widespread in the past. Soper's observations of the destruction of vegetation around water holes in Wood Buffalo National Park spring to mind in this regard. Soper said that such areas tended to become "wastes of naked earth." Certain historical sources suggest that when the plains bison were multitudinous, such wastes were more widespread and frequent in occurrence. While near Great Falls, Montana in mid-July, 1805, Lewis and Clark reported that their men were busy putting double soles on their moccasins in order to protect their feet against the sharp pinnacles of earth turned up by bison trampling grassland wet by recent rains. The pinnacles hardened and stood up in such numbers that the men found it impossible to avoid their hackle-like points. Such effects would be expected each time there was an appropriate combination of weather, clay soils and large numbers of bison.

The Beaver

Like the buffalo, the beaver was a major force behind the creation of a distinct type of landscape. It built innumerable dams and reorganized drainage over large areas. Ponds and swamps were widespread. These drainage changes also had their effect on vegetation, with marsh growth undoubtedly attracting certain animals, for example the moose.

References to such effects are fairly frequent in the Lewis and Clark journals.[14] For example, on May 8, 1805, while Lewis was travelling along the Missouri, near the mouth of the Milk River, he stated that there was "great appearance of beaver on this river, and I have no doubt but that they continue abundant, there being plenty of cottonwood and willow, the timber on which they subsist." Many beaver also were observed near Townsend, Montana, in late July, 1805. The animals dammed up the small channels between islands and caused the river to cut new routeways. Some channels eventually were filled with mud, sand, gravel and driftwood. This process compelled the beaver to move to another site. Lewis and Clark concluded that the beaver was very instrumental in adding to the number of islands crowding the river.

The beaver often made travel difficult. On July 30, 1805, while moving along the Jefferson River, a few miles beyond the forks of the Missouri, members of the Lewis and Clark expedition encountered many large beaver dams and "bayoes." In order to avoid these obstacles they had to climb up onto the plains and in the process were often submerged to their waists in mud and water. Not long afterwards, while still near the Jefferson River, Lewis saw "some very large beaver dams . . . several of which were five feet high and overflowed several acres of land." The dams were formed of willow brush, mud and gravel "so closely interwoven that they resist the water perfectly."

Excellent descriptions of the beaver landscape are available from places outside but close to the Cypress Hills area. For example, on October 22, 1754, while Anthony Hendry was in the plains-foothills fringe, not far from the present town of Red Deer, Alberta, he described the country as "Level land with poplars; and great many Creeks and ponds, with plenty of Beaver Houses." The next day his Indian companions killed ten beaver, but Hendry said that they might have slain two hundred if they had wished.

The Bison and Beaver Landscape

The foregoing makes it clear that the Cypress Hills country was far different in the years prior to the invasion of the white man than today. One can think in terms of two major landscapes. The first, that of the bison, was predominant, being characterized by numerous associated animals, much short grass, many wallows, extensive trail systems, great quantities of dung, bones, organic debris and a different set of sounds and smells as well. The second major landscape, that of the beaver, was concentrated in the valleys and beds of the rivers and creeks. It was marked by dams, extensive ponds in various stages of infilling with river sediment, marsh and swamp vegetation, and by associated animals such as moose and ducks.

Other Animals and Their Effects

While the bison and the beaver appear to have had the most profound effects on landscape, they were rivalled by other wildlife, particularly the various burrowing animals of the plains. The prairie dog and other ground squirrels all dug dens and extensive passages in the ground, as did the wolf, the coyote and the now nearly extinct kit fox. Lewis and Clark frequently refer to the effects of these animals, notably those of the prairie dog. The Americans called this animal "the barking squirrel" because of the noise it makes when disturbed. Described as light brick-red in colour, except for its lighter underside, the animal was said to weigh between three and three and a half pounds and to be about one and a half feet long. According to Lewis, these prairie dogs

> generally associate in large societies placing their burrows near one another and frequently occupy in this manner, several hundred acres of land . . . they feed on the grass and weeds within the limits of their village which they never appear to exceed on any occasion. As they are usually numerous they keep the grass and weeds within their district very closely grazed and as clear as if it had been swept.

The extent of the prairie dog villages was often remarkable. On September 17, 1804, while going up the Missouri near the mouth of the

White River, Lewis encountered a burrow-ridden plain which was about one mile wide and three miles long. On August 5, 1805, when a few miles below the Marias River, Lewis and Clark came upon a colony so large that they travelled for seven miles through "a skirt" of its territory.[15]

Another organism that undoubtedly had profound though periodic effects on the landscape was the locust. Sometimes these insects did not come for years, but when they struck they consumed much of the vegetation in their path. The members of the Palliser expedition observed one outburst in the eastern plains in early August, 1857. While camped near the Pembina River, they were visited by a violent southwestern wind and dense clouds, among which the lightning played vividly, without producing a thunder storm. One of the low clouds was found to consist of myriads of grasshoppers. A breeze from the east caused the insects to begin falling like snow. During the next day or so of travel, the expedition was handicapped by the effects of these insects. The soils in the area were reportedly poor, being sandy and stony, so that grass grew "only in swampy places;" but this herbage was further reduced by the ravages of the swarming grasshoppers and it became difficult to find enough feed for the horses.[16]

Fire

Fire had a far greater effect on landscape prior to white invasion than it does today.[17] Grass fires were caused by lightning or by man. The Indians set them accidentally or deliberately for signals, hunting, war or other purposes. White travellers set fires for similar reasons or in new ways, for example, by introducing wood- and coal-burning railroad engines which threw sparks along their route. The resulting conflagrations often were very extensive, covering thousands of square miles.

A grass fire of immense proportions was described by Henry Youle Hind in the eastern and central Canadian plains in the late 1850's. As he reported it:

> From beyond the South Branch of the Saskatchewan to the Red River all the prairies were burnt last autumn, a vast conflagration extended for one thousand miles in length and several hundreds in breadth . . . we traced the fire from the 49th parallel to the 53rd and from the 90th to the 107th degree of longitude. It extended no doubt to the Rockie Mountains.[18]

Grass fires were not always raging infernos, but could be rather gentle slow moving affairs, depending on fuel supply, wind and other variables. However, many of the fires generated sufficient heat to destroy or damage poplars and other trees, thereby contributing to the maintenance and at times to the extension of the grasslands into the surrounding parkland and forests.

A considerable amount of control over large grass fires was achieved in southern Alberta and the Cypress Hills country in the early 1900's, although substantial blazes still occur today in areas where the grass is unbroken for long distances by roads and cultivated fields. Some scholars have claimed that, as a result of fire control, areas which formerly were grassland have been invaded by trees, notably the poplars, whose sprouts are no longer removed from their suckering roots every few years by fire.

Grass fires also affected other parts of the landscape. The upper organic layer of the soil was sometimes severely burned. Animals also fell victim to the flames, especially in the spring when the flightless young ducks, hens, and other birds were especially vulnerable. Large mammals were affected as well; some early travellers came upon buffalo which had been killed, injured or blinded by fires. Perhaps the most vivid of these accounts is that of Alexander Henry (the Younger) who saw fire work its course through bison near Pembina Post in the Red River Valley on November 25, 1804. As he expressed it, the plains were

> burned in every direction and blind buffalo seen every moment wandering about. The poor beasts have all the hair singed off; even the skin in many places is shrivelled up and terribly burned, and their eyes are swollen and closed fast. It was pitiful to see them staggering about, sometimes running afoul of a large stone, at other times tumbling down hill, and falling into creeks . . . In one spot we found a whole herd dead . . . [19]

Significance to Some Long-Standing Problems

The foregoing discussion bears on a number of long-standing problems of interest to geographers, historians, biologists and other scholars. Among these are (a) the character of the so-called "pristine" landscape; (b) the impact of fire and bison on grassland and other vegetation; and (c) differences in the perception of the aridity of the Canadian plains among nineteenth-century white travellers.

(a) Some Comments on the Character of the Pre-European Landscape

Many early ranchers and settlers in the grasslands and parklands of southwestern Canada and the nearby United States remarked on the richness and length of the grass, which some said reached "the horses' bellies." During the late nineteenth and early twentieth centuries, however, as increasing numbers of livestock were introduced and cultivation spread, much ground was broken and long grass replaced by a shorter cover with a different species composition. Wind and other forms of erosion also increased in the 1920's and 1930's. The minds of men were stirred against "over-grazing" and "accelerated erosion." And so they should have been; not so much because such processes were new or "unnatural" as because they were excessive and threatened to damage or destroy grass, soil and other elements of the ecosystem valued by people for economic, aesthetic or other reasons. The bison was part of the pre-European ecosystem; indeed a predominant part of it. Yet this animal grazed heavily and probably contributed substantially to the maintenance of a short grass cover in much of southern Alberta and Saskatchewan until its depletion and near elimination allowed the growth of the mid and tall grasses which were viewed as "natural" by the early settlers. Through wallowing, and merely walking, the bison undoubtedly caused "accelerated erosion" over large areas, particularly along river valleys. Such erosion became more severe and widespread as a result of the introduction of livestock and the plough. Cattle were fenced in after the close of the open range and their concentration in growing numbers in confined pastures must have produced effects greater than those of the free-ranging bison. However, the difference between livestock and the bison appears largely to have been one of degree.

In sum, during the buffalo days in the northwestern plains there undoubtedly were areas of tall grasses and poplar trees, particularly along the river valleys or in highland areas where moisture was more plentiful and bison grazing may not have been common in summer. However, there were also hordes of bison and other animals chopping up the ground, raising clouds of dust as they grazed, walked, wallowed and manured the short grass landscape typical of much of their plains habitat.

(b) Some Comments on the Effects of Fire and Bison on the Grassland and Parkland

Over the years many observers have suggested that bison and fire were important agencies in maintaining the grassland and parkland and in changing their boundaries.[20] The numerous bison undoubtedly trampled and destroyed trees and shrubs, carving paths and open spaces in the aspen or poplar groves. The bison also rubbed against trees in the fashion described by Soper in Wood Buffalo National Park. Such activities could have reduced the rate of aspen encroachment onto the grassland, although the paucity of historical references to such effects suggests that they may have been minor overall.

On the other hand, at certain times and places the wallowing of the bison, and the burrowing of other animals, may have worked to promote the extension of the poplar onto the grassland. The seed of this tree has difficulty penetrating the prairie sod and so in taking root in the mineral soil, with the result that most trees develop from the suckering root system underlying poplar groves. However, seed will establish itself where the grass has been broken by animals and the soil colonized by a protective cover of snowberry, cinquefoil and other low shrubs.

Browsing animals such as the elk and the deer probably had a greater effect in preventing the extension of aspen than the bison. It is not generally realized that the elk was exceedingly numerous over much of the North American plains in pre and early European days. Traders and explorers such as Fidler and Lewis and Clark often referred to large herds of these animals along the South Saskatchewan and the Missouri in the late 1790's and early 1800's. One gains the impression that they were using almost every grove along these rivers at the turn of the nineteenth century.

The elk and the deer both browse on snowberry and other shrubs, as well as on the succulent buds and tips of the willow and poplar, especially in winter. Their browsing undoubtedly killed or damaged many trees and limited the growth and expansion of the groves just as it does today in areas such as the Porcupine Hills or Banff National Park. These effects could have been reinforced by the activity of the beaver, the rabbit and other animals. The attacks of the rabbit on the bark of the trees could have caused many deaths, especially during the peak of this animal's ten-year population cycle.

The effects of fire on vegetation also have been noted by some early travellers. For example, David Thompson, a voice of the late eighteenth and early nineteenth centuries stated that:

> Along the Great Plains there are many places where large groves of Aspen have been burnt the short stubs remaining; and no further production of trees having taken place, the grass of the Plains covered them; and from this cause, the Great Plains are constantly increasing in length and breadth, and the Deer give place to the bison.[21]

Similar observations could be quoted for later time periods. But, even with these, it is difficult to decide whether the grassland was expanding at the expense of parkland and surrounding woodland during the eighteenth and nineteenth centuries, for the poplar can re-establish itself very rapidly following fire, as shown by the observations of Henry Youle Hind, a visitor in the 1850's. To quote him, "a portion of prairie escapes fire for two or three years and the result is seen in the growth of willows and aspens, first in patches, then in larger areas, which in a short time become united and cover the country . . ."[22] Such rapid rates of regrowth make it difficult to determine how permanent and progressive the effects of fire were on the vegetation of many areas. In a given time period, conditions might be favourable to burning in one part of the prairies and not in another. The grassland border therefore could have expanded and contracted unevenly in space and in time.

In summary, it is difficult to isolate one element in the ecosystem and conclude that it was principally responsible for the nature and extent of the grassland and parkland of the Canadian prairies in pre and early European days. Vegetation was influenced by a number of interconnected elements in the system, including the rather obvious one of weather and climate which has not been referred to in the preceding discussion.

(c) Differences in Perception of the Aridity of the Canadian Plains

A relatively detailed understanding of the effects of animals on the landscape has significance for those interested in the varying perceptions of early visitors to the northwestern plains. The example that comes most readily to mind is Palliser's dry belt or triangle.[23] Although the strength of this concept may be as much a creation of his readers and critics as of Palliser himself, there is no doubt that a substantial part of the southern Canadian plains is relatively dry and unsuited for cultivation. Opinions on the degree of aridity have differed, however, among observers. John Macoun, who travelled through much of the southern plains in the 1870's and 1880's, twenty years after Palliser, expressed the opinion that the Irishman had exaggerated the area's dryness. Macoun himself thought much of the area was suitable for wheat and other crops.

Possible reasons for this difference in perception have been discussed for years and various explanations offered, ranging from the possibility of climatic variation to differing expectations among visitors. Thus, for example, it is pointed out that Palliser and his companions came to the plains in the late 1850's when much of the central United States was perceived as a great desert. What Palliser and his men "saw" may therefore have been influenced by this concept. Macoun came about two decades later when geographical knowledge was better and the idea of the central American desert was no longer so much in vogue. He therefore may have been less prepared than Palliser to see aridity in the southern Canadian plains.

But there is another possible explanation which is much more closely connected with the results of this study, that is that the differences in perception of aridity may have been due to the differing effects of bison and other animals on the landscape. In Palliser's day the bison were still relatively numerous. Moreover, they were very plentiful in what is now southwestern Saskatchewan during the 1850's when he visited that area. In contrast, twenty years later, when Macoun passed through the plains the herds had been depleted and he saw relatively small numbers of them. Under these circumstances grazing might have been lighter and grass more plentiful, giving the appearance of greater humidity. However, the role of the bison is unlikely to be the sole answer to this perception problem. Probably the explanation lies in the interaction of many of the factors considered by different thinkers.

Footnotes

1
J. G. Nelson, *The Last Refuge*, manuscript in final stages of preparation.

2
M. Lewis and W. Clark, *Travels to the Source of the Missouri River and Across the American Continent to the Pacific Ocean in the Years 1804, 1805 and 1806*, ed. T. Tees (London, 1814); and also Lewis and Clark, *History of the Expedition Under the Command of Lewis and Clark*, ed. E. Coues, 3 vols. (New York, 1965).

3
P. Fidler, "The Journal of 1800-1801 and 1801-1802," in *Saskatchewan Journals and Correspondence*, ed. Alice Johnston, Hudson's Bay Company Record Society, XXVI (London, 1967).

4
I. Spry, *The Palliser Papers* (Toronto: The Champlain Society 1968).

5
D. Thompson, *David Thompson's Narrative, 1784-1812*, ed. R. Glover (Toronto, 1962).

6
F. A. Larocque, "The Journals of François Antoine Larocque," in *The Frontier and Midland*, ed. R. Hazlett, XIV and XV.

7
Alexander Henry (the Younger) and David Thompson, *New Light on the Early History of the Greater Northwest*, ed. E. Coues, 2 vols. (Minneapolis, 1965), II.

8
M. Cocking, "An Adventurer from Hudson's Bay: Journal of Matthew Cocking from York Factory to the Blackfoot Country, 1772-73," ed. L. J. Burpee, *Proceedings and Transactions of the Royal Society of Canada*, Series 3, II (1908), Sec. II.

9
I. Cowie, *The Company of Adventurers* (Toronto, 1913).

10
J. Audubon, *Audubon and His Journals*, eds. J. J. Audubon and M. Audubon, 2 vols. (New York, 1960).

11
Personal Observation, Summer, 1967.

12
The following quotes and discussion are from J. D. Soper, "History, Range and Home Life of the Northern Bison," *Ecological Monographs*, 2 (1941), pp. 347-412.

13
F. Larson, "The Role of the Bison in Maintaining the Short Grass Plains," *Ecology*, 21, 2 (1940), pp. 113-121.

14
The following references to observations of beaver dams and the like by Lewis and Clark are from Raymond Darwin Burroughs ed., *The Natural History of the Lewis and Clark Expedition* (East Lansing, 1961), pp. 111-113.

15
Ibid. pp. 103-105.

16
I. Spry, *op. cit.* (August 1 and 2, 1857).

17
J. G. Nelson and R. E. England, "Some Comments on the Causes and Effects of Fire in the Northern Grasslands Area of Canada and the Nearby United States, ca. 1750-1900," *The Canadian Geographer* (in press, December, 1971).

18
H. Hind, *Narrative of the Canadian Exploring Expedition of 1857 and of the Assiniboine and Saskatchewan Expedition of 1858*, 2 vols. (London, 1860), p. 292.

19
A. Henry (the Younger) and David Thompson, *New Light on the Early History of the Greater Northwest*, ed. E. Coues, 2 vols. (Minneapolis, 1965), I.

20
See F. Roe, *The North American Buffalo* (Toronto, 1951), the Appendix, for a discussion of this topic.

21
J. Warkentin ed., *The Western Interior of Canada* (Toronto, 1964), or R. Glover ed., *David Thompson's Narrative, 1784-1812* (Toronto, 1962), p. 197.

22
Hind, *op. cit.*, p. 336.

23
See I. Spry, *op. cit.*, Introduction.

Isotherms and Politics:
Perception of the Northwest in the 1850's

G. S. Dunbar

"Geography," said Professor W. L. Morton, "is man's concept of his environment at any given time."[1] In other words, geography is what we perceive it to be, just as history is what historians make of it, so that geographies and histories are inevitably coloured by the individual experiences of the authors who create them. Historical geography, then, is concerned with the evaluation, or perception, of environment at any time in the past, or with changing perception through time. In this paper, I hope to assess the views held in the 1850's concerning the habitability and cultivability of Northwest British North America, especially the area of the present prairie provinces. The views of Red River farmers, Hudson's Bay Company traders, explorers, scientists, and Canadian journalists and politicians naturally reflected their varied backgrounds and interests. They saw in the Northwest what they expected to see, what they wanted to see, not always what the realities of the situation tried to force them to see. Of special interest is the role the young science of climatology was made to play by these various observers. There was a great paucity of meteorological data on the Northwest - indeed, this area represented one of the largest lacunae on the world climatic map - and so pseudo-scientific speculation was all the more rife. By 1850 the Northwest had been ranged over by explorers for more than a century and its agricultural possibilities tested for more than half that time, but there was still a wide variety of opinion regarding its ability to support large-scale agricultural colonization. The Honourable Company apparently favoured a westward transfer of Voltaire's famous indictment of Canada ("quelques arpents de neige"). Those who opposed the Company gained support from the publications of the American climatologist Lorin Blodget, whose monumental book, *Climatology of the United States and of the Temperate Latitudes of the North American Continent*, appeared in 1857 just as the Select Committee of the British House of Commons ended testimony on the Hudson's Bay Company's exclusive patent. My present paper is a study of the role of Blodget's works and other contemporary writings in reshaping the image of the Northwest in the 1850's. It is not a study of the physical climate so much as it is an essay on the climate of opinion.[2]

Agricultural Beginnings

Early agriculture in the Northwest has been described by Frank Gilbert Roe and the Professors Morton, but it would be instructive to review this topic briefly. It is important to keep in mind that the Northwest, including the Red River Settlement, all lay beyond the North American agricultural frontier until after 1870, and the sites of early agricultural experiments can be properly evaluated only if one views them in terms of conditions which prevailed at those times. Professor W. L. Morton's hierarchy of sites is useful in this discussion. The early sites were all what he would term "primitive site" and "squatter site," and it would be unfair to judge them by any other standard. Viewed in this light, these sites were rather successful in raising crops sufficient to supplement the needs of the fur traders. Gardening was attempted at all Hudson's Bay Company posts, and limited success was attained even on Hudson Bay and at the lower Mackenzie River post of Fort Good Hope. Evidence demonstrating the feasibility of growing cereal grains, especially wheat, however, was contradictory, and it was not until after 1870 that the future role of the southern part of the region as a great granary became clear. It was not until Morton's "homestead site," with attendant facilities to transport wheat to outside markets, became established that the destiny of the prairies was made manifest.[3]

Rather ironically, the first agricultural experiments were made in some of the least promising parts of the Northwest - the shores of Hudson Bay - and the limited success there might have been a deterrent to later attempts inland. Although we do not know the fate of the "kilderkin of virginia wheate" and the "2 bushells of buck wheate" sent as seed to Hudson Bay in 1683-1684, we can surmise that they failed but that the accompanying vegetables took root. Garden produce, for the Governor and officers at least, was grown at York Factory in the 1730's, and by 1749 it appears that a modest amount of horticulture was carried on, although Arthur Dobbs' extravagant claims for the fertility of the bayshore and shield lands should be heavily discounted. In the same years, La Vérendrye's forays into the interior, although they did not result in permanent settlements, at least demonstrated the possibility of agriculture, as when La Vérendrye gave some "pease and unripened corn" to hungry Indians near Fort St. Charles on Lake of the Woods in 1733.[4]

The first really important attempts to expand gardening into true

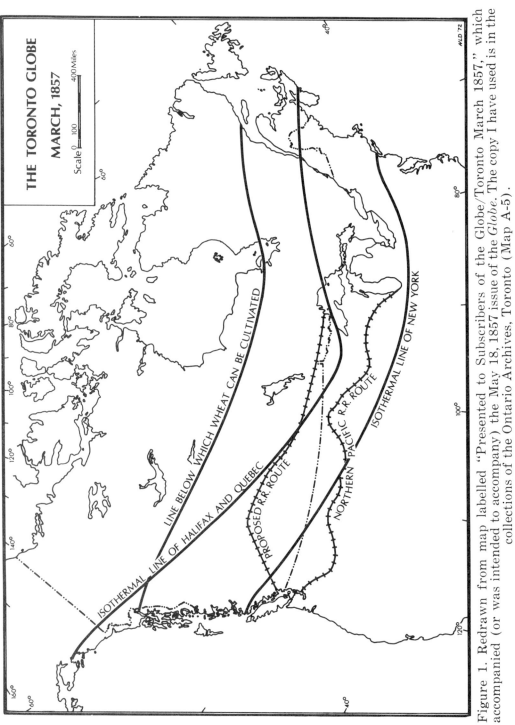

Figure 1. Redrawn from map labelled "Presented to Subscribers of the Globe/Toronto March 1857," which accompanied (or was intended to accompany) the May 18, 1857 issue of the *Globe*. The copy I have used is in the collections of the Ontario Archives, Toronto (Map A-5).

farming came after the beginning of the 19th century in the south-eastern part of the territory. Alexander Henry the younger met with notable success in farming, first at Pembina and then later at Portage la Prairie, from 1800 to 1808, and this experience might well have influenced the Hudson's Bay Company to accept Selkirk's proposal in 1811. Selkirk, who had entertained notions of settling redundant European peasants in different parts of North America as early as 1801, focussed his attention on the Red River after his marriage to Jean Wedderburn-Colvile in 1807 and his subsequent purchase of Hudson's Bay Company stock. It has been said that Selkirk's interest in the Northwest was aroused by reading Mackenzie's *Voyages* (1801), but Mackenzie's book made no great claims for the settlement possibilities of the Northwest, and Selkirk was then investigating several other regions as well.[5]

Although George Simpson recanted late in life and attributed his earlier enthusiastic statements on the agricultural possibilities of the Northwest to a "ghost writer," as a young man he was convinced of the necessity of promoting horticulture at the fur posts. In 1820 he urged the extension of gardening at Fort Wedderburn and other northern posts when he saw the importance of the Dunvegan potato gardens to the North West Company traders. He remarked, too, on the quality of the farm William Williams had established at Cumberland House. Williams was raising wheat, barley, and maize, but, despite these auspicious beginnings, Williams was followed by men of lesser zeal, and there were only ten acres of cultivated land at Cumberland House in 1858. Smaller gardens were maintained at the other posts.[6]

The agricultural history of the Red River Settlement can be interpreted in many different ways, depending on one's background and interests. Although the Settlement was initially sanctioned by the Hudson's Bay Company and was envisioned as another provision post, the market for local produce was saturated by 1832, and the Settlement thenceforth became "the anathema of the fur trade monopoly." Although the total cultivated area grew from over 2000 acres in the early 1830's to more than 8800 by 1856, Red River agriculture could only be characterized as "subsistent, riparian, and restricted," in W. L. Morton's words. In general, however, I should judge the Red River Settlement to be a qualified success, all the more remarkable because it existed for a half century in advance of the North American agricultural frontier. Its chief problems seem to have been connected with its relative isolation rather than with the physical properties of the region. However, until a thorough examination was made after 1870, it was convenient to blame the Settlement's poor showing on its physical attributes, particularly climate.[7]

Early Meteorological Observations

Although Canada had acquired a reputation for snow and severe winters before the time of Voltaire, most Europeans still adhered closely to the classical theory of the rigid latitudinal zonation of climate. They naturally believed that European climates were the "normal" ones and that North America was somehow aberrant if her climates failed to match those of European lands in the same latitudes. As a growing body of observations came in from travelers, European scientists began to distinguish between the climates of coastal and interior locations. The French naturalist Buffon termed the latter "excessive climates." Alexander von Humboldt said that his mentor, Georg Forster, a member of Cook's second expedition, was the first to describe the climatic difference between locations at the same latitude on the east and west coasts of continents, the latter being milder in all seasons. These differences could not be easily demonstrated until someone devised a method for their graphic portrayal. Although Simeon DeWitt of New York State had some sort of scheme in mind for a "climatological chart" as early as 1792, he did not follow through with his plan, and the first successful map of this sort came with Humboldt's invention of the isotherm in 1817. The isotherm was not the first isarithmic line, for Humboldt acknowledged the priority of Edmond Halley's magnetic lines of 1701. However, Humboldt's isarithms, unlike Halley's, were followed by numerous imitators, probably because such lines are especially useful in the field of climatology. The coinage of new terms for different kinds of isolines became very popular, but by mid-19th century there was a surfeit, and few worthwhile terms have been added in the last hundred years. Humboldt did not produce a true map, but his chart had a grid and numerous locations on it, and so it can be easily converted into a map. On it are shown six isotherms for a part of the Northern Hemisphere, from mid-North America eastward to China. The areas beyond reach of the isotherms in north-eastern Siberia and western North America (west of the Great Lakes) were not well known and had not yet yielded enough climatic data to be fitted into a generalized world pattern. These areas were of special interest to Humboldt, and he urged the governments involved to fill in the blank spots.[8]

Humboldt's invention of the isotherm, although seemingly a rather modest contribution, was actually a great scientific breakthrough and was just what was needed to establish the science of climatology on a sound basis. It enabled data to be organized and easily presented cartographically, and it facilitated the making of comparisons among different parts of the world.

Humboldt used the term "isotherm" for average annual temperature lines, and he coined the terms "isocheim" and "isothere" for winter and summer lines, respectively, but these terms fell into disuse after mid-century, and we now use "isotherm" for all temperature lines regardless of the time period being measured. Isotherm mapping was a popular exercise in the scientific world after 1817, and it is very instructive to compare maps made during the first four decades, down to the publication of Blodget's book in 1857.[9]

Humboldt used a rather miscellaneous assortment of data for his isothermal chart. The longest and most reliable series of data were from European stations, and Uppsala, Sweden, was cited as having the best record of all. The only North American stations he used were in the eastern half of the continent, and the records were rather short. In British North America he cited Nain, Labrador (two years of observations) and Quebec (four years). There was not as yet any network of weather stations for a systematic survey in North America. Such a system had been commenced in Europe in the late 18th century by the Societas Meteorologica Palatina, but no such network was established in North America until 1819, when the Surgeon General's Office of the United States Army began receiving meteorological data from the medical officers stationed at far-flung posts. The State of New York followed in 1825, and subsequently the states of Pennsylvania (1837) and Massachusetts (1849) established similar systems. In 1849 the recently founded Smithsonian Institution began the most ambitious programme of data collection under the direction of its Secretary, Joseph Henry, who had been involved with the New York programme twenty years earlier. In the same year Henry went to Toronto to confer with J. H. Lefroy, who was in charge of the Observatory there and who promised Henry the support not only of observers in British North America but in Bermuda and the West Indies as well. In 1853 the senior grammar schools in each county in Canada were supplied with instruments, and the observations were continued for several years.[10]

Actually, weather data had been collected for some time on an individual basis in Canada and the Maritimes, as well as in the eastern United States. There remained, however, large gaps, particularly in the interior of the continent. The United States was able, with its network of army posts, to fill in some of these lacunae fairly early, but the western interior of British North America long remained a meteorological problem area. The prairies remained little known even in the 1850's. The trading posts were naturally sited in or near the land of the furbearers, so that the Bay shores and far northern lands attracted a disproportionate share of the scientific observers who came to the country.

Although some information about weather was recorded rather

early on Hudson Bay, I have not been able to determine exactly when the use of instruments was begun there. Barometers and thermometers were in use no later than 1730, when Captain Christopher Middleton employed them on the Bay. Peter Fidler kept a daily weather record for most of his long career in the Northwest, 1788-1822. In 1800 a Company directive discouraged such observations, saying that "Diaries of Winds & Weather are to us useless & need not be kept." In 1814, however, the Company suffered a change of heart and ordered weather journals to be kept and sent instruments to some posts. They were then interested in determining "which of the productions of European cultivation" might be successfully grown at the fur posts.[11]

In 1819 John Franklin was despatched "to amend the very defective geography of the northern part of North America," and his subsequent expeditions produced a great deal of scientific information about the Northwest. Especially noteworthy were the observations of the medical officer, John Richardson. In the next thirty years Richardson was to provide more accurate and useful information about the climate and cultivability of the Northwest than any other individual. In his paper, "Remarks on the Climate and Vegetable Productions of the Hudson's Bay Countries," published in 1825 in *The Edinburgh Philosophical Journal*, Richardson discussed the weather and agricultural possibilities at Cumberland House, Fort Enterprise, Fort Chipewyan, and Little Lake. At Fort Chipewyan, he said, "barley, and I believe wheat, are advantageously cultivated, and the latter [Little Lake, 61° 12'N.] is the most northerly fur-post at which, as far as my information goes, barley has been tried, and succeeded." In 1835 Richardson was instrumental in having observations made on permafrost (which he believed to be directly related to average annual temperature) at a number of Hudson's Bay Company posts, and in 1839, with the aid of the Royal Geographical Society, he sent out twenty-six thermometers to take air and soil temperatures. Unfortunately, most of the thermometers were lost through accident, and Richardson was not able to draw any new conclusions with them. At the same time, extracts of his letters from fur traders were published in *The Edinburgh New Philosophical Journal*. In the January, 1841 issue were reprinted Murdoch McPherson's record of temperatures at Fort Simpson, 1837-40, and Peter Warren Dease's observations on the cultivation of cereal grains in the high latitudes. Dease reported that wheat, which took about four months to ripen, was very chancy at Forts Liard and Dunvegan, but barley, with a tree-month growing season, was "cultivated to advantage" at Forts Liard, Simpson, and Norman. Only turnips could be persuaded to grow at Fort Good Hope.[12]

In 1848-49 Richardson made meteorological and agricultural observations at Forts Confidence, Simpson, Norman, and Good Hope and concluded that "the 65th parallel of latitude may . . . be considered as the northern limit of *Cerealia* in this meridian." These observations were published in his remarkable two-volume work, *Arctic Searching Expedition* (1851). Richardson noted maize growing in Rupert's Land to 51°N., wheat growing somewhat precariously at Fort Liard, and barley ripening well "in good seasons" at Fort Norman. He believed that his scanty meteorological data were sufficient "for extending the lines of mean annual heat *(isothermal)*, mean summer heat *(isothaeral)*, and mean winter heat *(isocheimenal)* across the continent," but, unfortunately, he did not produce such a map. Although the winter temperatures seemed to decline directly with increasing latitude in the interior of North America, Richardson noted that the summer temperature lines trended northwestward from the Great Lakes. "The summer heats do not . . . decrease in the same ratio as we go to the north; on the contrary, the isothaeral lines nearly follow the canoe route, and run to the northward and westward." Using the data in Dove's "Temperature Tables" in the *Report of the British Association for the Advancement of Science for 1847*, Richardson could find little difference in the summer heat - and thus in the capacity to produce cereals - between North America and European lands in the same latitude.[13]

Richardson's works provide the most accurate summary of conditions in the Northwest by the early 1850's, and he must be given substantial credit for expanding the scientific awareness of the northern interior of North America. Professor Lewis Thomas has recently said that although Richardson "published some crop production data . . . he did not attempt a systematic survey of the agricultural potential of the North West," but I feel, after reading Richardson's works, that he did more than anyone else to publicize the region's agricultural possibilities. I should be inclined to say, without being able to document my statement, that Richardson's work was a major source of inspiration for Lorin Blodget. Perhaps Northwest British North America would not have attracted Blodget's interest had it not been for the work of John Richardson.[14]

Lorin Blodget

Lorin Blodget (1823-1901), the American climatologist and statistician, is best known as the author of *Climatology of the United States and of the Temperate Latitudes of the North American Continent* (1857). For this monumental work, Blodget has been called "The Father of American Climatology." He is virtually unknown to the present generation of students, but I should like to resurrect him long enough to demonstrate his contributions to the climatology and even to the settlement of Northwest British North America.[15]

Lorin Blodget was raised on a farm near Jamestown, New York and attended Geneva (now Hobart) College for a year before his father died in 1838. In the 1840's he taught school near Jamestown and engaged in local politics. Cleveland Abbe has said that Blodget's "interest in meteorology was aroused during the years 1841-1844 when traversing Wisconsin, Illinois, and Iowa for the purpose of examining and purchasing land." In 1849-50 he was a volunteer weather observer near Jamestown for the Smithsonian Institution and first came to the attention of Joseph Henry when he wrote to inquire about getting better instruments. Blodget was thereupon invited to Washington to serve as Henry's assistant, and he was given considerable latitude in building up the Smithsonian's collections. He served at the Smithsonian for three years, 1851-54, and then left after disagreement with Henry over the use of the Institution's records in his own publications.[16]

In June 1854 Charles Mason, Commissioner of Patents, wrote to Joseph Henry saying that he had heard of a manuscript by Blodget "on the climatology of the United States, compared with that of Europe and other parts of the world" and requested permission to publish it in the annual Agriculture volume of the *Report of the Commissioner of Patents*. Henry replied that the materials in Blodget's paper were collected under the direction of the Smithsonian, the State of New York, and the Medical Bureau of the Army and that they ought to be published first in a general report sanctioned by those bodies. However, he said that he would not stand in the way of the paper's publication since the Patent Office would give it immediate and wide circulation. Thus Blodget's first general climatological monograph was published - "Agricultural Climatology of the United States Compared with That of Other Parts of the Globe." In comparing the climates and capabilities of North America and the Old World Blodget was clearly influenced by the work of Alexander von Humboldt, "whose models were his guide, and whose tone of generalization his highest ambition to attain."[17]

With the publication of the "Agricultural Climatology," Blodget and Henry came to a parting of the ways. Blodget stayed in Washington until 1857 working on meteorological reports for the Pacific Railroad Survey and the Surgeon General's Office, both in the Department of War. These materials formed the basis of his *Climatology of the United States*, which was published in 1857 in Philadelphia after he moved to that city from Washington. He spent most of the rest of his life in Philadelphia where he was engaged in the compilation of commercial data. He kept up his climatological interests, however, for he wrote the climate section of various atlases edited by H. F. Walling (including

Tackabury's Atlas of the Dominion of Canada), wrote several meteorological papers, including essays on the climate of Alaska and the Great Plains, and maintained a bibliography of climatology into the 1890's.[18]

In the present paper I should like to concentrate upon Blodget's writings of the Washington period, culminating in the publication of *Climatology of the United States*, with special reference to the implications of these writings to the growing interest in the extension of settlement and cultivation in Northwest British North America.

In the 1850's Lorin Blodget was able to draw upon a large body of data for the United States east of the Mississippi and for Canada and the Maritimes as well, but the records were few and brief for the western half of the continent. Their brevity, however, did not deter him from using them in his bold generalizations. Blodget contended that even a one-month record was valuable, for he could extrapolate from it and fit it in with stations of longer record. He remarked upon the "symmetry" of the distributions of heat and precipitation and was convinced that he had evidence to illustrate their permanence. Among the 964 meteorological observers and correspondents of the Smithsonian in 1854, there were only six from British North America, and these were all from Canada and Nova Scotia, but Blodget was able to draw some data and inferences about lands to the west from his wide reading. In Richardson's *Arctic Searching Expedition* he found sufficient data to confirm his belief in the cultivability of Northwest British North America even beyond 65°N. Blodget, drawing on Richardson's experience, stated that the decreasing elevation of the land north of the sources of the Mississippi permitted the extension of wheat far to the northward. "The successful growth of both wheat and Indian corn near Lake Winnipeg is not so decidedly anomalous," he said, "as the temperature for the whole summer is higher at Fort Garry than at the sources of the Red river at the North and of the Mississippi."[19]

In 1855 there was published, in the latest of the Army Meteorological Registers, a "Report on the Prominent Features of General Climate in the United States" by Lorin Blodget. This report was illustrated with five "Isothermal Charts" and five "Hyetal or Rain Charts" showing the mean distribution of temperature and rainfall for each season and for the whole year. The charts covered the United States and the extreme southern part of British North America - to Lake Winnipeg in the centre of the chart. In this work Blodget mentioned temperature data for Canada and the Maritimes from the collections of Dove and Sabine, but for western British North America there were only Richardson's data. Blodget confidently asserted the comparative value of these data, even though the records were short.[20]

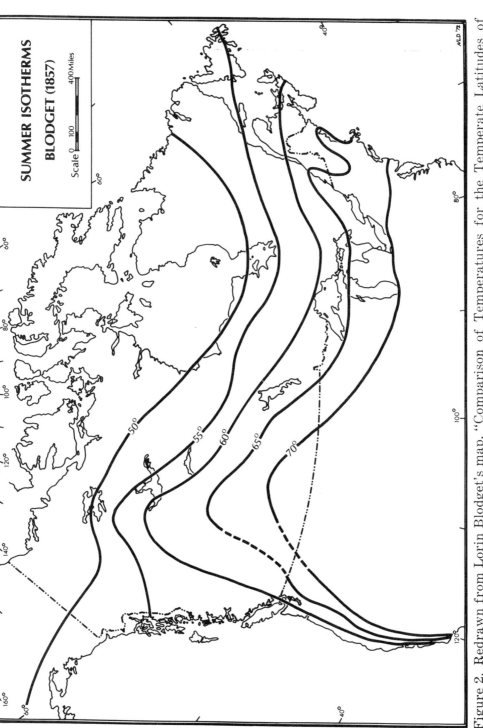

Figure 2. Redrawn from Lorin Blodget's map, "Comparison of Temperatures for the Temperate Latitudes of the Northern Hemisphere," accompanying his *Climatology of the United States* (1857). In the same volume he also had an "Isothermal Chart—Mean Distribution of Heat for the Summer," which extends only to about 51°N. in the centre. There are many important differences between the two maps, but here I am only interested in showing the trends of the isotherms.

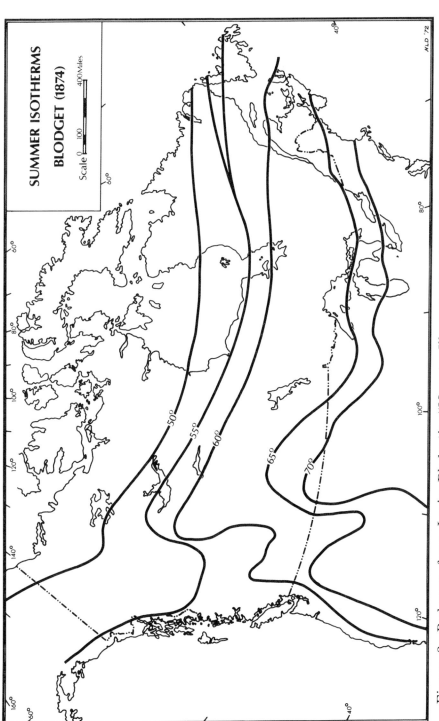

Figure 3. Redrawn from Lorin Blodget's "Map to Illustrate the Climatology of the Dominion of Canada" (1874), which was printed in *Tackabury's Atlas of the Dominion of Canada*, ed. by H.F. Walling (Montreal, 1875).

"We know very little," said Blodget, "of the quantity of rain falling in British America and other parts of the north, the measurement at Sitka, Russian America, being almost the only one beyond the Canadas." He believed that the northern Great Plains west of Fort Pierre (near present Pierre, South Dakota) were "uncultivable from the absence of summer rain." This statement showed the continued belief in the existence of "The Great American Desert." Even the early explorers had contributed to the desert legend, which became widely known after the Long Expedition of 1819-20. It was to be reinforced by Joseph Henry's paper, "Meteorology in Relation to Agriculture," in the 1850's but was then to be significantly modified, at least as far as western British North America was concerned, by the Palliser and other expeditions of the late '50's.[21]

Also published in 1855 was the first volume of the great railroad surveys - *Report of Explorations for a Route for the Pacific Railroad, near the Forty-Seventh and Forty-Ninth Parallels of North Latitude, from St. Paul to Puget Sound* by Isaac I. Stevens - a report to which Lorin Blodget contributed meteorological instructions and also six pages of "General Notes on the Climate." When Stevens' *Narrative and Final Report* was published in 1860, he had the benefit of Blodget's 1857 book and also Henry Y. Hind's first report. By 1860 the Great American Desert had definitely been stopped short of the 49th parallel, except for Palliser's Triangle. Canadian propagandists seized upon the desert notion to predict dire results for those so foolish as to settle south of the 49th parallel. Although there is some question about how widely such beliefs were held, there are indications that the desert concept caused promoters to look northwestward for their manifest destiny.[22]

In the late 1850's the Hudson's Bay Company's exclusive rights were again coming up for review, and in the first half of 1857 extensive hearings were held by a Select Committee of the British House of Commons to determine the Company's fitness to continue its monopoly. Commercial interests in Upper Canada, led by the Toronto *Globe*, wanted to see the Company's monopoly ended and Canadian jurisdiction extended westward, even to the Pacific. Accompanying the Select Committee Report was a "Map of the Northwest Part of Canada, Hudson's Bay & Indian Territories," drawn by Thomas Devine by order of Joseph Cauchon, Commissioner of Crown Lands, Toronto, in March 1857. The map is remarkable for the large number of isotherms shown. These isotherms were taken from H. W. Dove (1852), Johnston's *Physical Atlas* (1848), and the U. S. Army Meteorological Register of 1855.[23]

The case for the Company was put by George Simpson and his cohorts, but Simpson's attempt to denigrate the agricultural possibilities of the Red River Valley and lands westward was refuted by reference to his own book, *Narrative of a Journey Round the World* (1847). Simpson's statement to the Committee, "I do not think any part of the Hudson's Bay Company's territories is well adapted for settlement; the crops are very uncertain," was belied by passages in his book describing the richness of the lands around Red River and between Lake Superior and Lake Winnipeg.[24]

Early in 1857 there appeared newspaper articles by Lorin Blodget on the climate and settlement possibilities of the Northwest. In a letter to the *New-York Daily Tribune*, published 22 January 1857, Blodget stressed the adequacy of warmth and precipitation in the northern Great Plains, in contrast to the Great American Desert to the south. In a letter to a Philadelphia newspaper, *The North American*, in February, Blodget showed that he was interested in the proceedings of the Select Committee and that he was confident of the imminent end of the Company's control. "All the area here corresponding to France, Germany, the Baltic countries, and British islands, is but hunted for paltry furs, when its area, climate, and capacity are scarcely less than these areas of Europe."[25]

The Toronto *Globe*, meanwhile, was printing numerous accounts of Red River and the West, capped by a long article in the 18 May 1857 issue on "The Hudson's Bay Territory: Its History, Geology, Climate, Trade, and Natural Resources." The issue was accompanied by a map dated March 1857. The map showed two isotherms - one the "Isothermal Line of New York" and the other the "Isothermal Line of Halifax and Quebec" - and also a line indicating the northern limit of wheat cultivation. In the article several travelers, especially John Richardson, are quoted on the fertility of the Territory, and Lorin Blodget is cited on the increasing warmth and cultivability as one travels northward on the Great Plains.[26] (Figure 1)

The Select Committee did not wind up its business until the end of July 1857, and the *Globe* and other newspapers published a running account of the committee proceedings through the spring and summer. The Committee's recommendation to allow Canada "to annex to her territory such portion of the land in her neighbourhood as may be available to her for the purposes of settlement, with which lands she is willing to open and maintain communications" was disappointing to many Canadians who had hoped for immediate and unconditional annexation. The Hudson's Bay Company realized that its days were numbered, but it gained a new lease on life with the economic depression of the late '50's and the turning of Canadian interest in other directions.[27]

In the summer of 1857, as the Select Committee was concluding its business but not in time to be used as evidence, there appeared Blodget's *Climatology of the United States and of the Temperate Latitudes of the North American Continent.* The Canadian edition was briefly noted in the *Globe* on September 1, but the paucity of contemporary reviews is remarkable. In the only extended Canadian review I have seen, the reviewer gives no evidence of having read beyond page 164 in Blodget's 536-page book.[28]

For the present paper, the most interesting part of Blodget's book is the very last chapter, a brief (six-page) essay on the "Climate of the Northwestern Districts," which expands the ideas in his *New-York Daily Tribune* article. By "Northwestern" Blodget meant all the North American continent "west of the 98th meridian and above the 43rd parallel," a huge area then virtually unpopulated (by whites) but which Blodget likened in its climate and agricultural possibilities to western and northern Europe. (43°N. is the northern boundary of present-day Nebraska, and the 98th meridian runs near Gladstone, Manitoba, birthplace of W. L. Morton!)[29]

Blodget's last chapter almost has the appearance of after-thought, and it is quite different in character from the rest of the book, which is a rather straightforward discussion of the climatology of the United States. The terminal chapter has a propagandistic tone. Blodget begins by saying, "The great practical interest now felt in the northwestern areas of this continent requires that some distinct reference to their climate should be made . . . in a manner more acceptable to the general reader [than the 'scientific analyses' earlier in the book]. The whole climatological discussion bears more or less directly on this point throughout, but a compact statement of the advantages belonging to this territory, and having their basis in climate, is quite desirable." He compared the northwestern districts to "Gaul, Scandinavia and Britain . . . [in] the period of the earliest trans-Alpine Roman expansion." These lands "were regarded as inhospitable regions, fit only for barbarian occupation." "Climate is indisputably the decisive condition, and when we find the isothermal of 60° for the summer rising on the interior American plains to the 61st parallel, or fully as high as its average position for Europe, it is impossible to doubt the existence of favorable climates over vast areas now unoccupied." The "commercial and industrial capacity" of the Northwest "is gigantic," said Blodget, "and but for the pernicious views entailed by the fur traffic as to the necessity of preserving it as a wilderness, it would long since have been opened to colonization."[30]

In this work Blodget extended the isotherms farther north than he did in the Army Meteorological Register of 1855. "At the time those were drawn [1855] the number of observations beyond the limits of the United States was so small that the full expression was not given to the statistics then used, in the fear that some correction would ultimately be found to apply to them, reducing the extreme northward curvatures they indicated. But a farther collection and comparison warrants the positions now given to the thermal lines, placing them farther northward than before, and extending them in a course due northwest from Lake Superior to the 58th parallel." (Figure 2) Then, in a sentence that was often quoted, Blodget remarked, "The buffalo winter on the upper Athabasca at least as safely as in the latitude of St. Paul's, Minnesota, and the spring opens at nearly the same time along the immense line of plains from St. Paul's to Mackenzie's River."[31]

Blodget confidently stated that "for the small number of points observed above the 45th parallel, the statistics are very well distributed to define the climate." From Lake Superior, "in a line northwestward, there are Fort William, Pembina, Fort Garry, and the fine series of observations at Norway House ... Then Carlton House, Cumberland House, Edmonton House, Fort Liard, Fort Simpson, Sitka, and Yukon, - forming a crescent along the milder portions, and beyond which the still better observed points at Lake Athabasca, Great Bear Lake, and Hudson's Bay, confirm the distribution so as to leave no doubt of its general reliability."[32]

Although Blodget's book appeared too late to be used in the Select Committee hearings, it and his earlier works were cited by contemporary writers and travelers, notably James Wickes Taylor, the St. Paul propagandist, who extolled the virtues of "British Central America," as he called it, in order to stimulate American interest in its settlement and, possibly, annexation. Of the western explorers in the late 1850's, only Simon Dawson made much use of Blodget's writings. Dawson not only quoted Blodge extensively and favourably but went even farther in trying to affirm the climatic suitability of the Northwest. "According to the Isothermal charts of Lorin Blodget," said Dawson, "the lines of equal temperature for the summer should have a north-west direction from Red River. Now, admitting this theory to be correct, the climate of Red Deer River and Swan River, other circumstances being the same, should be equal to that of Red River Settlement. But I am of opinion that it is superior, inasmuch as that these rich valleys, while they are at but a very slight elevation above the valley of Red River, are removed from the influence of the cold winds from Lake Winnipeg, which prejudicially affect the latter in the spring." Dawson compared the climate of Red River with that of Kingston and said that the growing season at the former was "somewhat longer than in Canada, east of Kingston."[33]

Blodget's concern with the Northwest did not long survive his move to Philadelphia, but the basic points of the habitability and cultivability of the Northwest had been made, and there were others, such as James

Wickes Taylor, to carry on the promotional work. Blodget became occupied largely with commercial statistics in Philadelphia, but he demonstrated continuous interest in climatology. His involvement with the
atlas projects of H. F. Walling is most important, and we ought to take
particular notice of Blodget's climatic section of Walling's *Tackabury's
Atlas of the Dominion of Canada* (1875). The isotherms in the
Tackabury atlas show considerable southward migration from the positions they occupied on Blodget's maps in 1857.[34] (Figure 3)

Blodget's writings, especially the *Climatology*, have shown surprising durability over the years. Indeed, his *magnum opus* is still referred to as "the most important Climatology of North America to
date." Perhaps this is as much an indictment of climatologists for failing
to produce a comprehensive work on the climates of North America as
it is a tribute to Blodget's book. A modern climatologist, John Leighly,
has called the book "a rounded scientific and literary fabric . . . a flower
of the waning years of our intellectual golden day," but he objected
strongly to Blodget's isarithmic maps. "Blodget," he said, "evidently
had no notion of the character of isarithms as indices of the distribution
of a continuous variable over a surface; he permitted his to terminate
on the map, to bifurcate and anastomose." The book did not escape contemporary criticism, either from the scientific or the literary point of
view. We can sympathize with the reviewer in *Petermann's Geographische Mittheilungen* who said, "Der Styl des Buches ist manchmal
eigenthümlich und nicht immer klar." The longest and most penetrating review, unfortunately anonymous, appeared in *The American
Journal of Science and Arts*. The reviewer praised the book generally
but said that it "is loose in style and often obscure; it contains many
careless and somewhat erroneous statements: and the views which it
embodies respecting the causes of the most common meteorological
phenomena are radically erroneous." Blodget's isothermal and rainfall maps, however, were praised as definite contributions to
meteorology.[35]

These maps, based as they were on meagre data, particularly in the
interior of the continent, were only tentative and subject to change as
newer data were recorded. Those of us who hesitate to commit ourselves cartographically are in awe of Blodget's courage in drawing isotherms across the continent on the basis of only a few months' observations at scattered stations. This was a necessary first step, however, in
the climatic description of the continent. Most contemporary users of
Blodget's book probably regarded the isotherms as immutable scientific
constructs. They used the isotherms, and meteorological data
generally, to bolster their views of the settlement possibilities of the
Western interior. Alexandre Taché, Bishop of St. Boniface, was one of

the few who opposed the authority of the isotherms. He said, "The figures representing the mean temperatures of the months . . . have determined the isothermal lines, and greater experience proves that they are not to be depended upon. These lines are fundamentally wrong, for . . . a single night is sufficient to destroy all analogy with the climate of the country to which they refer." Most contemporaries, however, were beguiled by the isotherms and regarded them as infallible guides to agricultural possibilities.[36]

Concluding Remarks

The immediate influence of Blodget's writings cannot be exactly determined, but it seems that Professor W. L. Morton was not extravagant when he said: "Blodget . . . became the darling of the publicists of Toronto and St. Paul, and one of the actual openers of the Northwest to settlement. His quiet language had the sweep and style of the empire-builder."[37] Vindication of Blodget's grandiose judgments had to await the establishment of "homestead site" when the North American agricultural frontier reached Red River after 1870. However, a fair amount of scientific data had accumulated by 1857 so that his pronouncements were not wholly unjustified at that time. The wonder is, in retrospect, that Northwest British North America was not better known despite its small white population. John Richardson had laid a solid foundation for the scientific description of the Northwest by 1851, and within a few years Lorin Blodget was to take the scattered data and, in the Humboldtean manner, forge the grand generalizations that the propagandists were to find so useful. My aim in this paper has been to describe more fully the work of these men in shaping the image of the Northwest in the pre-Confederation years. We should be especially thankful that their efforts have culminated in this Western Canadian Studies Conference.

Footnotes

Research for this paper was supported by a grant from the American Philosophical Society. I wish to record my special thanks to Professors John Warkentin, W. L. Morton, Eric Ross, and Mr. Frits Pannekoek for their suggestions and encouragement.

1
W. L. Morton, "The Geographical Circumstances of Confederation," *Canadian Geographical Journal*, LXX (March, 1965), 74.

2

Cf. J. W. Watson, "The Role of Illusion in North American Geography: A Note on the Geography of North American Settlement," *The Canadian Geographer*, XIII (Spring, 1969), 10-27.

3

F. G. Roe, "Early Agriculture in Western Canada in Relation to Climatic Stability," *Agricultural History*, XXVI (July, 1952), 104-123; A. S. Morton, *A History of the Canadian West to 1870-71* (London, n.d.); W. L. Morton, "Agriculture in the Red River Colony," *Canadian Historical Review*, XXX (December, 1949), 305-321; W. L. Morton, "The Significance of Site in the Settlement of the American and Canadian Wests," *Agricultural History*, XXV (July, 1951), 97-104; W. L. Morton, *Manitoba: A History* (Toronto, 1957).

4

E. E. Rich, ed., *Minutes of the Hudson's Bay Company, 1679-1684: Second Part, 1682-84* (Toronto, 1946), pp. 101, 313; A. S. Morton, *op. cit.*, 180, 224; Roe, *op. cit.*, 107.

5

Elliott Coues, ed., *New Light on the Early History of the Greater Northwest. The Manuscript Journals of Alexander Henry... and of David Thompson... 1799-1814* (New York, 1897), I, *passim*; S. N. Murray, "A History of Agriculture in the Valley of the Red River of the North, 1812 to 1920" (unpublished Ph.D. dissertation, Department of History, University of Wisconsin, 1963), p. 61; P. C. T. White, ed., *Lord Selkirk's Diary, 1803-1804* (Toronto, 1958), xii-xxiv; Alexander Mackenzie, *Voyages from Montreal...* (London and Edinburgh, 1801), pp. lvii, lxv, 400.

6

J. S. Galbraith, *The Hudson's Bay Company as an Imperial Factor, 1821-1869* (Berkeley and Los Angeles, 1957), p. 334; E. E. Rich, *The Fur Trade and the Northwest to 1857* (Toronto, 1967), p. 290; E. E. Rich, ed., *Journal of Occurrences in the Athabasca Department by George Simpson...* (Toronto, 1938), *passim*; H. Y. Hind, *Narrative of the Canadian Red River Exploring Expedition of 1857 and of the Assiniboine and Saskatchewan Exploring Expedition of 1858* (London, 1860), I, 448.

7

Galbraith, *op. cit.*, 311; W. L. Morton, "Agriculture in the Red River Colony," *op. cit.*, 321.

8

Alexander von Humboldt, *Kosmos* (Stuttgart and Tübingen, 1845), I, 345-347; H. E. Landsberg, "Early Stages of Climatology in the United States," *Bulletin of the American Meteorological Society*, XLV (May, 1964) 269; A. von Humboldt, "Des lignes isothermes et de la distribution de la Chaleur sur le globe," *Mémoires de physique et de chimie, de la Société d'Arcueil*, III (1817), 462-602 [translated and reprinted as "On Isothermal Lines, and the Distribution of Heat over the Globe," *The Edinburgh Philosophical Journal*, III (1820), 1-20, 256-274; IV (1821), 23-37, 262-281; V (1821), 28-39]; A. H. Robinson and H. M. Wallis, "Humboldt's Map of Isothermal Lines: A Milestone in Thematic Cartography," *The Cartographic Journal*, IV (December, 1967), 119-123; W. Horn, "Die Geschichte der Isarithmenkarten," *Petermanns Geographische Mitteilungen*, CIII (1959), 225-232; J. L. M. Gulley and K. A. Sinnhuber, "Isokartographie: Eine terminologische Studie," *Kartographische Nachrichten*, XI (August, 1961), 89-99.

9

See especially W. Meinardus, "Die Entwickelung der Karten der Jahres-Isothermen von Alexander von Humboldt bis auf Heinrich Wilhelm Dove," *Wissenschaftliche Beiträge zum Gedächtniss der hundertjährigen Wiederkehr des Antritts von Alexander von Humboldt's Reise nach Amerika am 5. Juni 1799* (Berlin, 1899).

10

Humboldt, "On Isothermal Lines," *op. cit.*, V, 32-33; Landsberg, *op. cit.*, 268; *Scientific Writings of Joseph Henry* (Washington, 1886), II, 25-26, 449; Thomas Coulson, *Joseph Henry: His Life and Work* (Princeton, 1950), p. 196.

11

Christopher Middleton, "Observations on the Weather, in a Voyage to Hudson's Bay in North-America, in the Year 1730 . . .," Royal Society, *Philosophical Transactions*, XXXVII (March-May, 1731), 76-78; R. P. Stearns, *Science in the British Colonies of America* (Urbana, Illinois, 1970), pp. 250-251; A. B. Lowe, "Canada's First Weathermen," *The Beaver*, Outfit 292 (1961), 4-7; A. M. Johnson, ed., *Saskatchewan Journals and Correspondence* . . . (London, 1967), p. lxxvii.

12

J. Franklin, *Narrative of a Journey to the Shores of the Polar Sea* . . . (London, 1823), p. xii; J. Richardson, "Remarks on the Climate and Vegetable Productions of the Hudson's Bay Countries," *The Edinburgh Philosophical Journal*, XII (1825), 212; Richardson, "Notice of a few Observations . . . ," *Journal of the Royal Geographical Society of London*, IX (1839), 117-120; Richardson, "Note on the best Points, in British North America, for making Observations . . .," *ibid.*, 121-124; Richardson, "On the Frozen Soil of North America," *The Edinburgh New Philosophical Journal*, XXX (1841), 110-123; Murdoch McPherson, "Register of the Temperature of the Atmosphere, kept at Fort Simpson . . .," *ibid.*, 124-126; "On the Cultivation of the Cerealea in the High Latitudes of North America," *ibid.*, 123-124.

13

J. Richardson, *Arctic Searching Expedition* (London, 1851), I, 165-166; II, 258-259, 267-269; H. W. Dove, "Temperature Tables," *Report of the . . . British Association . . . 1847* (London, 1848), 373-376, with twenty-three separately numbered pages of tables. The only data from Northwest British North America in Dove's tables were from Cumberland House.

14

L. H. Thomas, "The Mid-Nineteenth Century Debate on the Future of the North West," *Documentary Problems in Canadian History*, I, *Pre-Confederation*, ed. by J. M. Bumsted (Georgetown, Ontario, 1969), p. 220.

15

W. J. Humphreys, "Lorin Blodget," *Dictionary of American Biography* (New York, 1929), II, 379; [Cleveland Abbe] "Lorin Blodget," *Monthly Weather Review*, XXIX (April, 1901), 174; "Lorin Blodgett's [sic] Life is Ebbing," *The*

Philadelphia Inquirer, March 24, 1901, p. 1; J. K. McGuire, "The Father of American Climatology," *Weatherwise*, X (June, 1957), 92-94, 97.

16
Abbe, *op. cit.*, 174; National Archives (Washington, D. C.), Record Group 27, III, Letters 309 and 310; *Ninth Annual Report of the Board of Regents of the Smithsonian Institution* . . . (Washington, 1855), pp. 19-20.

17
Report of the Commissioner of Patents for the Year 1853. Agriculture (Washington, 1854), pp. 327-432; L. Blodget, *Climatology of the United States* . . . (Philadelphia, 1857), p. x.

18
H. F. Walling, ed., *Tackabury's Atlas of the Dominion of Canada* (Montreal, 1875), pp. 6, 98-101; L. Blodget, "Alaska. What is it Worth?" *Lippincott's Magazine*, I (1868), 185-191; Blodget, "Forest Cultivation on the Plains," *Report of the Commissioner of Agriculture for the Year 1872* (Washington, 1874), pp. 316-332; "Catalogue of Works on Atmospheric Physics and Climatology. Library of Lorin Blodget," American Philosophical Society, *Proceedings*, XXXII (1893), 248-269.

19
Smithsonian Archives (Washington), "Letters Sent. Metr. Dept. No. 1. Written by Lorin Blodget 1853-4," pp. 182-183, 277, 442; L. Blodget, "1854 - Washington. Observers & Correspondents of the Smithsonian Institution," MS volume in library of the American Philosophical Society, Philadelphia; *Report of the Commissioner of Patents for the year 1853. Agriculture* (Washington, 1854), p. 391.

20
Army Meteorological Register, for Twelve Years, from 1843 to 1854, Inclusive, Compiled from Observations Made by the Officers of the Medical Department of the Army . . . (Washington, 1855), pp. 679-763.

21
Ibid., 747, 760; G. M. Lewis, "Three Centuries of Desert Concepts in the Cis-Rocky Mountain West," *Journal of the West*, IV (July, 1965), 457-468; G. M. Lewis, "Regional Ideas and Reality in the Cis-Rocky Mountain West," Institute of British Geographers, *Transactions and Papers*, Publication no. 38 (1966), 135-150; *Scientific Writings of Joseph Henry*, II.

22
A. C. Gluek, *Minnesota and the Manifest Destiny of the Canadian Northwest* (Toronto, 1965), p. 132; M. J. Bowden, "The Perception of the Western Interior of the United States, 1800-1870 . . .," *Proceedings of the Association of American Geographers*, I (1969), 16-21.

23
Report from the Select Committee on the Hudson's Bay Company . . . (London, 1858); H. W. Dove, *Die Verbreitung der Wärme* . . . (Berlin, 1852); A. K. Johnston, *The Physical Atlas* (Edinburgh, 1848).

24
G. Simpson, *Narrative of a Journey round the World, during the years 1841*

and 1842 (London, 1847) I, 36-37, 45-46, 53, 55-56; *Report from the Select Committee*, pp. 45, 50, 77, 107.

25
New-York Daily Tribune, January 22, 1857, p. 3; *Daily Minnesotan* (St. Paul), January 3, and February 13, 1857; *Littell's Living Age*, XVII (April 18, 1857), 159.

26
Globe (Toronto), May 18, 1857, p. 2.

27
Report from the Select Committee, pp. iii-iv.

28
Globe, September 1, 1857, p. 2; "G. T. K." (G. T. Kingston, Professor of Meteorology, University College, Toronto) in *Canadian Journal of Industry, Science, and Art*, III (January, 1858), 28-34.

29
Blodget, *Climatology*, 529.

30
Ibid., 529-530, 533.

31
Ibid., 530. In his "Preliminary Chapter," p. 28, Blodget had forewarned the reader that he was interested in the "industrial and commercial results" no less than in the meteorological aspects of his work, and he drew attention to "the plains of the Missouri, Saskatchawan [*sic*], Athabasca, and Mackenzie Rivers."

32
Ibid., 534.

33
Gluek, *op. cit.*, 133; H. Bowsfield, ed., *The James Wickes Taylor Correspondence, 1859-1870* (Winnipeg, 1968), pp. xviii-xxv; S. J. Dawson, *Report on the Exploration of the Country between Lake Superior and the Red River Settlement, and between the Latter Place and the Assiniboine and Saskatchewan* (Toronto, 1859), pp. 22-23.

34
Walling, *op. cit.*

35
R. A. Bryson, Professor of Meteorology and Geography, University of Wisconsin, in letter, September 20, 1968; R. DeC. Ward, "Lorin Blodget's 'Climatology of the United States': An Appreciation," *Monthly Weather Review*, XLII (January, 1914), 23-27; Ward, *The Climates of the United States* (Boston, 1925), *passim*; J. B. Leighly, "Climatology," *American Geography: Inventory and Prospect*, ed. by P. James and C. Jones (Syracuse, 1954), pp. 336-339; *Petermann's Geographische Mittheilungen*, 1857, no. 12, p. 545; *The American Journal of Science and Arts*, XXV (1858), 247.

36
A. Taché, *Sketch of the North-West of America* (Montreal, 1870), p. 17.

37
W. L. Morton, *The Critical Years. The Union of British North America, 1857-1873* (Toronto, 1964), p. 33.

Steppe, Desert and Empire

John Warkentin

My title is adapted from Alexander von Humboldt's essay "Steppes and Deserts," published in Tübingen in 1808 in a little book called *Ansichten der Natur* and re-issued in much expanded form in two English editions in 1849 and 1850. Humboldt was essentially looking at steppes and deserts as landscape, or physiognomy as he called it, and was especially interested in analyzing their impact on man's aesthetic feelings and emotions. Only incidentally - though Humboldt's passing remarks can never be taken lightly - did he view them in their potential resource value, as the possible basis of economic development and empire.

It seems appropriate to draw the connection with Humboldt in this talk because when I first read his essay I kept associating his ideas with the western interior of Canada, where images of steppe and desert have also prevailed and become vital factors in determining strategies of colonizing and developing the land. Of course the natural landscape of the plains of interior Canada is not all steppe or desert or even prairie. The interior is a region where grass and forest meet, so that there are in fact three great vegetation zones: grassland; transition of grasslands and woodlands; and woodlands. Among the names that have been applied to one or another of these areas are: barrens, plains, prairies, meadows, steppes, desert, Fire Country, parkland, aspen-grove, fertile belt, strongwoods, and Great Western Forests. Some-times the areas have been viewed as landscape in the Humboldtian sense of physiognomy, sometimes in the sense of resource capability. This has resulted in confusion and misinterpretation. Images or myths of good land and bad land have been established, held sway for a time, and eventually been replaced by other appraisals. Meanwhile the course of empire-building was affected by particular images during their periods of tenure.

In this talk, I want to examine how the grasslands and the transition zone immediately to the north were viewed, described and interpreted, from the time of the first written records to the late nineteenth century when general settlement began. I will be concerned with the conceptions of men far away as well as those on the spot, and in particular I want to look at how terms such as desert, steppe and fertile belt came to be applied to specific zones, what such phrases meant to various observers, and what they came to mean to others.

The earliest reports we have of the area come from Henry Kelsey, who as a youth just out of his teens travelled in 1690-2 alone with a group of Indians from York Factory to the present The Pas and then into the country between the Saskatchewan and Assiniboine rivers. In both verse and prose he provided a picture of the landscape. The essential elements of the area's physiognomy were identified once he passed the Saskatchewan river: first woods, then clumps of trees amongst grass, and finally plains of grass as the woods were left behind. Kelsey introduced terms which were to be applied time and again in the future. "Desert" was used, in the sense of a lonely, empty area not as a sandy waste; "plain" seemingly in both the sense of flat terrain and as a synonym for grasslands; "poplo ridges" and "poplo island" for the aspen-grove park belt; and "barren ground" probably in the sense of bare of trees, though this term could have resource connotations as well.[1] In his entry of August 12, 1691, Kelsey caught exactly what countless observers after him have had to say about the man-made appearance of the parklands:

> Now we pitch again & about noon ye ground begins to grow barren [struck out in original] heathy & barren in fields of about half a Mile over Just as if they had been Artificially made with fine groves of Poplo growing around ym.[2]

Kelsey's complete journals did not see the light of day until 1929, but in 1749 a Committee of the House of Commons appointed to inquire into the affairs of the Hudson's Bay Company published excerpts from them, and in 1752 Joseph Robson referred to Kelsey's journey and the country he had seen, so that a few of Kelsey's descriptions of the land became public knowledge.

Subsequent explorers tended to echo Kelsey's observations on landscape rather than make appraisals of resources. The French explorers in the early eighteenth century remarked on the vast plains and prairies of the interior. Taken together the French had a knowledge of a vast expanse of territory extending from Lake Winnipeg to the Gulf of Mexico, but none of them, including the La Vérendryes, seem to have generalized on the character of the plains or attempted to define the area covered by prairie. The word "prairie" likely had various meanings, including both marshland and dry short grass country. Over sixty years after Kelsey's journeys the British made a spectacular re-entry into the interior, when Anthony Henday travelled in 1754-5 all the way from York Factory to the Saskatchewan and westward to where he probably could see the Rocky Mountains. In one season he spanned the full width of the "dry inland country, called by the Natives, the Muscuty Tuskee,"[3] conveying in his journal for the first time a sense of the vast dimension and scale of the grasslands. Henday travelled along the margins of the park belt with a group of Indians and by and large was highly impressed with the country. The Indians told him that the land to the south was named "Arsinee Warchee (i.e. dry country),"[4] a clear indication that the recognized significant regional differences within the interior. Henday's journal was not published until this century so that his observations were not widely known.

Henday's successors, Smith, Pink, Tomison, Cocking, and other servants of the Hudson's Bay Company, frequently used the term "Barren Grounds" in their journals, but they were well aware that the area was a fine provisioning ground for the Indians,[5] and once Hudson's Bay Company posts were established in the interior in 1774 the traders began to obtain food supplies there as well. Resource appraisals were thus made of the barren grounds, and the land was found to be rich in buffalo meat, so that "barren" clearly was a landscape term for grassland in this particular context, not a wasteland. None of these observations were printed but were kept with the business records of the Hudson's Bay Company. However, the first book on the interior by a man who had lived there was published in 1790 by Edward Umfreville. He praised the land along the North Saskatchewan, where he had lived, very highly, but he knew nothing of the South Saskatchewan Country so he could not make regional comparisons. As it happened, a reference in the correspondence of some Hudson's Bay Company officials to Umfreville's activities on the North Saskatchewan led to the recording of a distinctive regional term for that transition zone, the "Fire Country,"[6] indicating how the traders regarded the border land of forest and grassland, where it was thought that the woodlands were retreating in the face of frequent fires. Again, this information did not reach a wider public.

After the Conquest, British and American-born traders from Montreal began to enter the interior and compete with the Hudson's Bay Company for furs. Like the French they had the direct experience of entering the area from the Great Lakes, and they also possessed some knowledge of the plains west of the Mississippi. Perhaps it is this background which encouraged these men to place the plains in a continental context, viewing them in wide perspective and even delimiting their extent on manuscript maps and describing them in published books. On a manuscript map prepared in 1775 by Alexander Henry the elder a line showing "The Course of The Great Plaines" is marked, evidently intended to indicate the boundary between wooded country and grassland.[7] In 1775-6 Henry wintered in the interior, and in his account of his experiences, published in 1809, he stated that the plains, or prairies, extended from the Athabaska river to the Gulf of Mexico.[8] Peter Pond, in a map dated 1785, marked with a dotted line the eastern boundary of "immense Plains" stretching from north of Slave Lake to the forks of the Mississippi and Ohio rivers.[9] In 1801, Alexander Mackenzie, the most famous Nor'Wester of all, described the plains as extending across an area conforming reasonably to what Henry and Pond had shown on their maps.[10] This description appeared in a book recording his travels which had a wide circulation. Discerning readers now could know the continental extent of the plains, though there was no attempt to differentiate their varying internal characteristics.

Finer distinctions, akin to those recognized by the Indians with whom Henday had travelled, began to be made by David Thompson about 1800 when he was with the North West Company, and by some Hudson's Bay Company traders. Thompson said that the country on the North Branch of the Saskatchewan had "a fine deep black vegetable mould," but that the southern branches had a "very Sandy Soil."[11] Regional resource comparisons also began to be made. In 1815, James Bird, Chief Factor for the Hudson's Bay Company at Edmonton, wrote that the plains on the Saskatchewan were "more fertile than the larger plains of the South."[12] This is a clear anticipation of resource appraisals made forty to fifty years later by scientific exploring expeditions. Bird's conception of the plains is revealed in a map prepared at Carlton Post in 1815, attributed to Bird but more likely drawn by J. P. Pruden who was stationed there at the time (figure 1).[13] The map reveals how the plains were perceived by a man living on the North Saskatchewan in the aspen-grove area. "Woody Country" and "wood & Small Plains" are shown north of Carlton; these are succeeded southward by "Patches of small woods" and even a "last tuft of woods," and then in the receding distance beyond the South Saskatchewan river "Wide Plains" are marked again and again. The distant wide plains near the Bow river were visited shortly after the map was drawn by a Hudson's Bay Company brigade in 1822-3. The area was described as "an immense barren plain," with the soil near the Rockies considered to be better than the land farther away which was "poor and Sandy," though it was thought that gardens would succeed on the banks of the rivers.[14] This information, as so often before, was only available to Hudson's Bay Company officials in London.

A resource appraisal contradictory to those made by Hudson's Bay Company men at this time, in that it favoured the southern plains over the northern country, was published in 1820 by Daniel Harmon, a Nor'West fur trader. In his book of reminiscences he said that there were two main regions in the interior: one, extending from 44° to 52°, was plain or prairie country, almost entirely destitute of timber and sufficiently dry for any kind of cultivation; but the other area, from 52° to 70°, was rougher, with thinner soil and more water, and was perhaps one quarter to one third suited to cultivation.[15] The contrast of dry and wet seems to have been based on surface water. Hereafter it was public knowledge that a dry prairie existed in the interior, though the exact nature of the possible agricultural resources would still be obscure to readers. Further knowledge was slow in coming, even though a wide variety of observers began to visit the interior.

Practised scientific observers, attached to the two Franklin overland expeditions, entered the area for the first time in the 1820's. However, Dr. John Richardson and Thomas Drummond added nothing to what the fur traders had remarked on, nor did David Douglas, the famous botanical explorer who travelled along the North Saskatchewan in 1827. These visitors stayed within the parklands, and did not make any personal observations of the plains in the southern interior. Things were different in the United States. Investigators from east of the Mississippi were entering the plains, and from their observations a new image of the grasslands developed which was to have profound effects on how the plains of British North America were viewed.

Fur traders travelling up the Missouri in the 1790's had considered the country sterile, and Lewis and Clark on their exploration of 1804-6 called a restricted district on the Missouri "desert and barren."[16] Zebulon Pike in the published report of his 1806-7 exploration of the Arkansas river referred to a "sandy sterile desert."[17] But it was Stephen H. Long, after exploring the country along the Platte river in 1819-20, who wrote the decisive condemnatory interpretation of the region, backed up with the words "Great Desert" printed on the map accompanying his report, which created a conception of the plains east of the Rockies as a physical desert in the minds of the American public over the next few decades.[18] Thus the image of the Great American Desert, a perception of the plains which contrasted with that of the Hudson's Bay Company and North West Company traders, came into existence.

The traders had used terms such as barren grounds, prairie, plains, and even desert in the sense of empty and desolate, and some had recognized that the land on the North Saskatchewan was more fertile than that lying to the south, but they also knew that the southern interior was a great buffalo-meat producing region and not one had described it as a desert wasteland. But if continent-wide generalizations on the extent of the plains would continue to be made, as they had been made in the past by the Nor'Westers, then the new strongly expressed American views that an arid desert existed in the United States would have to be taken into account in describing the character of the British

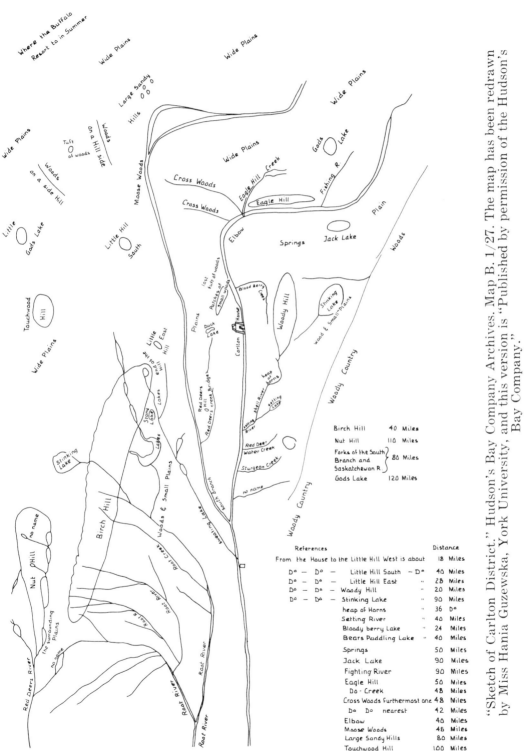

Where the Buffalo Resort to in Summer

Wide Plains

Wide Plains

Large Sandy Hills

Wide Plains

Wide Plains

Wide Plains

Woods on a Hill side

Tuft of woods

Moose Woods

Cross Woods

Cross Woods

Eagle Hill Creek

Eagle Hill

Gods Lake

Fishing R.

Plain

Woods

Woods on a side Hill

Little Gods Lake

Little Hill South

Elbow

Springs

Jack Lake

Touchwood Hill

last tuft of woods

Patches of small woods

Blood Berry Creek

Woody Hill

Stinking Lake

wood & Small Plains

Wide Plains

Little Hill East

Plains

Duck Lake

Carlton House

Waddy Country

heap of horns

hill to hill

Stony Lake

Lakes

Red Deer's creek Bridge

Setting Lake

Little Woods & Small Plains

Stinking Lake

Birch Hill

Red Deer Water Creek

Sturgeon Creek

no name

Setting River

Woody Country

Birch Hill   40 Miles
Nut Hill   110 Miles
Forks of the South
Branch and   } 80 Miles
Saskatchewan R.
Gods Lake   120 Miles

no name

Nut Hill

Red Deers River

Root River

Root River

Root River

Root River

the surrounding Plains

no name

References

From the House to the Little Hill West is about   18 Miles

Do — Do — Little Hill South — Do   40 Miles
Do — Do — Little Hill East   "   28 Miles
Do — Do — Woody Hill   "   20 Miles
Do — Do — Stinking Lake   "   90 Miles
            heap of Horns   "   36 Do
            Setting River   "   40 Miles
            Bloody berry Lake   "   24 Miles
            Bears Paddling Lake   "   40 Miles

            Springs   50 Miles
            Jack Lake   90 Miles
            Fighting River   90 Miles
            Eagle Hill   50 Miles
              Do - Creek   48 Miles
            Cross Woods Furthermost one 48 Miles
              Do Do nearest   42 Miles
            Elbow   40 Miles
            Moose Woods   48 Miles
            Large Sandy Hills   80 Miles
            Touchwood Hill   100 Miles

Distance

"Sketch of Carlton District." Hudson's Bay Company Archives. Map B. 1/27. The map has been redrawn by Miss Hania Guzewska, York University, and this version is "Published by permission of the Hudson's Bay Company."

North American plains. The grasslands of British North America had always been visited and viewed from the secure familiar base of the northern and eastern woodlands; now for the first time there was an opportunity for an entirely new image of a desert bad land, born in lower latitudes, to be diffused northwards if there was some medium for conveying it in that direction. It was some decades before this happened. In the meantime American scientific explorers roamed the trans-Mississippi plains, and some of their observations were also to affect the way in which the plains of British North America would be perceived.

American scientific observers entered the Missouri River Country in the 1840's mainly to collect natural history specimens for scientific museums such as the Smithsonian Institution. They were interested in collecting, not in regional resource appraisals. Only in the next decade was impetus given to general regional evaluations through the search for the best route for the proposed United States transcontinental railroad. The expeditions which looked for routes in the three more southerly latitudinal belts "confirmed" the existence of the Great American Desert west of the Mississippi river. Only Governor I. I. Stevens, carrying out the railroad survey along the most northerly belt through the Missouri River Country, did not use that generalization, though he did isolate areas of poor as well as good land. Many other surveyors and scientific explorers were in the field as well in the 1850's. G. K. Warren, who had previously explored the very dry Green and Snake river areas, emphasized that the desert character of the plains was not like that of the deserts west of the Rockies. Geologists began to carry out comprehensive investigations in this decade. F. V. Hayden prepared a report on the geology of the Missouri river area in 1857, in which he classified the Cretaceous strata and also attempted to draw relationships between particular geologic formations and potential agricultural capability.[19] Two other famous geologists, James Hall and James D. Whitney, in a survey of Iowa made a careful distinction between "prairie" and "plain."[20] A great deal of both empirical and interpretive geological and landscape information was thus being published by field investigators in the United States. And some of this data was applicable to the plains of British North America.

As information of various kinds accumulated, particularly meteorological data, grand generalizations on the resources of the western part of the continent which had some basis of fact began to be made by scientists in the eastern United States. Joseph Henry of the Smithsonian Institution, in a report on the physical geography of the United States printed in 1856, suggested that the 98th meridian was a crucial climatalogical dividing line, with the territory between that meridian and the Rocky Mountains a barren waste which would dissipate some of the dreams of extending settlement over the western part of the United States.[21] This was a repetition of the views held long since by Pike, Long, and many others but coming from the pen of one of the most respected scientists in the United States such an opinion carried weight. However, the climatologist L. L. Blodget swung the interpretation of agricultural potential a somewhat different way in his famous *Climatology* of 1857. As has been ably demonstrated by H. Bowsfield and G. S. Dunbar,[22] Blodget was the first person to drive home the point that the relatively warm climate of northwest interior North America would be of great significance in the agricultural development of that part of the continent. Blodget worked at a very broad scale, but since his remarks on the relation of temperature zones to agricultural development in the North West have proven roughly correct he has been given full credit by succeeding writers for his ideas, and has almost come to be regarded as a prophet. A grand classification of the physiography of North America into major regional units was attempted also at this time by another American savant. In the 1856 edition of A. K. Johnston's magnificent *Physical Atlas* the noted American geologist H. D. Rogers described the map of "Physical Features of North America."[23] On this map a "Great Central Plain" is designated in the interior of the continent. Within it the "Western Steppes" extend from the Peace river to the Rio Grande along the foot of the Rockies, and the "Great American Desert" is shown as a smaller unit within the Steppes. From the accompanying letterpress it is quite evident that Rogers applied the term Steppes to the high plains surface sloping eastward from the Rockies, broken by a succession of terraces or escarpments.

Thus a very important body of information on the American plains was accumulating: some of it descriptive; some of it carefully recorded and classified scientific data; some of it interpretive, speculative and contradictory; but all available in print. There seems to have been little spill-over of this information into British North America before the 1850's, perhaps because the British views were still filtered through the forest country surrounding the grassland. Moreover, the grasslands of British North America were hardly penetrated by the men based in the Red River and Saskatchewan Countries, except by the *Métis* on their annual buffalo hunts, so that the American studies likely did not appear very relevant. In short, thinking at this time was still in east-west latitudinal channels, not in north-south continental terms. Perhaps, indeed, Blodget made such a marked impact because he was one of the first men to deliberately attempt to transcend the latitudinal lines and follow isothermal belts in his thinking, cutting across conventional national frames of reference.

There were few empirical reports on interior British North America in the half-century before 1857 to match those in the United States. Trade became more and more routine once the Hudson's Bay Company was in exclusive control of the fur trade after 1821, and the regular reports by traders on their activities were housed in the Company's London offices and did not see public light. Only a few accounts of special journeys appeared in print. Thomas Simpson on his way to explore the Arctic coast travelled in winter from Fort Garry to Carlton in December of 1836, and the image of a desolate winter landscape comes through very explicitly in his writing.[24] By contrast, his uncle, Governor George Simpson, in a book on his journey around the world in 1841-2 paints a very pleasant picture of the fertile lands along the North Saskatchewan river in the summer of 1841.[25] West of present Portage la Prairie Governor Simpson ascended a terrace cut by the waters of Lake Agassiz in the Assiniboine delta, and referred to "one of Nature's steps from a lower to a higher level," a tantalizing, albeit fleeting, reference to two of the great relief surfaces of the plains.[26] The rarely visited Bow river area was probably described for the first time in print when Father P. J. Smet's letters referring to his short mission visit there in 1845-6, after a hard journey across the Western Cordilleran from Oregon, were published in 1847. He talked about travelling through "deserts," but seemed to use the word as a synonym for unknown country and wilderness, not a physical desert.[27] In any event, Father de Smet praised highly the land at the base of the Rockies.

One of the few other early sources we have to turn to on that area is David Thompson who in the 1840's was writing his reminiscences of the fur trade. Unfortunately Thompson's geographical descriptions only became readily available to readers in this century, because they were not published until 1916 and some not until 1962, though a few people had access to some of his papers in the 1850's and '60's. His narrative includes splendid regional interpretations of various parts of the British North American interior, making him one of the first important regional geographers in Canada. He noted that dews and rains were more copious on the North Saskatchewan than in the land to the southwest, and distinguished between plains and meadows on the basis that the grass on the plains was too short for cutting with a scythe, but that on meadows the grass was sufficiently long so that hay could be made.[28] He also looked at the interior in a continental perspective. The eastern side of the plains contained extensive meadows, but south of 44° to the Gulf of Mexico the plains were barren for great spaces, even of coarse grass.[29] Thompson considered the plains along the North

Saskatchewan and the wooded country north of the Assiniboine suited for agriculture, but the country extending to the Missouri river was deemed only adequate for pastoral uses, not agricultural, except in a few places.[30] In 1842, in a letter to the secretary of the Governor-General of British North America, Thompson made a very broad but generally valid resource appraisal of the interior which serves to summarize his views. He stated that fully one third of the land along the 49th parallel was fertile soil of the first quality, and the rest was part of the grassy plains extending to the mountains.[31] Deserts by name had not entered Thompson's mind, despite the fact that he was looking as far south as the Gulf of Mexico, and writing in the 1840's when the image of the Great American Desert was current.

The general geographical compilations and accounts on the country actually published about the time Thompson was writing did not nearly measure up to the old fur trader and geographer's narrative, even though some of the books were written by very able men. Admittedly, source material on British North America was very sparse, and even if information on the United States was available there was great difficulty in relating those conditions to the lands across the 49th parallel. In 1829, Hugh Murray, a capable Scottish compiler of historical and geographical works wrote a general book on North American exploration and landscape which contained an excellent description of the interior plains of the United States based on Stephen H. Long, including the account of the desert, but absolutely nothing on British North America.[32] Dr. John Richardson included accounts of the physical geography of British America in various publications. In one book he said the prairie lands of British North America were similar to those on the Missouri and Arkansas rivers, and cited Pike and Long in his bibliography, but he did not explicitly extend the Great American Desert into British North America.[33] In another report he compared, in a passing comment, the prairies of British North America to the Siberian steppes near Lake Aral.[34] This is perhaps the earliest analogy comparing a part of British North America with a district in Russia. In 1851, Richardson wrote the best account of the physical geography of British North America published to that time. He used terms such as prairie and plain, prairie plateau and prairie slope, but not steppe or desert.[35] Richardson, however, never did really come to grips with the interior plains as a region as Thompson had done, nor did he ponder over the desert concepts of Pike and Long, and thus did not add much illumination on the special qualities of the British North American grasslands.

Other writers fell far short of even Richardson's efforts, as books on Rupert's Land containing visions of empire began to appear in various quarters. Despite a lack of factual information, great sweeping resource appraisals of the interior were made as men began to see that the Selkirk Colony at Assiniboia might be a forerunner of a wider colonization. Some authors were primarily concerned with the question of whether the Hudson's Bay Company should be permitted to retain control of Rupert's Land. R. M. Martin wrote a book in 1849 defending the Company's monopoly and playing down the possibilities for settlement, but those views were shortly contested by J. E. Fitzgerald, assisted by Alexander Isbister, in another book.[36] Obviously these men followed set policy positions in formulating their resource evaluations.

Agricultural resources could only be developed and these speculations on the lands beyond Red River tested if there were improvements in accessibility. Comprehensive schemes for building transcontinental communications lines across British North America, using the motive force of the steam engine to drive either boats or railroad locomotives, were proposed in print at least as early as 1829 and pamphlets and books advocating various schemes continued to pour forth right through to the 1850's and '60's. By the nature of these things the plans of the MacTaggarts, Carmichael-Smythes, Synges, and others were based upon visions not knowledge, and the character of the terrain was normally an incidental factor in their speculations. Sources on the interior tended to be the writings of Sir Alexander Mackenzie and the two Simpsons; but once a few books were written the transportation planners and colonizers also cheerfully cited one another as authorities. A few of the later schemers were aware of American scientific explorations and of the concept of the Great American Desert and reasoned that the land in British North America was of a different, that is better, nature, and argued all the more strongly for a northern route. All the proposals were speculative, and nothing whatsoever was begun on the ground. Most of the writers were British, primarily concerned with such matters as emigration from Britain, colonization of British North America, development of resources and commerce, and the need for military defence against the United States. Almost inevitably the Hudson's Bay Company came under attack in these works.

Other expansionists also were critical of the Company. Beginning in the 1840's growing attention was given in Canada West to Rupert's Land. This partly was an acquisitive interest in the agricultural potential of the area, a matter of mounting urgency as the best land was taken up in Canada West, and partly an intention to extend the commercial influence of Canada, and particularly Toronto, into Rupert's Land.

Increasingly in the 1850's the question turned to whether Rupert's Land could be colonized: that is, was farming possible; what could be the region's role in the development of British North America and the

Empire; and, depending on answers to these questions, how should the area be administered. Since the British House of Commons had to formulate policy on the future of Rupert's Land, a Select Committee of Enquiry on the Hudson's Bay Company met at Westminster in 1857 to consider these matters. Many witnesses appeared before the Committee. Most thought that only the southern districts, if any, would be suited for settlement, though Dr. Richard King, who had travelled through the interior in the course of an overland Arctic expedition, thought that the fertile areas lay north of the Saskatchewan river.[37] Surprisingly, despite the fact that many witnesses were willing to damn the agricultural potential of the area, no one equated the southern interior of British North America with the alleged Great American Desert, or even mentioned the desert. Governor George Simpson expressed negative opinions on the possibilities of colonizing the interior, and a study of his private correspondence with other Hudson's Bay Company officials at this time indicates that his opinion was quite genuine, and that he truly believed that only a few favoured districts could be settled.[38] Nothing conclusive on the potential of the land emerged from the Enquiry except an awareness that there was a pressing need to obtain more information. A very much smaller but similar Committee of Enquiry established by the Canadian government a few months after the British Select Committee had met plainly revealed that there existed in Canada an expansionist thrust to push westward, and a pronounced tendency to exaggerate the possible resources of Rupert's Land.[39]

Even before the Committees of Enquiry had begun to meet there had been a plan brought forward in Britain in 1856 to send a scientific exploring expedition to Rupert's Land. It started as a private venture but soon turned into a government-sponsored exploration. The Canadian government responded in the spring of 1857 with its own expedition. The contradictory evidence which the Committees had heard on the resources of the interior demonstrated convincingly the need for all objective information which such explorations could provide on possible transportation links between Rupert's Land and Canada, on the geology, climate and vegetation of the area, and the potential for colonization based on agriculture.

Captain John Palliser, who led the British expedition, had hunted buffalo on the Missouri and Yellowstone rivers in 1847-8 and written a routine traveller's account of his experiences which would not have inspired any perspicacious person to entrust a scientific expedition to the author. Fortunately, he was accompanied on the exploring expedition by some extraordinarily able scientific observers, James Hector, a geologist, Eugene Bourgeau, a botanist, and Lieutenant Thomas Blakiston who carried out magnetic observations.

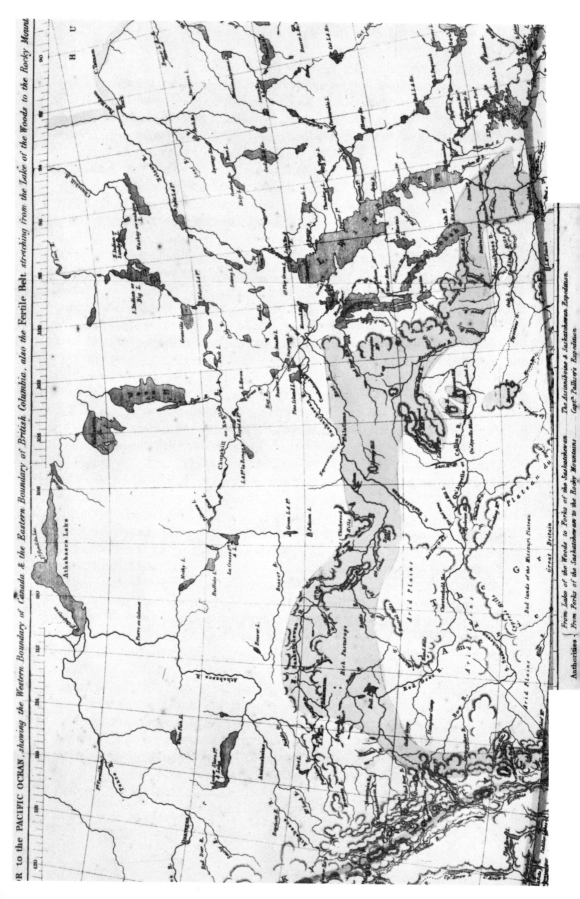

Canadian Pacific Railway Route Survey at the Elbow of the North Saskatchewan River in 1871.
[Published by permission of the Public Archives of Canada]

H. Y. Hind, who taught geology and chemistry at Trinity College, Toronto, was the geologist on the Canadian expeditions of 1857-8, and S. J. Dawson, a competent civil engineer, was the surveyor. L. L. Blodget's ideas on the resources of the North West were current in Toronto in the mid-1850's, and at least one of the explorers was aware of various American conceptions of the plains. Even before the Canadian expedition was planned Hind had been reading about the Great Plains and the Great American Desert, and had written a short speculative article, published in 1857, on the potential resources of the interior of the continent, in which he displayed an awareness of the thinking of Joseph Henry and Blodget on those matters. Hind even referred to the Great American Desert, and suggested that the thrust of westward settlement would be deflected northward by it into the valleys of the Red and Saskatchewan rivers.[40]

In the field seasons of 1857-9 Palliser and his men gathered evidence on the topography and resources of the interior from Red River to the Rocky Mountains, though the central area extending from the Cypress Hills north to the South Saskatchewan river was not visited. In their interim reports and maps, published in 1859 and 1860 as *Papers* and *Further Papers*, great vegetation zones and relief surfaces were identified.[41] Already on the general map produced in 1859 and published in the *Papers* the "Northern limit of true Prairie land - Sterile or with scanty pasture . . ." is shown, bounded to the north by a "Zone of Ancient forest cleared by fire - Soil fertile and rich - Vegetation luxuriant - Partially wooded with Poplar Willows & a few Pines," and north of this again the "South limit of the Thickwoods." Great vegetation zonations and terse resource appraisals were combined in these descriptions. In the printed material in the *Papers* there were brief comments on different districts confirming the generalizations made on the map. A geological report by Hector was also included in the *Papers* in which he distinguished three "prairie levels" marking the step by step rise in elevation of the plains from Lake Winnipeg to the Rockies.[42] The identification of these successive levels, of course, became a classic generalization, at a regional scale, on the relief features of the interior. The generalization seems to have been based on observed field data, though there is a chance that before he left England Hector might have seen H. D. Rogers' 1856 map of the physical features of the North American continent, and got some idea of the major relief surfaces in the interior from it. However, Hector did not use the term "steppes" at this time as a synonym for the prairie levels.

In the 1860 *Further Papers* many of the above observations were bolstered with further field evidence. Of great new interest is the fact that Blakiston in a separate report, which he submitted after leaving the expedition following a dispute with Palliser, showed that he clearly was aware of some American sources on the interior. He wrote that the plains, which were generally called the "High Central Plains" in the United States rose from Lake Winnipeg to the Rocky Mountains by successive steps, and that the Coteaus were the steps of the plains as they gained altitude.[43] The ideas are similar to Hector's interpretations of the major relief features of the interior plains, but they are not as fully or as clearly stated. Blakiston used American precedents in classifying the prairie into "dry arid," "arable," and "willow" prairie, and suggested that the southern part of the Saskatchewan Country had seldom more than a couple of inches of vegetable mould, "which tract stretching southward beyond the Missouri has in parts not inaptly been termed 'desert'."[44] Further, Blakiston drew attention to the same general zones of poor land and land of greater fertility as appeared on the map drawn by Palliser and Hector.

The *Papers* and *Further Papers* are very significant documents, not only because of the factual material they contain, but because great spatial generalizations were emerging, though an appropriate terminology had not been worked out. As yet the references to the American images of prairie and bad land were almost "thrown away" remarks by Blakiston, and Hector had made no direct references to American sources on these matters.

We must now turn to the work of the Canadian expedition. The explorers from Canada did their own field observing but they also had access to the data collected by Palliser and his men as it appeared in the *Papers*, which helped them in preparing their final reports.

S. J. Dawson spent much of his time investigating the route between Lake Superior and Red River, but in 1858 he made a quick journey to the Lower Saskatchewan river by Lakes Manitoba and Winnipeg, and returned by the Assiniboine to Red River. Dawson divided the country into three topographic divisions, identifying two of the three levels recognized by Hector, but distinguishing the Manitoba Escarpment as a separate unit. In assessing the possibilities for settlement he embraced Blodget's views on climate, once again showing the influence of Americans on the explorers of British North America,[45] but did not set down his interpretations in any detail. It is regrettable that Dawson did not travel farther westward than the Upper Assiniboine so that we could have had his opinions on the character of the plains of the central interior.

In 1857, his first field season, Hind did not travel west of Portage la Prairie, but obtained some information at second hand from local informants on the country extending to the west. He did not use a consistent terminology in referring to the topography of the lands he himself had not visited, but it is significant that neither his informants, as recorded by Hind, nor Hind himself used the term desert in describing the plains stretching westward to the South Saskatchewan and the Missouri rivers.[46] In the summer of 1858 Hind entered the country visited by Palliser and Hector the previous year, and travelled to the South Saskatchewan. This was before Palliser's first interim report was available to him. Just as with Palliser and Blakiston the concept of a sterile southern plain juxtaposed to a more fertile cultivable area to the north and east formed in Hind's mind, based on his field observations, as recorded in his *Report* of 1859.[47] He thought, however, that the southern lands were reclaimable if the annual fires which devastated the grasses were to cease for a few years.[48] Hind at this time did not explicitly refer to the extension of the Great American Desert into British North America, but towards the end of the *Report* he threw together some observations on the arid interior east of the Rockies, contained in the main text, with a lengthy footnote containing related quotations from his own remarks on the Great American Desert as they had appeared in the *Canadian Almanac* two years earlier.[49] Thus the arid interior plains of British North America were indirectly linked with the Great American Desert, though the connection was not carefully spelled out. Hind soon remedied this.

A firm, decisive depiction of the Great American Desert in southern Rupert's Land together with a fertile zone arched around it on the north and west, appeared on a map dated August, 1860, in the British Parliament's printed version of Hind's account of his exploring expeditions. The written part of the report is a close reproduction of the Canadian document with only minor editorial differences, but the British report contained this new map drawn by John Arrowsmith, the well-known London cartographer. It not only showed "The Great American Desert" printed boldly across the southern plains of British North America and extending into the United States, but a "Fertile Belt" stretching in a great arc from the Lake of the Woods to the Rocky Mountains, passing through the Red and Saskatchewan River Countries and ending in the foothills at the 49th parallel (see figure 2).[50] Quite clearly much of the field data on which the western part of the map was based came from Palliser as acknowledged by Hind. Arrowsmith, who was also drawing maps for Palliser's reports, had access to Palliser material and it appears that some Palliser data was incorporated by Arrowsmith on the map intended for Hind's British report even before it had appeared in print in the Palliser *Further Papers*. The map prepared by Arrowsmith for Hind's British Parliamentary report was also reproduced in Hind's narrative account of his expeditions which he prepared for popular distribution and published in November, 1860.[51] In the *Narrative*, Hind had the opportunity to discuss in detail the potential importance of the presence of a desert and a Fertile Belt in British North America on the economic development of the interior. He immediately saw the importance of these conceptions as images of bad and good land in the West. Hind also introduced the words "prairie" and "plain" to Rupert's Land in the usages defined by the American geologists Hall and Whitney. The prairie, Hind suggested, was the tall grass area east of the Missouri Coteau, and the plains comprised the area of shorter grasses and the more sterile region forming the plateau of the Grand Coteau.[52] But these terms did not take hold. They disappeared under the new conceptualizations of Fertile Belt and Great American Desert stressed so strongly elsewhere in the *Narrative*.

Palliser and Hector were home in Britain in the summer of 1860, and likely they were not exposed to the new terminology until they came across it in Hind's map and his text in the *Narrative*. The fact that they did not use such publicist's terms as Fertile Belt and Great American Desert in addressing a general meeting of the Royal Geographical Society on their explorations in June of 1860, despite the fact that they mentioned the existence of good and bad country,[53] would indicate that they probably had not yet encountered the terms. Furthermore, one gets the impression from an incidental but revealing comment written by Hector in 1861 stating that Palliser's expedition was the first to recognize the "fertile belt,"[54] but not claiming that Palliser's group named it, that Hector was perhaps attempting to stake out credit where credit was due. Once the terms "Fertile Belt" and "desert" were in circulation Palliser and Hector did use them in their later reports.

In 1863 the results of the Palliser expedition were presented to the public in a final massive *Report*. The major findings are stated bluntly in the introduction. The great regional generalizations on vegetation and relief are presented, and terms such as "fertile belt" and "central desert" are used. Further, in the body of the *Report* these words occasionally appear in the pages describing the field traverses made in 1857, '58 and '59, but one must bear in mind that the manuscript copy for the printer was prepared after the return of the expedition to England and after Hind's map and *Narrative* were issued. Unfortunately most of the field books of the Palliser expedition are lost or destroyed so that there is at present no way of checking whether the terms "fertile belt" and "central desert" were used in the field.[55] In any event Hind would not have had access to the field books and the terms did not appear in the *Papers* and *Further Papers*, so we have to credit him with the public introduction of the terms "Fertile Belt" and "Great

American Desert" to designate two special conceptual regions and images of good and bad land within British North America.

An innovation in nomenclature was introduced by Hector when he substituted the word "steppe" for "level" in referring to the "three prairie levels." "Steppe" was first used in this way by Hector in a paper read before the Geological Society of London in 1861,[56] and it is possible that he may have followed H. D. Rogers' prior usage of it as a physiographic term, though Hector does not cite Rogers. Nowhere does Hector justify this use of an inappropriate vegetation term for a physiographic feature. We have already noted that Sir George Simpson and Blakiston employed the word "step" in referring to a break in slope in the general rise of the plains, and the word "steppe" occasionally blurs over towards the meaning in the Palliser *Report*.[57] Generally, however, it is used to refer to the great erosion surfaces of the interior plains, and in that sense it was widely adopted by subsequent writers.

The generalizations of Fertile Belt and Great American Desert were great overriding classifications for looking at the vast resources of the interior at a regional scale. The scientific explorers were well aware that there were many districts of poor land in what they called the Fertile Belt, and of good land in the desert. In fact, Hector even said in a section on meteorology towards the end of the 1863 *Report* that the true desert of the United States did not extend into British North America, thus contradicting some of the generalizations in the introduction of that volume.[58] Hector, however, did make observations on the nature of parent materials which brought the level of field investigation to a finer level of detail than the grand climatic generalizations. He noted that in the south, where Tertiary and Cretaceous clays formed the surface, hard clay soils of a barren nature prevailed, but that to the north on the Pleistocene deposits the soils were more varied.[59] He thought that summer moisture was adequate to support vegetation in Rupert's Land, and attributed the extension of arid plains into such high latitudes to the presence of the Cretaceous clays. He may have been guided in these observations by F. V. Hayden's work in the Missouri Country just to the south. Whatever his inspiration Hector did make a vital distinction between the soils of the northern and southern interior, placing on a more scientific basis similar but unpublished observations already made by David Thompson and James Bird.

It has been necessary to examine the broad findings of the British and Canadian scientific exploring expeditions in some detail because their observations and classifications set the style in which the interior was perceived for some decades to come, and in selected instances, such as the three prairie steppes, in the way they are conceived today. The phrases Fertile Belt and Great American Desert effectively broadcast images of great regions of good and bad land in the West. Hind made explicit public pronouncements on the implications for future settlement of these zones, and got much of the early public attention. There were reviews in British journals emphasizing the resource appraisals made by Hind, and also giving some attention to Palliser's observations on vegetation zones. Yet in the long run, Palliser's name has become more securely identified with the images of good and bad land than Hind's, especially with the idea of the existence of an alleged desert in the interior. The various terms, of course, appeared in the Palliser *Report*, but perhaps the most effective instrument in imprinting these ideas on the public's mind was the Palliser map intended to accompany the *Report* but not published until 1865. This was not just a simple map of the interior designating the Fertile Belt and the Great American Desert, as in Hind's map of 1860, but a fine detailed cartographic representation of the area which served as a fundamental source of information and a base map of the region for many years. On this map the three prairie levels or steppes, "Arid Plains," zones of vegetation, and areas of rich land are designated, but the terms Great American Desert and Fertile Belt do not appear. Yet from the annotations on the map there was no mistaking the change in quality of the land in going from south to north, and it is this Palliser map, together with the introduction to the *Report*, which made such a long lasting impact.

Prior to Palliser's and Hind's expeditions to the interior, there had been a generally passive, largely uninformed, yet on the whole positive, appreciation of the nature of the land. After the expeditions a myth of good land in the North Saskatchewan Country was reinforced, and established more strongly than before, and a myth of bad land in the southern interior was started. In fact, the tag of desert could now be applied to the latter at any time to make the idea of sterility all the more potent. Thus the Palliser and Hind expeditions really established the background and set the conditions for a succession of new appraisals of the interior. Their work marked the beginning of a direct, not just a speculative, concern with the resources of the region, and the problems of devising strategies for administering the area, building transportation links, and colonizing the land.

The critical evaluations which were to shape the future of the region were made by outsiders, not by residents of the area, because the views and the images presented by concerned outsiders effectively influenced the governmental and financial institutions interested in developing the resources of the region and also affected possible migrants to the interior. Local residents did not tend to praise or damn districts in the way external examiners did, but took a much more placid view of the potential resources of the interior. Neither the contemporary histories

of Red River nor the weekly *Nor'Wester*, published at Red River beginning in 1859, convey any sense of a physical desert existing somewhere westward of the Colony. In fact, in the 1850's, Edward Denig, an
experienced American trader living on the Missouri in the area of the
alleged desert, wrote "Notwithstanding the unquestioned dull and
dreary appearance always presented by naked and extensive plains
there are no places that could reasonably be termed deserts."[60] In the
evidence submitted to the Select Committee on the Hudson's Bay Company in 1857 there was no hint from any of the witnesses that a desert
was thought to exist. Indeed, in the testimony of Rev. G. O. Corbett and
John McLaughlin there was indirect evidence against such a view.[61]
Thomas Cook, a mixed-blood missionary stationed at Fort Ellice, went
on buffalo hunts with the Indians and *Métis* in the 1860's and early '70's.
It is apparent from Cook's journals that he was aware that the southern
interior had its advantages and disadvantages as a place in which to
live, but to someone like Cook who knew the land it was a region in
which man could live a nomadic life, and the plains were not a forbidding wasteland.[62]

Travellers who entered the area in the 1840's, '50's and '60's, such as
Paul Kane, the Earl of Southesk, Lord Milton and Dr. Cheadle, and Dr.
John Rae, made few illuminating comments on the region in comparison
to what Palliser and Hind had reported. The Earl of Southesk, the most
observant of these travellers, thought the barren prairie was scarcely
even suited for grazing purposes,[63] but most travellers were non-com-
mittal about resources and at best might hazard a comment on the arid
and desolate appearance of the landscape in the southern interior.

Such neutrality ceased in the 1860's when the terms for the transfer of Rupert's Land to Canada were negotiated. Surprisingly, the
Palliser-Hind term of "Fertile Belt" became a technical phrase with
its own special meaning in the negotiations carried on amongst the officials of the British Colonial Office, the Hudson's Bay Company, and
the Government of Canada. The accepted position became that the
northern part of Rupert's Land was suited for the fur trade, whereas
the land to the south, extending from the North Saskatchewan river
to the 49th parallel, was largely fit for settlement. Consequently
the whole southern interior began to be designated the "fertile
belt" in the negotiations. This delineation did not correspond with the
Fertile Belt as defined by Palliser or Hind, but the negotiators rarely
referred to those explorers in their memoranda; they were thinking
at a mid-continental scale and did not choose to draw fine distinctions within the relatively small area south of the North Saskatchewan river not suited for producing furs. Once the negotiations for
the transfer of Rupert's Land were completed in 1869-70 the special

usage of "fertile belt" was lost to sight, except insofar as the terms continued to affect the transfer of land from the Crown to the Hudson's Bay Company.

Generally there was a return to the more restricted delimitation as defined by Palliser and Hind, but by no means everyone adopted their location of the fertile land. Indeed the attempts to identify and locate a Fertile Belt and decide whether or not a desert existed in the southern interior were just beginning. There were great latitudinal shifts in the location of the Fertile Belt, and the very idea of the existence of a desert was to come and go.

One person who early deemed that it was necessary to investigate the reliability of the Palliser-Hind conceptions of the quality of land in the interior was A. J. Russell, Inspector of Crown Timber Agencies in Canada. In 1869 he published a book on the Northwest based on wide reading but no field observation in which he suggested that fertile pockets of land extended north of the Saskatchewan river into the lake country, and warned against making sweeping adverse generalizations about the agricultural potential of the prairie land to the south, saying the land might very well have been underrated by Palliser and Hind.[64]

The view that the fertile lands lay to the north of the Saskatchewan river within the forest region was strongly advocated in 1870 by Bishop Taché, who had a quarter of a century of experience in the country. He accepted the extension of the Great American Desert into British North America, but was sceptical of the praise lavished on the Fertile Belt, and stated that the zone had been overrated.[65] A considerable part of his life had been spent in mission work on the Upper Churchill river, so he was praising the very areas with which he was familiar. In 1873, Captain William F. Butler, soldier, indefatigable traveller and acute topographical observer, who visited the North Saskatchewan Country in the winter of 1872-3, reiterated Taché's views even more strongly, stressing that the centre of the true Fertile Belt lay north of the Saskatchewan river.[66] He criticized the southern lands by inference only, since Butler had not visited them. Men such as Samuel Anderson of the International Boundary Survey of 1872-5, and the officers of the North West Mounted Police, who traversed the southern interior regularly after 1874, tended to follow the lead of Palliser and Hind and view that area as forbidding and barren, even if not quite a desert, despite the fact that they lived and survived quite successfully on the plains.[67] Even the Dominion Lands Survey regarded the southern plains as a desert when it began its cadastral surveys in the interior in the 1870's.

But a direct reappraisal of the Palliser-Hind conception of the existence of a desert in the southern interior came with the arrival of G. M.

Dawson, a young scientist from Montreal, on the plains to work as a geologist on the International Boundary Survey. Dawson took surface materials and soil into account in evaluating the land, factors which F. V. Hayden, the American geologist, and James Hector of the Palliser expedition had already considered. Most of the third steppe, Dawson said, was not as good as the best parts of the first and second steppes, but he expressed the very telling judgement that

> the explorations in connection with the Boundary Survey have served to show, that this country, formerly considered almost absolutely desert, is not - with the exception of a limited area - of this character; that a part of it may be of future importance agriculturally, and that a great area is well suited for pastoral occupation and stock farming.[68]

When men began to look closely and carefully at the ground and did not just base their thoughts on the generalizations of others the idea of a desert in the interior was ready for dissolution. Dawson had pointed the way.

The attack on the concept of the desert continued with the surveys for the Canadian Pacific Railway carried out under the direction of Sandford Fleming. Even here there was no concerted opinion of what was good and what was bad land, because various engineers and observers took different positions on just where the most fertile areas were located. Fleming accepted the Palliser-Hind formulations on good and bad land as a working basis for considering the resources of the interior, and projected the C.P.R. railroad route through the Fertile Belt on the North Saskatchewan towards Yellow Head Pass. But there were strong advocates for very different interpretations on where the good land lay and on which routes to follow. The northern area beyond the Saskatchewan extending towards the Peace river had its enthusiastic supporters amongst the railroad group, including Charles Horetzky, employed as a surveyor, the botanist John Macoun, and the Deputy Engineer-in-Chief of the C.P.R., Marcus Smith. Smith vigorously promoted a northern route, shifting the Fertile Belt northward to Lac la Biche, Lesser Slave Lake and the Peace river, to be in line with Pine Pass through the Rockies which he was advocating. Meanwhile John Macoun was strongly instrumental in revising the prevailing view that the southern interior was an arid plain not suited for agricultural development, even though he continued to believe in the fertility of the Fertile Belt and Peace River Country as well. Macoun made numerous reconnaissance resource surveys for the C.P.R. and the government, and as early as 1876 before he had even visited the southern plains he was suggesting on the basis of the reports of Palliser and G. M. Dawson that there were many good areas within the "Desert," though he also stated that on the evidence available to him at that time he could not give limits to the desert.[69] In the next year he followed G. M. Dawson's ideas even more closely in discussing the southern country, and ended by stating that only a limited area in the southern interior was desert.[70] Thus on the basis of the existing literature Macoun had begun to do away with the idea of a desert, and advocated this position even more strongly once he travelled in the southern interior in 1879 and 1880. He continued to follow the lead of Dawson in attributing much of the aridity to the nature of the surface materials and soil.

Macoun has been accused of propagandizing in favour of the southern plains in order to lend support for a southern railroad route.[71] The evidence is against this, because Macoun was already following Dawson in exploding the myth of the desert before the C.P.R. route was shifted south in 1881 by the C.P.R. syndicate, away from the route Fleming had projected. It is true, however, that Macoun was an optimist, and easy and a bit reckless in his generalizations about the quality of land. Also he had a great belief in plants as indicators of fertility, and he may have been carried away by the fact that he was in the interior during the wet decade of the 1870's, when the vegetation on the plains was likely deceptively verdant. Macoun's work had considerable impact. The Dominion Lands Branch already reported in 1880 on the basis of Macoun's surveys for the government that the "portion of the so-called American Desert which extends northerly into Canadian territory, is proved to have no existence as such," and Macoun himself said in a speech in 1881 that there was no such thing as a fertile belt, "it was all equally good land."[72] In his large book, *Manitoba and the Great North-West*, published in 1882, Macoun was a deliberate publicist and established to his satisfaction that most of the interior was habitable, and he explicitly stated that he was revising views previously held by others which were counter to his own more favourable interpretations.[73]

It is difficult to say to what extent policy decisions on railroad-building and resource development were related to the new interpretations of the quality of the land in the southern interior. Certainly the politicians in Ottawa were concerned about the resource potential of the plains and in the years from 1879-82 debated about the number of arable acres in the West, and voiced concern about whether the desert actually existed. Proponents of the transcontinental railroad such as Sir Charles Tupper, the Minister of Railways, drew support from Macoun's rosy generalizations, and Tupper even talked about a "garden of the world" in the West.[74] The Liberal opposition in the House of Commons was sceptical about the quality of the land in the south and tried to find out why Marcus Smith's proposed northern route was not adopted, and wondered whether the desert did not eliminate much land from future settlement.[75] The Conservatives in power wanted to think that all the lands were generally fertile, clutched the Fertile Belt and turned to Macoun's reports to demonstrate that the desert conditions in the south were merely local. Many of these interpretations were based on partisan politics, but also there was genuine perplexity and concern about the quality of the resources in different parts of the plains and the best location for the railroad line.

The latter problem was taken out of the hands of the politicians when the Canadian Pacific Railway Syndicate was formed in 1880 and in the following spring made the decision to shift the route from the Fertile Belt, Fleming's choice, to go through the southern plains, the erstwhile desert of Palliser and Hind. Probably the change was made for a variety of reasons, including, I expect, a belief that there was good as well as bad land in the south (likely Macoun had some influence here); that the shortest most direct route to the Pacific Ocean was preferable over the long run; that traffic would be generated in supplying the special needs of future settlers in the more arid area; and that a southern line would help prevent American railroads from invading Canadian territory. Surprisingly, the change of routes was hardly discussed in the House of Commons and even the question of the resource potential of the southern country tended to fade away once the whole project was in the lap of the Syndicate. There seemed to be an unconscious acceptance that a railroad would by its mere existence improve the country and that the matter of the aridity of the southern plains need no longer be raised.

Yet, even if the politicans stopped debating over the resources of the interior, other observers still had much doubt about the nature of the land. In 1879, Alexander Munro, a caustic New Brunswick surveyor, furiously attacked the rosy pictures of the interior painted by so many writers, including the many rave comments on the rich lands of the Fertile Belt.[76] The Rev. D. M. Gordon that same year sensibly suggested that fertile or infertile areas did not exist in vast continuous belts in the interior, so that grand generalizations were misleading.[77] In 1881 the lands of the interior received a wonderful public relations endorsement when the Governor-General, the Marquis of Lorne, travelled through the area and pronounced the land fine, thus lending his prestige, and the avenues to wide publicity that his office enjoyed, to dispelling the myth of the arid interior.[78] Yet even while the railroad was being constructed through the southern plains in 1881-3 there was still much doubt about the true character of the land.[79] Perhaps the most revealing comments came from Sir Sandford Fleming, who travelled through the interior by the new railroad in 1883 and recorded that in his opinion the land improved relatively in going from the plains of the United States northward to the North Saskatchewan river. He still was somewhat sceptical about the quality of the land in the southern interior near the 49th parallel, certainly in comparison to the Fertile Belt, though the idea of a desert had been eradicated from his mind.[80]

With the railroad built, settlement began, and the future of the region was to be decided by the actual experiences of farmers. No railroad, of course, was built through the northern Fertile Belt recognized by Taché, Butler, Marcus Smith and others, so that the question of whether that country was fertile or not remained an academic problem. The first actual test of widespread agricultural colonization west of Manitoba came in the southern interior. Detailed land surveys closely followed the railroad tracks, and as the surveyors' field notes flowed into Ottawa the annual reports of the Department of the Interior stated ever more firmly that the former idea of a large area of relative desert or barren land in the southern plains was contraverted, though admittedly it was still hard to appraise the exact potential of the land. In the Report of the Department of the Interior for 1882 there was a very illuminating statement on perception of the land:

> newcomers are inclined to underrate the fertility of prairie soil. A surveyor on his first trip to the North-West, will classify as third and fourth class land, what another, more experienced will call first and second class. It should be remembered that with the same quality of land, the prairie of the west cannot have as good an appearance as the highly cultivated meadows of the east.[81]

Quite quickly then in the early 1880's John Macoun's optimistic views of the southern plains got authoritative support and documentation from the land surveyors so that the desert image began to be expunged from official literature. The C.P.R. did its best to foster this by placing ten experimental farms near the right-of-way on its main line in 1882, and established, to its satisfaction at least, that farming was possible. Such information quickly hit the immigrant guide books and soon the desert was heard of no more except in the words of far away writers who had not yet received the latest dogma, or of some boosters of Canada who it seems found it expedient to acknowledge the existence of a Great American Desert so that they could say that it extended in less malignant form across the border.

Even as the railroad and settlement eroded the image of the desert, they also spelled the ultimate demise of the Fertile Belt in the way Rev.

D. M. Gordon had foreseen. It would not do to single out a northern zone for special distinction, when, following the construction of the railroad, the southern plains were actually being occupied. The wider conceptualizations of a large desert and extensive Fertile Belt were abandoned in the 1880's, and in their place emerged a recognition of the specific qualities, good and bad, of the smaller districts within which settlers moved and lived, and could directly comprehend. By what they achieved farmers recorded indelibly the quality of the land and their own management ability, and images of extensive desert zones and fertile belts proved delusive against such potent evaluations. This freed the word "fertile" to be used for other unknown and untried areas within Canada into which optimists wanted to entice farmers, such as various "clay belts" and the Canadian North Land. After 1880 the views and words of outsiders on the land had less and less significance on determining the resource images of the interior plains. What counted were the aspirations, accomplishments, and conceptions of the people who lived in the many communities within the region.

However, the underlying physical circumstances of a dryer southern area and a moister northern land with associated soils and vegetation types noted by James Bird, David Thompson, John Palliser, H. Y. Hind, Sandford Fleming and many others remained a reality, and special farming techniques such as conserving moisture by summer fallowing, irrigation, or turning from arable farming to ranching were devised to overcome deficiencies in moisture. In some years the climatic conditions approached so close to aridity that the image of the arid desert of Palliser and Hind was reinvoked, as happened in the 1930's. But such crisis conditions did not even always have to prevail to get an occasional return to the desert image. There was a chance that this could happen whenever a comprehensive objective view of the natural environment was suspended. For instance, in the 1890's when land surveyors were attempting to promote irrigation in the southwest portion of the interior, they emphasized the arid conditions they wished to overcome to such a degree in their official government reports that a carefully phrased retraction was published in a subsequent official statement.[82] This is only another instance of how difficult it is to be objective about the potential use of a marginal area, especially when there are changing resource demands. Each observer tends to have blinders which channel and limit his particular perception of an area.

In the interior grasslands of Canada there has been a wide variety of interpretations of the potential of the land for agricultural resource use, but over all the idea has prevailed that the more dependable area for farming is in the north and that the south is less well-endowed. Yet even today the images of garden and desert come into play when overriding changes in natural conditions affect large zones for many months on end, upsetting the existing equilibrium of farm life. As Humboldt suggested, areas of low precipitation, such as steppes and deserts, are indeed distinctive habitats for man.

Footnotes

1

[Henry Kelsey] *The Kelsey Papers*. With an Introduction by Arthur G. Doughty and Chester Martin. Published by the Public Archives of Canada and the Public Record Office of Northern Ireland. Ottawa: King's Printer, 1929.

2

Ibid., p. 11.

3

L. J. Burpee, ed., "York Factory to the Blackfeet Country. The Journal of Anthony Hendry, 1754-55." *Proceedings and Transactions of the Royal Society of Canada*, Third Series, Vol. I (1907), p. 325.

4

Andrew Graham, "Observations on Hudsons - Bay." Entry of October 29, 1754. Hudson's Bay Company Archives. E.2/6. p. 44. Information in this paper from the Company's Archives is "published by permission of the Hudson's Bay Company."

5

Joseph Smith, "York Factory Journal 1757/58. By Joseph Smith." Hudson's Bay Company Archives. B.239/a/45. fo. 3r.
William Pink, "William Pink's In-Land Journal 1767 & 8." Entries for August 18, November 13, 1767. Hudson's Bay Company Archives. B. 239/a/58. fos. 8r, 17v.
William Tomison, "Journal Book inland to the Muscoutte Country Anno Domi 1769." Entry of November 9, 1769. Hudson's Bay Company Archives. B.239/a/64. fo. 9v.
Matthew Cocking, "Journal of a Journey Inland with the Natives by Matthew Cocking Second at York Factory, commencing Saturday 27th, June 1772, and ending Friday 18th June 1773." Entry of August 7, 1772. Hudson's Bay Company Archives. B.239/a/69. fo. 9r.

6

John Kipling, "The Abstracts from Mr. Kipling's Journal." Entry of August 3, 1786. "Albany Letters Inward." Hudson's Bay Company Archives. A.11/5. fo. 43r.
Governor and Committee to Edward Jarvis, Chief at Albany House. May 23, 1787. Hudson's Bay Company Archives. A.5/2. fo. 161v.

7

The map is in the Map Library of the Public Archives of Canada, Ottawa. It is titled "A Map of the North West Parts of America. With the Utmost Respect. Inscribed to His Excellency Sir Guy Carleton, Knight of the Bath: Captain General and Governor of the Province of Quebec: General and Commander in

Chief of His Majesty's Forces In the Said Province, and Frontiers thereof. &c. &c. &c. By his Most Obedient Humble Servt. Alexr. Henry."

8

Alexander Henry, *Travels and Adventures in Canada and the Indian Territories, Between the Years 1760 and 1776* (New York, 1809), p. 265.

9

Henry R. Wagner, *Peter Pond Fur Trader & Explorer.* Yale University Library: 1955. A copy of Pond's map is included in a portfolio accompanying the volume. It is titled "Copy of a Map presented to the Congrès by Peter Pond a native of Milford, in the State of Connecticut." "New York I. March 1785." It is a facsimile of the St. John de Crèvecoeur copy in the Bibliothèque du Service Hydrographique de la Marine, Paris. Professor Malcolm Lewis first drew my attention to this important boundary in his paper, "Apperceptual Geographies: British Contributions to the Emergence of Ideas about the Cis-Rocky Mountain West." Mimeographed copy of paper read to Section E, British Association for the Advancement of Science, September 7, 1970, p. 10.

10

Alexander Mackenzie, *Voyages from Montreal* (London, 1801), pp. lxiii, lxix, 402-3.

11

Quoted in John Warkentin, "David Thompson's Geology: A Document." *Journal of the West*, Vol. VI, No. 3 (July, 1967), p. 483.

12

James Bird, "A short Account of Edmonton District 1815." Hudson's Bay Company Archives. B.60/e/1. fo. 1v.

13

"Sketch of Carleton District." Hudson's Bay Company Archives. Map G.1/27.

14

Francis Heron to Governor George Simpson. Bow River District, May 1st., 1823. Hudson's Bay Company Archives. B.34/e/1. pp. 197-8.

15

Daniel W. Harmon, *Sixteen Years in the Indian Country, The Journals of Daniel Williams Harmon 1800-1816*, ed. W. Kaye Lamb (Toronto, 1957), p. 238.

16

Elliott Coues, ed., *History of the Expedition under the Command of Lewis and Clark . . . Performed during the years 1804-5-6, by Order of the Government of the United States,* 4 vols. (New York, 1893), Vol. I, p. 329. Entry of May 26, 1805. (The Lewis and Clark Journals were first published in 1814.)

17

Elliott Coues, ed., *The Expeditions of Zebulon Montgomery Pike; To Headwaters of the Mississippi River, through Louisiana Territory, and in New Spain, During the years 1805-7,* 3 vols. (New York, 1895), Vol. II, p. 428.

18
Edwin James, *Account of an Expedition From Pittsburgh to the Rocky Mountains, Performed in the Years 1819, 1820.* 3 vols. (London, 1823), Vol. II, pp. 156, 170, 173; Vol. III, pp. 236-7, 276-89.

19
F. V. Hayden, "Notes Explanatory of a Map and Section Illustrating the Geological structure of the country bordering on the Missouri River, from the mouth of the Platte River to Fort Benton, in lat. 47° 30' N., long. 110° 30' W." *Proceedings of the Academy of Natural Sciences in Philadelphia* (May, 1857), pp. 112-3.

20
James Hall and James D. Whitney, *Report on the Geological Survey of the State of Iowa.* Vol. I, Part I (1858), pp. 18-9.

21
Joseph Henry, "Meteorology In Its Connection with Agriculture." *U.S. Patent Office Report. Agricultural Report.* 34 Congress, 3rd Session. Sen. Ex. Doc. 53, pt. 4. pp. 481-3.

22
Hartwell Bowsfield, *The James Wickes Taylor Correspondence 1859-1870.* Altona: Manitoba Record Society (1968), p. xviii.
G. S. Dunbar, "Isotherms and Politics: Perception of The Northwest in the 1850's," pp. 80-101.

23
A. K. Johnston, *The Physical Atlas of Natural Phenomena* (Edinburgh and London, 1856), Plate 7.

24
Thomas Simpson, *Narrative of the Discoveries on the North Coast of America; Effected by the Officers of the Hudson's Bay Company During the Years 1836-39* (London, 1843), pp. 26-48.

25
George Simpson, *Narrative of a Journey Round the World, During the Years 1841 and 1842,* 2 vols. (London, 1847), Vol. I, p. 79.

26
Ibid., p. 62.

27
Pierre Jean de Smet, S. J., *Oregon Missions and Travels over the Rocky Mountains in 1845-46,* R. G. Thwaites, ed., *Early Western Travels 1748-1846* (New York, 1966), Vol. 29, pp. 171, 209, 244-5. (First published in 1847).

28
Richard Glover, ed., *David Thompson's Narrative 1784-1812* (Toronto: The Champlain Society, 1962), pp. 53, 141.

29
Ibid., pp. 141-3.

30
Ibid., pp. 54, 142-3, 181.

31

David Thompson to Captain H. Bagot. Montreal, February 12th, 1842. Public Records Office, London. C.O. 42/490. fo. 97v.

32

Hugh Murray, *Historical Account of Discoveries and Travels in North America; Including the United States, Canada, the Shores of the Polar Sea, and the Voyages in Search of a North-West Passage; with Observations on Emigration*, 2 vols. (London, 1829), Vol. II, pp. 293-4.

33

John Richardson, *Fauna Boreali-Americana; or the Zoology of the Northern Parts of British America* (London, 1829), pp. xvii, xxvii.

34

John Richardson, "Report on North American Zoology." *Report of the Sixth Meeting of the British Association for the Advancement of Science*. Held at Bristol in August, 1836. Vol. V (London, 1837), p. 153.

35

John Richardson, *Arctic Searching Expedition*. 2 vols. (London, 1851), Vol. II, pp. 164, 200.

36

R. Montgomery Martin, *The Hudson's Bay Territories and Vancouver's Island* (London, 1849), p. 15.
James E. Fitzgerald, *An Examination of the Charter and Proceedings of the Hudson's Bay Company, With Reference to the Grant of Vancouver's Island* (London, 1849), pp. 116, 119.

37

Great Britain: Parliament. *Report from the Select Committee on the Hudson's Bay Company, 1857*. Ordered printed, July 31, August 11, 1857, p. 313.

38

Sir George Simpson, "Notes on Trade and Territory of H.B.C. drawn up by Sir George Simpson." Hudson's Bay Company Archives. E.18/8. fos. 34v, 35v, 39r. This statement was sent to the Hudson's Bay Company in January, 1857.
Sir George Simpson to John Shepherd: Lachine, November 25th, 1857. Hudson's Bay Company Archives. A.12/8. fo. 631v.

39

Canada: *Report*. "The Select Committee appointed to receive and collect evidence and information as to the rights of the Hudson's Bay Company under their Charter, the renewal of the license of occupation, the character of the soil and climate of the Territory, and its fitness for settlement, have the honor to present their First Report as follows." June 8th, 1857.

40

The Canadian Almanac and Repository of Useful Knowledge, For the Year 1857. Toronto: Maclear & Co. Article on "Our Railway Policy - Its Influence and Prospects," p. 31.
The Canadian Almanac and Repository of Useful Knowledge, For the Year 1858. Toronto: Maclear & Co. Article on "The Great North-West," pp. 28-9.

I am indebted to Professor W. L. Morton for guiding me to these important articles. He mentions them in a forthcoming biography of H. Y. Hind.

41

John Palliser, *Papers Relative to the Explorations by Captain Palliser*. Presented to both Houses of Parliament by Command of Her Majesty, June 1859 (London, 1859).
John Palliser, *Further Papers Relative to the Exploration by the Expedition Under Captain Palliser*. Presented to both Houses of Parliament by Command of Her Majesty, 1860 (London, 1860).

42

Palliser, *Papers*. [James Hector] "First General Report on the Geology of the Country examined by the Expedition under the command of John Palliser, Esq., during the Season of 1857, pp. 19-23.

43

Palliser, *Further Papers*, p. 35.

44

Ibid., pp. 35, 59.

45

S. J. Dawson. *Report on the Exploration of the Country Between Lake Superior and the Red River Settlement, and Between the Latter Place and the Assiniboine and Saskatchewan*. Printed by Order of the Legislative Assembly (Toronto, 1859), pp. 3-4, 15-7, 22-3.

46

[H. Y. Hind and others] Canada: Legislative Assembly. *Report on the Exploration of the Country Between Lake Superior and the Red River Settlement*. Printed by Order of the Legislative Assembly (Toronto, 1858), pp. 275, 298-9, 353-60.

47

H. Y. Hind, *North West Territory. Reports of Progress; Together with a Preliminary and General Report on the Assiniboine and Saskatchewan Exploring Expedition Made Under Instructions from the Provincial Secretary, Canada*. Printed by Order of the Legislative Assembly (Toronto, 1859), pp. 9, 31, 44, 48. Professor W. L. Morton in his forthcoming biography of Hind states that the report did not appear until 1860.

48

Ibid., pp. 31, 52.

49

Ibid., pp. 124-6.

50

H. Y. Hind, *British North America. Reports of Progress, Together with a Preliminary and General Report, on the Assiniboine and Saskatchewan Exploring Expedition* (London, 1860). Map titled "Map of the Country from LAKE SUPERIOR to the PACIFIC OCEAN, showing the Western Boundary of Canada & the Eastern Boundary of British Columbia, also the FERTILE BELT stretching from the Lake of the Woods to the Rocky Mountains."

134

51
H. Y. Hind, *Narrative of the Canadian Red River Exploring Expedition of 1857 and of the Assiniboine and Saskatchewan Exploring Expedition of 1858.* 2 vols. (London, 1860), Vol. II, bound between pp. 222 & 223.

52
Hind, *Narrative.* Vol. I, pp. 348-51.

53
John Palliser, "Latest Explorations in British North America: By Captain J. Palliser, with Dr. Hector and Mr. Sullivan." Read June 25, 1860. *Proceedings of the Royal Geographical Society*, Vol. IV, Session 1859-60 (London, 1860), pp. 231-2.

54
"Lord Ashburton's Anniversary Address, read by Sir Roderick Murchison, May 27, 1861." *Proceedings of the Royal Geographical Society*, Vol. V. Session 1860-61 (London, 1861), pp. 200-1.

55
The title of the full report is: John Palliser, *The Journals, Detailed Reports, and Observations Relative to the Exploration, by Captain Palliser, of That Portion of British North America, which, in Latitude, Lies between the British Boundary Line and the Height of Land or Watershed of the Northern or Frozen Ocean Respectively, and in Longitude, Between the Western Shore of Lake Superior and the Pacific Ocean During the years 1857, 1858, 1859, and 1860.* Presented to both Houses of Parliament by Command of Her Majesty, May 19, 1863 (London, 1863).
The report has been reprinted in: Irene M. Spry, ed., *The Papers of the Palliser Expedition 1857-1860* (Toronto: The Champlain Society, 1968). The reader should refer to the magisterial introduction by Mrs. Spry for an illuminating account of the work of the expedition, including invaluable descriptions of the backgrounds of the various members of the expedition, and an acute analysis of concepts such as Fertile Belt and the three prairie steppes.
Professor Spry who has made an extraordinarily thorough search for Palliser expedition material has not been able to locate most of the field books. Some of Hector's books have survived but I have not seen them.

56
James Hector, "On the Geology of the Country Between Lake Superior and the Pacific Ocean," *Quarterly Journal of the Geological Society of London*, Vol. 17 (1861), pp. 391-2.

57
Palliser, *Report.* p. 6.

58
Ibid., p. 270.

59
James Hector, "Physical Features of the Central Part of British North America, with Special Reference to its Botanical Physiognomy," *Edinburgh New Philosophical Journal*, N.S., Vol. 14 (1861), pp. 221-2, 233.

60

Edwin T. Denig, *Five Indian Tribes of the Upper Missouri*. Edited with an introduction by John C. Ewers (Norman, 1961), pp. 65-6.

61

Great Britain. *Select Committee*, 1857, pp. 140, 275-7.

62

Thomas Cook [Journal While on a Buffalo Hunt, June 1 - July 10, 1869]. Archives of the Society for the Propagation of the Gospel in Foreign Parts, London. S.P.G. Archives M ssionary Reports 1870-71. E. 26. pp. 649-72. By permission of the S.P.G. I am editing this journal for publication.
Cook [Report for the Quarter Ending 1870]. S.P.G. Archives Missionary Reports 1870-71. E. 26. p. 674.
Cook, "Journal Aug. 1st, 1864, Fort Ellice, S. River District N. America." Entry for October 20, 1864. S.P.G. Archives Missionary Reports. E. 22. p. 1277.

63

Earl of Southesk, *Saskatchewan and the Rocky Mountains. A Diary and Narrative of Travel, Sport, and Adventure, During a Journey Through the Hudson's Bay Company's Territories, In 1859 and 1860* (Edinburgh, 1875), pp. 78, 332.

64

A. J. Russell, *The Red River Country, Hudson's Bay & North-West Territories, Considered in Relation to Canada* (Ottawa, 1869), pp. 5, 32, 43-6, 65-7.

65

Mgr. Taché, *Sketch of the North-West of America*. Translated from the French by Captain D. R. Cameron (Montreal, 1870), pp. 10, 13-6, 19-20, 28.

66

William Butler, *The Wild North Land*, 10th ed. (London, 1896), pp. 357-8. (First edition, 1873).

67

Samuel Anderson, "The North-American Boundary from the Lake of the Woods to the Rocky Mountains," *Proceedings of the Royal Geographical Society*, Vol. XX, Session 1875-76 (London, 1876), pp. 274-302.
Frank Carruthers to Zell Carruthers, Fort McLeod, Nov. 10th, 1876. Public Archives of Manitoba. Carruthers Ms., Letter No. 3.
Colonel Macleod's statement quoted in Sandford Fleming, *Report in Reference to the Canadian Pacific Railway 1879* (Ottawa, 1879), p. 121.

68

George M. Dawson, *Report on the Geology and Resources of the Region in the Vicinity of the Forty-Ninth Parallel* (Montreal, 1875), p. 299.

69

Canada. *Journals of the Senate*, Vol. 10 (1876), Appendix 8, p. 26.

70

John Macoun, "Sketch of that portion of Canada between Lake Superior and the Rocky Mountains, with special reference to its Agricultural Capabilities," in Sandford Fleming, *Report on Surveys and Preliminary Operations on the*

Canadian Pacific Railway up to January 1877 (Ottawa, 1877), Appendix X. p. 324.

71

F. G. Roe, "Early Opinions on the 'Fertile Belt' of Western Canada." *Canadian Historical Review,* Vol. XXVII (1946), pp. 131-49.

72

Canada: *Sessional Papers 1881* (No. 3). Annual Report of the Department of the Interior for the Year Ended 31st December, 1880 (Ottawa, 1881), Part I, pp. vii-viii.
Macoun quoted in the *Manitoba Daily Free Press,* April 7, 1881.

73

John Macoun, *Manitoba and The Great North-West* (Guelph, 1882), pp. 56, 142-4.

74

Canada: Debates of the House of Commons. Vol. VII, 1879. Sir Charles Tupper, May 10, 1879, p. 1893.

75

Ibid., S. J. Dawson, May 10, 1879, Vol. VII, pp. 1920-2; Alexander Mackenzie, May 12, 1879, Vol. VII, p. 1967; Edward Blake, April 16, 1880, Vol. IX, p. 1454; Alexander Mackenzie, April 19, 1880, Vol. IX, pp. 1534-5.

76

Alexander Monro, *The United States and the Dominion of Canada: Their Future* (Saint John, N.B., 1879), pp. 65-9.

77

Daniel M. Gordon, *Mountain and Prairie; A Journey from Victoria to Winnipeg, via Peace River Pass* (London, 1880), p. 289.

78

Marquis of Lorne, *The Canadian North West* (Ottawa, 1881), pp. 8, 10. From a speech given on October 10, 1881 to the Winnipeg Club.

79

For example, *Manitoba Daily Free Press,* August 12, 1881.

80

Sandford Fleming, *England and Canada* (London, 1884), pp. 409-13.

81

Canada: *Sessional Papers 1883* (No. 23). Annual Report of the Department of the Interior for the Year 1882. Part I, pp. 8-9.

82

See *Canada: Sessional Papers, 1896.* Report of the Department of the Interior (No. 13). Report on Irrigation in Canada, dated March 15th, 1895, p. 6.
Canada: Sessional Papers, 1897. Report of the Department of the Interior (No. 13). General Report on Irrigation, dated July 2nd, 1896, p. 1.

Struggles, Triumphs and Heartaches with Western Wheat

Grant MacEwan

Wheat is big business, both for Canada and the world community. Over the years single grain has been Canada's biggest earner of foreign exchange and Canada's leading contribution to world needs. We boast about oil and gas and iron ore and wood pulp - and well we might because these products have become important in export - but wheat has lost none of the importance which placed this country on the world map. In the international community the Canadian symbol is wheat. And to the world's people, wheat has emerged as the most important single food product. It is now the most widely cultivated of all grains, surpassing rice and corn. World production in 1969 was over eleven billion bushels of which Canada's 684 million bushels were about six percent. World trade in wheat now comes close to two billion bushels per year. It should be noted that according to a recent United Nations report, wheat is now first among all foods in furnishing *both* calories and protein.

While Canada, in 1969, produced six percent of the world's wheat, it was the second biggest exporter or supplier in world trade. That has been this country's position quite consistently over the years. It is true that overseas markets have fluctuated greatly and at this time last year Canadian growers were discouraged and depressed; the outlook was so bad that the Government saw fit to institute an acreage reduction plan which led to total seeded area in 1970 falling to about 12½ million acres, less than half of what it was in earlier years. Canada came to the end of the official crop year, July 31, 1970, with a carry-over of 987 million bushels. To that could be added the 1970 production of 390 million bushels making a total of over 1,300 million bushels for disposal somewhere. It was an all-time record and looked like an all-time headache. But if we have learned anything about wheat we should know that it is a most unpredictable crop. When wheat fortunes are high they can be expected to drop; when they are low they can be expected to improve. In the 1969-70 year, our exports fell to a low point of 318 million bushels. This year we have seen the wheat market perform one of its spectacular reversals. The current crop year, ending July 30, 1971, instead of being one of the poorest for

Canadian wheat exports, may be one of the best. There was drought in Australia, poor production in Argentina, a decline in the United States corn crop, some seeding disappointments in Europe and Canadian wheat began to move more briskly. On October 27 last there was an announcement of a new sale for 98 million bushels to Mainland China and rather suddenly there loomed the prospect of a 1970-71 export of 500 million bushels with enough barley and rapeseed to bring total grain exports to 700 million bushels. If that was achieved it would make 1970-71 the biggest export year in Canadian history.

It would also add to the already amazing story of wheat in Western Canada. Wheat, let it be noted, is Canada's best success story. When the early struggles are considered, wheat was Canada's "Ugly Duckling" that became a beautiful "Swan." The history of wheat in the western half of Canada begins for all practical purposes with the Selkirk Settlers who arrived at the confluence of Red and Assiniboine Rivers late in 1812. They were carrying a bushel and a half of seed wheat because no matter how abundant the buffalo meat might be, these Anglo-Saxons wanted some bread. The wheat was planted on poorly prepared land beside the Red River but it was winter wheat and the seed was lost. For the spring of 1814 they had more seed but the small plots of wheat were frozen. There was violence in the colony in 1815 and '16 and no crops were harvested. The wheat of 1817 was frozen; the crops of 1818, '19 and '20 were destroyed by grasshoppers but determined settlers trekked into the United States to secure more seed. There was a good return in 1824, but it was too soon to be very cheerful because the crop of 1825 was largely destroyed by mice, and the season of 1826 was marked by severe flooding of the Red River and the loss of a crop year. Why the West's first farmers did not give up and forget about wheat is difficult to understand but their sheer determination was admirable and they succeeded in growing in most years thereafter enough wheat to meet gristing needs.

Farming at Red River did not change much in the next fifty years and nobody was greatly surprised when the grasshoppers were back to feast upon the little wheat fields in 1874 and 1875. After the former year of hopper onslaught, the good mothers of Red River were able to glean enough heads of wheat to provide some seed for the next season. But when the hoppers left nothing in 1875, and there was nothing to glean, certain members of the colony were delegated to travel south to buy wheat seed for 1876 planting. Arriving back with a raft load of wheat from Wisconsin, soon after the ice went out in the spring of 1876, those who bought it reported that it was a variety of which they had not heard previously. It was called Fife wheat and present-day students should pause, digress and consider its Canadian origin.

It was at Peterborough, Ontario, where an early Scottish settler, David Fife, resolved to obtain better spring wheat for his planting. He sent to Scotland for some new kinds but the result was less than satisfactory. He sent again, this time to a friend at Glasgow: "Please get me a sample of wheat from the Continent." There was a boat load of wheat from Danzig at the dock. The friend strolled on the deck on a Sunday afternoon and by chance his hat fell into the hold. He pursued his hat and in the struggle some kernels of wheat became trapped in the lining of the hat. At home, the seeds were removed from the hat and mailed to David Fife in Canada. Hopefully, Fife planted the new seed but it did not respond well either - except for one seed that produced an especially vigorous plant. It stooled and gave five heads. It looked good and Fife was elated. But one day at noon, while Fife was having lunch, his ox broke into the garden and was devouring the green wheat when Fife rushed from the house and drove the brute away. The critter had eaten four of the five heads; one remained. Fife fenced it and threshed the seed with his fingers. It looked good. Next year the seed from the head was planted with care and it was still excellent. The neighbours begged a few seeds and because both the wheat and Fife's hair were red, they called it Red Fife wheat. The new kind spread across the spring wheat belt of Ontario, into Michigan, into Wisconsin, and this was the wheat the Red River Settlers brought back in the spring of 1876.

On the Manitoba soil the Fife wheat responded magnificently and the yield was high. In Ontario, at the same time, the wheat crop was a failure and Steele Brothers, seed merchants, Toronto, needed supplies which were unobtainable in that province. A junior member of the firm decided to try Manitoba, took train to Chicago and St. Paul, stage and riverboat north and finally arrived at Winnipeg by team and wagon. The word got around that an Ontario man was there, prepared to buy up to five thousand bushels of wheat and pay eighty-five cents per bushel in cash - of all things. Farmers who had traded wheat for pemmican but had never sold any for cash, scooped up all they could spare and brought it to MacMillan's Mill in Winnipeg and collected their money. But the striking fact is that the West of ninety-five years ago could not furnish enough wheat to fill an order for five thousand bushels. The Toronto man, after buying all the wheat available, had 856 bushels and 10 pounds. Steele's wheat was taken upstream on the Red River, overland to Duluth and across the lakes to Toronto, there to fill the eastern buyers with astonishment. "Can we get more wheat like that?" they asked, and "When will we get a railroad to that western wheat country?"

Twenty-five years later, the western soil yielded 60 million bushels;

another twenty-five years and it was close to 400 million bushels. Another twenty-five years, it was at 552 million bushels.

It was a fantastic expansion but it was not a steady one. Some years there was failure due to frost or rust or drought or hail or something else. Red Fife wheat which loved the western soil and made the world's best bread, had one major shortcoming: it was late in maturing and too often the homesteaders saw an otherwise good crop ruined by an early fall frost. Again and again homesteaders remarked: "If only we had a variety like Fife but about a week or ten days earlier."

William Saunders who was the first director of Canada's Experimental Farms heard that cry and he and his sons began a search for something more suitable. They made numerous crosses between Red Fife and earlier kinds and in 1903 when Charles Saunders became Dominion Cerealist, he embarked upon a testing program, planting wheat from various crosses out in rod rows. One cross looked better than the rest; it was earlier than its Fife parent by more than a week and from the chewing test, Saunders believed it would be a good milling grain. Eager to have it tested right on western soil, he sent all he had to Angus Mackay, of Indian Head and in 1906 it was the best wheat grown on the Experimental plots at Indian Head. In 1907, '08 and '09 it was still the best and Mackay reported to Saunders that this could be the answer to a lot of homesteaders' prayers. Saunders called it Marquis and released it and it rapidly displaced the parent variety.

Marquis wheat was the equivalent of the Red Fife parent for bread making and it had an attractive appearance. Just two years after its release as a variety, a little farmer at Rosthern, Seager Wheeler, sent a sample of it to the International Show at Chicago and won the World's Wheat Championship. The sceptics said it was a fluke and wouldn't happen again but he repeated it in 1914, 1915, 1916 and for the fifth time in 1918. Wheeler's championship in 1911 marked the beginning of a long and amazingly consistent series of such championships. Between 1911 and 1970, wheat championships at recognized international shows have shown Alberta exhibitors winning thirty-eight times and Saskatchewan entries winning thirteen times. Only nine times did exhibitors from other parts win championships over Western Canadian exhibitors.

But wheat was never able to escape from all the forces working to destroy it and humble the growers. Marquis dealt a blow to the frost hazard but in 1916, while Marquis was still a young variety, the wheat crop of the West fell a victim of a plant disease, stem rust, and much of it was ruined. Losses in that year were placed at two hundred million dollars. Farmers felt helpless in coping with this mysterious new enemy but the plant breeders came forward with a proposal. Dr. W. P. Thompson of the Biology Department, University of Saskatchewan, suggested taking some selected wheat varieties apart, genetically, and reassembling the desired parts or genes and perchance making a variety with built-in resistance to rust. It was not something that could be done in a hurry but the plant breeders succeeded and brought forth one new rust-resistant variety after another, all of them tracing to Marquis and Red Fife and to a single seed which became entangled in a Scotsman's hat in Glasgow.

Plant breeders came to grips with the saw-fly menace the same way, creating Rescue and then Chinook varieties with solid stems in which the flies could not complete their life cycle. But the plant breeders could not do much about drought, drifting soil and ruinous prices which came together in the '30s. Wheat prices fell to a low point of 39⅜ cents a bushel for No. 1 Northern wheat at Fort William on December 16, 1932 - making it worth about half as much at some Alberta points - and yields in Saskatchewan plunged to an average of 2½ bushels per acre in 1937.

There was every reason for pessimism and some writers were ready to believe that wheat production would never flourish again on the Canadian prairies. The soil was finished some said. But the western soil was still productive and when the rains came again, western wheat production soared to productive levels unknown in earlier years. Western Canada's wheat fields in 1963 produced 703 million bushels, then 578 million bushels in 1964, and 661 million in 1965 and a nigh unbelievable 824 million bushels in 1968. The new problem was one of surplus and in 1971, even with a greatly increased movement of wheat to overseas countries, surplus is still a worry. Western Canada's wheat industry will have more ups and downs but its national and international importance is not in doubt. Moreover, the wheat story is one with which every Canadian should be familiar.

Agricultural Settlement in Alberta North of Edmonton

Bruce Proudfoot

That great wave of agricultural settlement which swept westwards across the United States in the nineteenth century, and westwards and northwards in Canada into this century, finally died out in the aspen poplar forest and muskeg of Alberta. In this remote Canadian province we reach the northernmost limits of continuous agricultural settlement on the American continent. We might, therefore, expect the region within which these limits lie to be marginal for agriculture in either, or both, of two ways. Firstly, the region might be marginal in a physical, especially climatic, sense, in which case crop losses would be considerable, or even total, at least in some years, as a result of such hazards as frost. Secondly, the region might be marginal economically, in which case additional increments of effort would be rewarded by smaller, and decreasing, increments of output. Moreover, we would expect the limits of settlement to fluctuate in response to changes in either economic or physical factors. If the prices of agricultural produce were high, for example, and all other factors remained equal, the limits should be pushed outwards, that is, northwards. Conversely, with low prices the limits should contract, southwards. Similar contraction might occur if agricultural prices were not in themselves low, but opportunities elsewhere were superior, for example, in the cities. Expansion might occur if climatically, or economically, one area were favoured in relation to other areas.

All these, and other, conditions have applied in Alberta north of Edmonton during the eight decades since the area was first occupied to any considerable extent by agricultural settlers. In this area there were few, if any, early group settlements in the sense that this term can be used in more eastern parts of the Prairies. The settlers came individually or as families, sometimes, but not always, joining others from the same source area in North America, Britain or Europe. Today there is little tangible evidence in the agrarian landscape of the ethnic background of those who settled the area. The township and range system with its quarter-section subdivision and its rectilineal layout of boundaries and roads has impressed a uniform pattern on the landscape. Some Roman Catholic and Orthodox churches are probably the clearest indices for the French or French Canadian, and some of the East European settled areas, respectively. There seem to be no clear associations between particular ethnic groups and distinctive types of farm buildings. Log cabins and barns were originally common throughout the formerly wooded areas but few of these have survived. They were early replaced by prairie-type farm houses and barns in styles common to considerable tracts of the American Midwest and Great Plains. Today many of these have in turn been replaced by characterless, functional structures common to both rural and urban areas.

In terms of the population itself assimilation rather than the preservation of distinctive, exclusive, cultural traits and social patterns, has been characteristic. By the end of the first initial phase of settlement at the beginning of World War I there were few districts of any size which were exclusive to any one ethnic group. However isolationist in original intent, the peoples of different ethnic backgrounds have been increasingly integrated into a commercial economy symbolized by English language educational systems and the railway and road networks which have linked the different parts of the area with each other and with the distant markets of the outside world. Even in such an area as the south-eastern Peace River Country, which has a uniquely high percentage of people of French-Canadian descent, patterns of economic activity today are as much a function of distance as of ethnic origin. In another area, in eastern Alberta, the county of St. Paul, where people of French-Canadian descent form one of the largest groups in a mosaic descended from other Canadians, British, American, German and Slavic peoples, only the patterns of church allegiance suggest the ethnic diversity. At least among the most innovative farmers in the county, patterns of social and economic behaviour, both within and outside the county, cut across ethnic origins.

At the time of settlement, the population of the whole agricultural area north of Edmonton was ethnically diverse. It was also as far as we can tell from contemporary and later descriptions, economically and technically diverse. Some settlers brought with them relatively large amounts of capital, others arrived with virtually nothing. Some already had agricultural expertise but many came from the manufacturing towns of Britain, Europe or North America. Of those with farming experience, immigrants from eastern and northern Europe had come from a broadly similar physical environment but one that was very different socially and economically. Only a few American immigrants had had previous experience in a roughly similar physical and human environment. Interestingly, many contemporary sources stress the importance to the new immigrant of some capital and some skill. The skills, if not in farming, should be in such trades as carpentry. In this way farm income might be supplemented, especially during the first few years, when only limited areas had been cleared for cultivation and the financial returns from farming were small.

Over much of the area land had to be cleared for agriculture, for the northern boundary of the true grassland prairie lay far to the south, and Edmonton marked the northern and western limits of the aspen parkland with its association of grassland, aspen groves and tree-fringed watercourses. There is no reason to doubt that the composition of the vegetation varied from place to place and time to time, but, in general, tree cover became more continuous northwards and west-wards. On the drier sandy ridges pine was common, on wetter slopes and in poorly-drained hollows spruce and willow were frequent. Willow was also found along the minor water courses, birch and larch on some muskeg areas. Aspen and white spruce occurred on the drier areas, sometimes as continuous tree stands, less often as groves interspersed with grassland. Lodgepole pine and white spruce dominated the area west of Edson, and the Swan Hills, south of Lesser Slave Lake. Muskeg and black spruce occurred widely through the areas north of Athabasca. True aspen poplar and spruce forest was found in the northernmost parts of the province. There were grassy meadows along some of the streams and bordering some of the lakes, many of them clearly maintained by fire. When burning was prohibited in some of these areas after World War I, as near Lac La Biche where they were being used as grazing land, the aspen rapidly colonized the formerly open areas. The largest expanses of grassland or prairie were in the southern Peace River Country, but this whole region was isolated from the agricultural areas further south by difficult upland terrain which has never been settled for agriculture. (See map on page 150.)

The generally wooded nature of the area probably surprised many of the early settlers. By the end of the nineteenth century when settle-ment was spreading into the area, the notion that all western Canada was rolling prairie, once grass but now vast wheatfields, providing food especially for Britain, was, I suspect, widespread. The early promo-tional literature designed to attract settlers emphasized the ease with which prairie could be converted into farmland, and commented little on the difficulties of clearing continuous woodland in the more north-ern areas. Persons used to the urbanized and cultivated landscapes of western Europe, or to the long-settled rural landscapes of eastern Europe were unlikely to appreciate the subtle, complex, patterns of vegetation that made up the Fertile Belt to the north of the drier grass-lands. Certainly not all the settlers were immediately impressed with their new surroundings, and many who attempted to settle on quarter-sections which were unsuitable for agriculture by reason of their poor soils or drainage moved to other areas, or into the small towns which developed to serve the needs of the rural population.

Fortunately for those studying the settlement process detailed observations on the nature of the area were recorded in the notebooks kept by the surveyors who were laying out the township and range system by which the land was being settled. Vegetation was noted in a systematic manner along the lines of transect which were run at one mile intervals north-south and at two mile intervals east-west. Using this information it has proved possible to compile some detailed maps of the vegetation at the time of survey, immediately prior to settlement. Such maps are most reliable for areas of considerable topographic variability, for vegetation is in part a reflection of topography. Where there are, for example, well-marked ridges of glacial deposits, extensive patches of blown sand, and ill-drained hollows filled with muskeg, it is a straightforward task to extrapolate vegetation boundaries between the north-south and east-west transects. Moreover, in many areas of such strongly differentiated terrain considerable areas of the original vegetation pattern may have survived until the present for muskeg has rarely been drained, nor have the steepest ridges and areas of sand been cultivated. It is, therefore, possible to check the pattern of reconstructed vegetation against the present pattern and ensure that the earlier pattern is ecologically reasonable in terms of the present pattern. For the area surrounding Athabasca, D. N. G. Stone, using these techniques, was able to prepare a map of the reconstructed vegetation at time of settlement, delimiting areas of broadleaf, needleleaf, and mixed needleleaf-broadleaf woodland, as well as open areas of grassland and swamp, windfall, and burnt-over woodland or brulé.

In areas of little topographic variation where the vegetation was mixed grassland an alternative method had been developed by C. J. Tracie who applied it successfully in the Grande Prairie region of the Peace River Country. The surveyors' information was used to obtain proportions of different types of vegetation along the transects and the quarter-sections on either side of the transects were then classified according to the varying proportions of different vegetation types present. These data were used both as the basis for maps and for comparison with other information about the individual quarter-sections. The availability of computers has made the task of handling these large amounts of information practicable, although the labour of converting the information in the surveyors' notebooks into a useable form is still considerable - in an area fifty miles square, there would be nearly four thousand miles of transects and ten thousand quarter-sections. If the information relating to vegetation is to be compared with such other information as dates of settlement there are similar problems of data conversion. On the basis of the information he collected and analyzed Tracie was able to show the extent to which early settlers in the Grande Prairie region preferred grassland over other vegetation types, and the relative importance of such other factors as distance from established centres.

Sources of data relating to the settlement process itself are many and varied. Because of the problems of handling so much information relatively little use has been made of these sources so that it is useful to indicate here the kinds of information available, and some of the types of results that may be obtained. Much of the usefulness of the records derives from the fact that the area was settled under a series of Land Acts whereby settlers applied to the Crown in whom the land was vested, for entry to particular quarter-sections on which they wished to settle. The basic framework was established in the Land Act of 1872, although later, greater flexibility was introduced with the possibility of land leases, homestead sales, and special concessions to War Veterans. Payment of a registration fee was required, and after the completion in the following years of certain statutory requirements relating to land improvement and residence on the quarter-section, the homesteader could file a claim of ownership and obtain title or patent to the land. The Township General Registers record for each quarter-section the date of initial entry, and any subsequent entries made after the withdrawal of the first entrant, together with information concerning the title of the land prior to its being obtained by an occupant. There is information on the kind of entry (for example, homestead, lease, or sale); the number, and in many cases the dates of cancellations; the name of the person making application, and the date of the patent or issue of title, if applicable. Any permanent restrictions on agricultural settlement are noted on unoccupied land; for example, if quarter-sections are reserved for Crown Forest or Grazing Leases. After patenting, a complete record of all changes in land ownership, and the documents relating to such changes are preserved in Land Titles. The third source is the Homestead Files containing records of every entry by a homesteader on a quarter-section, and also providing much useful social and economic information. On record are the date of homestead entry; the entrant's age; the size of his family, and often the ages of his wife and children; his birthplace; place of last residence and previous occupation. In addition, applications for patent record the acreage of land cleared, broken and cropped on each homestead, as well as the value of farm improvements.

Comparison of the dates when a quarter-section was first and last entered upon or the number of times a quarter-section was abandoned and re-occupied before it was finally patented, are some measure of the success of individual farmers and of the ease with which the land could be settled and made profitable. Such information provides a useful basis for the comparison of one area with another. If the Edson area, for example, is compared with the Grande Prairie area it is clear that the former was much more difficult to settle successfully than the latter. Another indicator of success in settlement is the length of time that elapsed between the date of last entry and date of patent. Interestingly in both the Edson and Grande Prairie areas the time was significantly shorter for land entered upon during and before World War I than afterwards. In both areas the easiest land to settle was taken up early. (See chart on page 151.)

The data sources just described enable the factors which influenced the initial settlement of the area to be analyzed in objective fashion. Such analysis can be supplemented by other information, for example, from local newspapers, and accounts of the process of settlement by the first settlers themselves. However, very few of the original settlers are to be found living in the area today for the initial settlement started on a substantial scale at least sixty years ago. On the date of settlement will depend in part the makeup of the present population, and the length of time the present farmers have been on their land. In the Goodfare area in the South Peace River Country west of Grande Prairie more than half the farmers living there in 1969 had been on their farms less than twelve years. They had taken over these farms by inheritance or purchase when the first or even second generation settlers had died or retired. Within this next decade those who settled in the 1930's will have almost all retired from active farming.

Apart from these changes brought about by the aging of the population, other major changes of an economic or technological sort have resulted in the movement of farm people from the land into the towns and cities. The initial concept of the quarter-section family farm was that such an acreage was as much as one family could cultivate, and that it would enable the farm family to support itself and produce a modest surplus. Whereas this may have been so earlier in the nineteenth century and in physically more favourable areas, it was realized during the settlement of the Canadian West from the 1870's and 1880's that such an acreage was inadequate to produce the volume of grain needed to supply the farmer with an adequate return on his labour and on the capital invested in his homestead. Legislation in 1879 and 1904 permitted a settler to "pre-empt" or acquire an additional quarter-section adjacent to his homestead at a cost of one dollar per acre. In many areas there was relatively rapid turnover of settlers. There were those who entered upon a quarter-section but were unable to fulfil the requirements necessary before they could patent it.

There were also those who were successful in patenting their holding who then sold it, often to a neighbour, and moved either to another homestead or to one of the developing service centres. There is some evidence that British immigrants and eastern, non-French, Canadians were more likely than others to sell their patented land and move into the towns. Conversely, as it were, many of the immigrants from eastern Europe who arrived relatively late in many areas settled on the poorer lands and with great persistence developed them into viable farm enterprises.

By world standards the degree of mechanization of the farms in the area with which we are dealing has always been relatively high. One result of this, is that there has always been pressure to occupy more than the original quarter-section at least in part to provide more income with which to pay for mechanization. Although mechanization began early the most substantial effects were not felt until the mid-1940's when horse-drawn machinery was replaced by larger tractor-drawn equipment. Similarly, horse-drawn rural transport was replaced by automobiles and trucks. The new more powerful machinery enabled larger areas to be cultivated in the same time by fewer people, and there was no longer any necessity to devote land to feed for horses. Equally important, the new machinery represented a much larger capital investment and usually involved regular cash payments to machinery dealers, far greater than the cash payments that had previously been common in paying hired labour. The outcome was further incentives to increase the size of individual holdings from the traditional quarter or even half-section. This whole process was intensified by the increasing expectations of farmers, more aware through radio, and later through television, of the standards of living and the expectations of other Canadians, now predominantly urban. In most parts of Alberta, including the area north of Edmonton, there were many older farmers who were able to retire in the immediate post-World War II period so that consolidation took place without the major social dislocations which might otherwise have been expected. Since that time the social problems have tended to increase, partly because of the inflation that has been general throughout the whole economy and affected all those who have retired. Other problems have also occurred as the costs of farm production have risen while the unit price of many farm products has remained about stationary, or even declined. To offset these tendencies farm output per acre and per person has continued to rise, the increases being most marked on the larger farms. The larger farms, too, have tended to grow at the expense of the smaller. Of the 104 most innovative farmers in St. Paul County none had less than 160 improved acres, and half had 660 acres or more in 1969. The largest had 3600 improved acres. In addition to their improved land most of these farmers had some unimproved land so that the size of holdings has increased far beyond the quarter or half-section that formed the basic homestead unit. Although these operators make up only 8.2 percent of the total number of farmers in the county they utilize 23.7 percent of the total improved farmland. The majority of these large operations are specialized, primarily in the production of beef cattle, and secondarily in the production of grain or hogs. There is every indication that the types of extensive land use now practised will continue in future.

The changes in degree of mechanization, farm size and farmer's aspirations have affected the small towns, villages and hamlets as well as the farms of the area. No longer could the single village store provide the goods the farm family wanted. Moreover the family could drive by automobile on graded and often paved roads to larger centres where a greater variety of goods and services was available. The original pattern of small service centres developed especially around the elevators built at seven or eight mile intervals along the railroads, and serviced the rural population within a radius of about ten miles, for that seemed normally to be the economic limit for grain delivery by wagon. The ideal railway network would then have consisted of lines some twenty miles apart, but it is only in a limited area east of Edmonton that such a close network developed. Elsewhere, the few railroads radiated outwards from the city, and many areas, especially in the North Peace River Country, were very far from the railroad. High Level, for example, was some 180 miles from the railway at Grimshaw, until the completion of the Great Slave Lake line in the 1960's. Even with such a restricted rail net in the area north of Edmonton, there were over three hundred small service centres, many of which had never had more than one hundred inhabitants. Many of the smaller centres, like many of the rural areas, lost people to the larger centres, particularly to Edmonton, after World War II. However, with some capacity for the expansion of settlement into unoccupied areas, the region north of Edmonton has lost population less rapidly than more southern regions. Some areas and some small centres have shown an absolute decline in their population numbers, but more commonly, the population total has remained static or increased only slowly as migration of the younger members of the community has been at a rate similar to that of the rate of natural increase. The result of this migration has been the development of a network of personal connections between the rural areas and the towns and cities, which has replaced the limited and dense network of economic and social connections between the rural areas and small service

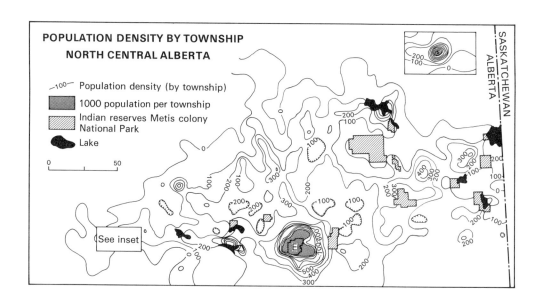

POPULATION DENSITY BY TOWNSHIP
NORTH CENTRAL ALBERTA

—100— Population density (by township)

1000 population per township

Indian reserves Metis colony
National Park

Lake

0   50

See inset

SASKATCHEWAN

ALBERTA

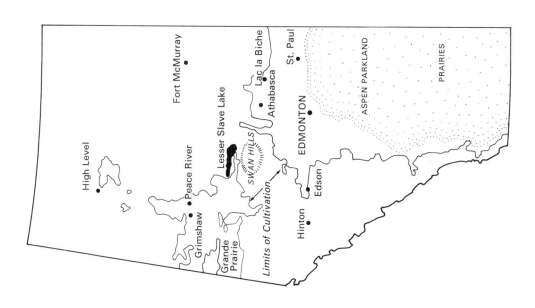

High Level

Fort McMurray

Peace River

Grimshaw

Grande Prairie

Lesser Slave Lake

SWAN HILLS

Limits of Cultivation

Lac la Biche

Athabasca

St. Paul

EDMONTON

Edson

Hinton

ASPEN PARKLAND

PRAIRIES

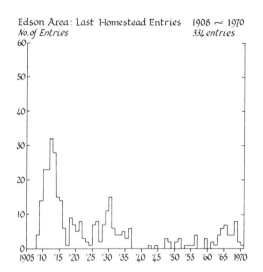

Edson Area: Last Homestead Entries 1908 ~ 1970
No. of Entries   334 entries

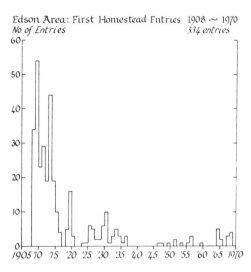

Edson Area: First Homestead Entries 1908 ~ 1970
No. of Entries   334 entries

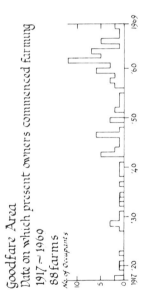

Goodfare Area
Date on which present owners commenced farming
1917 ~ 1960
88 farms

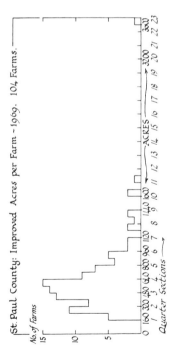

St. Paul County: Improved Acres per Farm - 1969. 104 Farms.

centres that existed prior to the widespread use of the automobile in the last twenty-five years.

With the exception of the development of such new resource towns as Hinton for forestry, and Fort McMurray for exploitation of the Athabasca Tar Sands, the most rapid rate of population growth in this period has occurred in Edmonton which has grown from a population of 120,000 in 1946 to a current population of 450,000. Although much of this growth can be attributed to the development of the oil and gas resources of the Province, and to the presence of the Provincial Government in the city, Edmonton is still the major economic centre serving rural northern Alberta and the outstanding focus of economic activity in the region. This is well shown in the local country newspapers in which advertisements from Edmonton firms often outnumber even those from firms in the town in which the paper is published.

For the area of north central Alberta which includes the continuously settled agricultural area north of Edmonton, but excludes the Peace River Country, the impact of distance from Edmonton on rural economic activity is strong indeed. The census sub-divisions which show, for example, the highest percentages of commercial farms, the largest average value of sales of products per farm, and the highest ratios between average sales and average capital value per farm, are ranged around Edmonton, and all these indicators of economic activity decline with distance away from the city. The population density similarly declines, but data are sufficient to show that the rate of decline is less along the major routeways which stand out like ridges radiating outwards from Edmonton. The significance of communications in the rural settlement pattern is thus as clear today as it was at the time of initial settlement.

Bibliography

The classic sources for information about, and interpretation of, the settlement of Western Canada remain the volumes in *The Canadian Frontiers of Settlement* series edited by W. A. Mackintosh and W. L. G. Joerg. In the present context see especially:

C. A. Dawson, *The Settlement of the Peace River Country: A Study of a Pioneer Area* (Toronto: Macmillan, 1934).

C. A. Dawson, *Group Settlement, Ethnic Communities in Western Canada* (Toronto: Macmillan, 1936).

C. A. Dawson and E. R. Younge, *Pioneering in the Prairie Provinces: The Social Side of the Settlement Process* (Toronto: Macmillan, 1940).

W. A. Mackintosh, *Prairie Settlement, The Geographical Setting* (Toronto: Macmillan, 1934).

Chester Martin and A. S. Morton, *History of Prairie Settlement and "Dominion Lands" Policy* (Toronto: Macmillan, 1938).

The chapter on "The Prairie Region" by H. G. Richards in *Canada: A Geographical Interpretation,* edited by J. Warkentin, (Toronto: Methuen, 1968) is a recent perceptive overview of the Prairies in their geographical and historical setting.

There is a wealth of detailed information historical and contemporary in *The Atlas of Alberta,* edited by J. J. Klawe (Government of Alberta and the University of Alberta, Edmonton, 1969).

This paper also draws in part on work done by a number of graduate students in geography at Edmonton, and I am particularly indebted to them for their enthusiasm, persistence and stimulus during the past few years.

A. Gill, "Off-farm employment and mobility in the Goodfare District, Alberta," unpublished M.A. thesis, Department of Geography, University of Alberta, 1971.

W. J. Hozack, "The spatial pattern of farming near Lac La Biche, Alberta," unpublished M. A. Thesis, Department of Geography, University of Alberta, 1969.

W. Jackson, "Ethnicity and areal organization among French Canadians in the Peace River District, Alberta," unpublished M.A. Thesis, Department of Geography, University of Alberta, 1970.

G. Pich, "Agricultural Innovations, County of St. Paul, Alberta," unpublished M.A. Thesis, Department of Geography, University of Alberta, 1970.

D. N. G. Stone, "The process of rural settlement in the Athabasca area, Alberta," unpublished M.A. thesis, Department of Geography, University of Alberta, 1970.

C. J. Tracie, "An analysis of three variables affecting farm location in the process of agricultural settlement: The South Peace River area," unpublished Ph.D. Thesis, Department of Geography, University of Alberta, 1970.

I am indebted to Mr. G. Lester for cartographic assistance and to Mrs. Donna Ferguson for secretarial help.

Postwar Migration and the Canadian West: An Economic Analysis

James Seldon

Throughout Canada's history, a number of writers have concerned themselves with various aspects of Canadian migration and migration policy. Some have argued that Canada (or more precisely, the Canadian economy) was already "full," and should severely restrict inflows; others have claimed that Canada was underpopulated and stood to gain significantly from a larger population.[1] Some have argued that Canada ought to be selective in her policies, admitting only the skilled and the educated; others have suggested that Canada has a responsibility to the rest of the world to accept also the unskilled and uneducated. Internally, there have been arguments in favour of increased mobility and of support for the immobile, as well as for increased education and training, and for subsidization of the unskilled. At the provincial, regional, and local levels, there are regular complaints about the "brain drain" - the loss of educated and skilled individuals - to other provinces, regions, or to "the big city."

In fact, it seems that one can identify almost as many suggestions for "correct' policies as there have been writers on the subject. Most have had one element in common, however: a belief that current policies were not the best available. It will be one goal of this paper to set the stage for a preliminary test of that presumption, focussing our view upon the later postwar period and upon the Canadian West.

The investigation follows three major paths: a look at the types of policies Canadian authorities have been pursuing; an attempt to explain migration flows; and an evaluation of the potential costs and benefits to be derived from flows of migrants, referring specifically to Western Canada.

Canadian Immigration Policy

The "new" Canadian immigration regulations,[2] which became law in 1967, define three classes of persons admissible to Canada as immigrants: sponsored dependents, nominated relatives, and independent applicants.

The first of three classes assigns priority of entry to dependents of persons already in Canada as Canadian citizens or having permanent resident status. Nominated or non-dependent relatives (including such persons as sons or daughters over twenty-one years of age, parents or grandparents under sixty years of age, and other normally non-dependent relatives) are required to meet slightly higher standards of education and occupation, but less stringent than those applied to independent applicants.

For all groups, major emphasis is placed upon the ability of the individual to obtain employment; a possible fifty "points" may be assigned to an individual on the basis of education and demand conditions in the individual's employment field. Since the required number of points for admission of independent applicants is fifty, it is obvious that a highly-educated applicant could qualify on those grounds alone.

The immigration regulations, plus the statements of immigration authorities, make it evident that present policy places great weight on the skills an immigrant possesses, but the reasoning behind this attitude on the part of Canadian authorities is not altogether clear.[3] The pubicly-expressed reasoning is that an individual coming to Canada must be able to support himself (with or without the aid of relatives in Canada) by obtaining employment. That is, the guiding principle appears to be a negative one, designed to prevent expense to current Canadian residents rather than to generate benefits for them. However this argument, as will be noted later, may simply be a "political" justification for a policy seen by the authorities to be economically desirable.

For Western Canada, and particularly for the Prairie Provinces, the emphasis of policy on directing flows to areas of high labour demand (areas to which those flows would naturally tend to gravitate in any event) has meant that immigration has been somewhat less than would otherwise have been expected. Further, the emphasis on educational achievement and industrial skills has tended to generate immigration to the larger Canadian cities, and to retard immigration to regions such as the Prairies.

In order to gain a better understanding of official reasoning, it is useful to look at the oft-quoted statement by Prime Minister Mackenzie King to the House of Commons in 1947. Paving the way for all subsequent policy on immigration in Canada, Mr. King stated:

> The policy of the government is to foster the growth of the population of Canada by the encouragement of immigration. The government will seek ... to ensure the careful selection and permanent settlement of such numbers of immigrants as can advantageously be absorbed in our national economy.

... the fear has been expressed that immigration would lead to a reduction in the Canadian standard of living. This need not be the case. If immigration is properly planned, the result will be the reverse.[4]

The Prime Minister was speaking at a time when the postwar economy was expected to suffer a severe slowdown, and which, through the depression and war years, had not accepted many immigrants, so that his attempts to soothe the fears of the Canadian people were understandable.

King, however, unlike recent speakers on the matter, did refer publicly to one potential benefit from immigration: an increase in the nation's standard of living. (Whether recent officials have accepted King's pronouncements as the final word or merely have not seen the need to make a more complete justification of their policies is a matter which might warrant further investigation.)[5] More recent statements have spoken of immigration as a means of filling Canada's manpower "needs" - hardly a great advance over the "absorptive capacity" of old!

Pressures on the immigration authorities from various interest groups seem to have subsided somewhat in recent years, but it is not yet clear whether this is due to the prolonged period of relative prosperity Canadians have enjoyed for most of the postwar period (so that it is now felt that the Canadian economy can "afford" immigration), or to the recognition of a gain to Canada from that inflow. It is clear, however, that in the past such pressures have played an important role in determining policy, and it is at least plausible that the same situation may arise once again in the future. The Prime Minister's statement, as Corbett makes quite clear, was ". . . one of the judicious compromises for which Mr. King was famous."[6]

Where pressures from regional interests within Canada are concerned, the demands appear to have increased in volume in recent years. Disparities in regional per capita income levels and rates of unemployment have led to requests for both direct and indirect compensation, the former via grants (for example, interprovincial equalization payments, the Canadian equivalent of Robin Hood according to the wealthy provinces), the latter in the form of assistance to education and training of the labour force. The degree of concern has been particularly strong on the Prairies (and in the Maritimes) where large numbers of skilled and educated individuals have been "lost" to regions of more rapid industrial growth, thus giving rise to the argument that, say, British Columbia is being subsidized by the Prairies. (It is hardly coincidence that this complaint usually surfaces when the provincial education budget is presented!) The point has not yet been reached where attempts are made to regulate inter-regional "immigration" and "emigration," by means of legal restrictions on flows of migrants, but this may be a reflection on the difficulties, constitutional and practical, involved in such policies rather than in a lack of desire on the part of the provinces. Campaigns such as Ontario's "Is there any other place you'd rather be?", while related to provincial elections, do give evidence of a willingness to compete for population as well as industry.

An Explanation of Migration Flows

In order to "explain" flows of migration to and from Western Canada, it is useful to utilize a simplified model of the world in which individuals desire to move from one location to another in response to higher real income levels. (By hypothesizing that it is *real* income which matters to an individual, rather than money income, we can take account of such factors as price differentials, the level of public services provided and the level of taxation, amenities such as climate or "atmosphere" for which there are no market prices, and so on.)

Whether or not an individual actually will move, of course, will depend upon a variety of factors other than income levels - government policy, the costs (both out of pocket and psychic) of moving, and the individual's assessment of his opportunity to *obtain* the higher real incomes characteristic of his destination, for example. Either an individual must expect to obtain employment in his new location at an income level higher than that which he previously received, or he must expect that the benefits he receives while unemployed in the new location will exceed the income he received in the old, whether or not be held a job. The relatively large number of unemployed in Vancouver who come from locations outside the city is evidence that this type of thinking may be at work. If one is to be unemployed, and if unemployment insurance and welfare payments are similar across Canada, then it is perhaps not at all surprising that a large number of individuals should prefer to be unemployed in Vancouver. If the chances of obtaining employment there are at least as great as those in alternative locations, this will be particularly likely. Similarly, the thought of a hard winter on the Prairies may prove to be the push factor which motivates migration.

In its simplest mathematical form, the model can be expressed as follows:

$$M_{ij} = M_{ij} \left[\frac{y_j}{y_i}, \frac{P(e_j)}{P(e_i)} \right]$$

where M_{ij} is the level of migration from location i to location j,

y_j is the per capita income in location j,

y_i is the per capita income in location i,

$P(e_j)$ is the perceived (subjective) probability of obtaining employment in location j,

$P(e_i)$ is the perceived probability of employment in i.

Now since $P(e_j)$ is likely to be a function of the level of population in location j (the larger the city, the more chance the individual may think that he has of finding a job), we can apply the concept of a gravity model to the prediction of migration flows. By analogy with the physical law of gravitation, we hypothesize that interaction between any two masses (for example, of population) will be directly proportional to the size of the masses, and inversely proportional to the distance between them.

For Western Canada, this interaction implies that larger centres such as Vancouver, Winnipeg, Calgary and Edmonton will serve, other things (incomes and unemployment rates) being equal, as both receptors and generators of significant migration flows. Further, the same sort of behaviour can be expected at the regional and provincial levels, with British Columbia exerting a strong attraction, Alberta a somewhat weaker pull, and Manitoba and Saskatchewan a pull factor so weak that it is likely to be overbalanced by the push factors.

Because $P(e_i)$ and $P(e_j)$ are subjective probabilities, any attempt to verify empirically the postulated relationship must make use of proxy variables that are felt to reflect those probabilities. Tests have been carried out using recorded rates of unemployment as the independent variable on the assumption that the expectations of an individual about his ability to find employment will be conditioned by the overall level of unemployment in the location under consideration.

For the purposes of carrying out empirical tests, the model has been simplified further by making the assumption that as long as the value of $\left(\dfrac{y_j}{y_i}\right)$ is greater than unity, migration from i to j will take place, subject again to policy regulation and to the costs of migration. The following table summarizes the relationships between flows to and from Canada and the rate of unemployment in Canada for various categories of migrants.

Table I - SUMMARY OF REGRESSION ANALYSIS:
MIGRATION TO AND FROM CANADA, 1951-1967*

Dependent Variable	Independent Variable	Simple Correlation Coefficient	Level of Significance
All Immigrants	% Unemployed in Canada	—0.79	.999
	U.S. % Unemployed minus Canadian % Unemployed	0.50	.95
	Annual Change in Canadian % Unemployed	—0.24	—
All Immigrants, one year lagged response	% Unemployed in Canada	—0.81	.999
	U.S. % Unemployed minus Canadian % Unemployed	0.64	.99
	Annual Change in Canadian % Unemployed	—0.49	.95
Professional Inmigrant Workers	% Unemployed in Canada	—0.31	—
	U.S. % Unemployed minus Canadian % Unemployed	0.23	—
	Annual Change in Canadian % Unemployed	—0.21	—
Sponsored Immigration, One Year Lag	% Unemployed in Canada	—0.62	.98

Table I - continued

Dependent Variable	Independent Variable	Simple Correlation Coefficient	Level of Significance
Sponsored Immigration, One Year Lag (continued)	U.S. % Unemployed minus Canadian % Unemployed	0.64	.99
	Annual change in Canadian % Unemployed	−0.24	—
Emigration to the U.S. of non-Professional Workers	U.S. % Unemployed	0.35	—
	Canadian % Unemployed	0.52	.95
	Time	0.61	.98
	Annual change in U.S. % unemployed	0.12	—

*Source: Seldon, J. R., "Some Aspects of Canadian Immigration Policy in Theory and in Practice," unpublished Ph.D. dissertation, Duke, 1969, Statistical Appendix II.

Given that the higher the level of training or education the less likely the average rate of unemployment will be in influencing an individual's decision to move, then the correlations shown in *Table I* between rates of unemployment and levels of migration to Canada tend to support our explanation of population movements. *Table II* shows the year-by-year unemployment and immigration figures. (See following page.)

There is, of course, some difficulty in interpreting the causal relationship which apparently exists between the flows and the rate of unemployment in Canada. It is probable that Canadian policy, which has been aimed at restricting inflows of lower-skilled individuals when rates of unemployment were high, and stimulating inflows when the

Table II - UNEMPLOYMENT RATES AND CANADIAN IMMIGRATION, 1951-1970*

Year	Total Inflow	Inflow to Western Canada	Canadian Unemployment Rate
1951	194,391	39,599	2.6
1952	164,498	38,527	3.0
1953	168,868	40,326	3.0
1954	154,227	38,835	4.6
1955	109,946	27,129	4.4
1956	164,857	35,769	3.4
1957	282,164	74,700	4.6
1958	124,851	29,156	7.2
1959	106,928	23,848	6.0
1960	104,111	23,493	7.0
1961	71,689	16,009	7.2
1962	74,586	15,759	5.9
1963	93,151	18,215	5.5
1964	112,606	22,646	4.7
1965	146,758	33,148	3.9
1966	194,743	43,396	3.6
1967	222,867	55,286	4.1
1968	183,974	47,979	4.8
1969	161,531	42,099	4.7
1970	147,713	39,623	5.9

*Sources: *Immigration Statistics*, various years. *Labour Force Survey*, various years.

economy was close to full employment, has been at least partly responsible for the close correlation which appears.

There are three basic pieces of evidence which bear on the above argument: the (slight) improvement in correlation brought about by the use of lagged variables; the higher correlation coefficients for lower skill and education levels; and the evidence provided by the analysis of inter-regional flows within Canada. The first two of these are under the potential influence of policy, although the use of (time-series) data for the years 1951-1967 represents an attempt to minimize the resulting biases. The last is largely policy-free.

A recent study of interprovincial migration by Tom Courchene[7] provides the relevant evidence on internal flows. Courchene makes use of Census and Family Allowance information (though the lack of detailed data on internal Canadian migration serves as a severe constraint on attempts to work in this field) to test the relationships between flows of migrants and a variety of other variables, including income levels and rates of unemployment in source and destination provinces. Income levels, rates of unemployment, and migration are found to be significantly correlated, suggesting that even in the absence of policy regulation, migration responds fairly readily to economic conditions.

For interprovincial migration, rates of unemployment in source regions appear to play a "push" role in generating outmigration. The higher the rate of unemployment on the prairies, for example, the more likely is migration to British Columbia to take place, other things being equal. (The fact that unemployment rates for the Prairies are likely to have been cyclically understated due to the large potential for underemployment of labour in the agricultural sector during recessionary periods makes this observation all the more striking.) Preliminary investigations have shown this factor to be insignificant internationally, although some doubt is cast upon the international results. Since these relationships were investigated through the use of single equation multivariate analysis, it is likely that the close correspondence between rates of unemployment in Canada and the United States biased downwards the tests of significance. Further, the fact that most outmigration from Canada is of skilled or educated individuals tends to reduce the relevance of average rates of unemployment.

The evidence available at present, then, tends to support the model which has been developed to "explain" migration movements for Canada, both interprovincially and internationally. Migration tends to occur from regions of lower per capita incomes to regions with high average income levels; from areas of high unemployment to regions with low unemployment; and from regions with small aggregate income and population to areas with larger aggregate income and population.

A much more complete test of the model awaits the results of the 1971 Census of Canada.

The Economic Effects of Migration Flows

It has become standard procedure in recent years to calculate the benefits from immigration and the costs of emigration by adding up the value of "human capital" (which is nothing more than the total cost, including foregone earnings, of the education and training an individual has received) embodied in those flows, and to subtract one from the other to obtain a net measure of benefits. According to this reasoning, for the period 1953-70, Canada as a whole obtained gross benefits from the inflow of professionals alone which amounted to well over two billion dollars, and net benefits of approximately one and one quarter billion dollars.[8] Attempts have been made to carry out a more sophisticated analysis by taking into account the human capital values embodied in Canadian students receiving training abroad and the costs of educating foreign students in Canada,[9] but the overall evaluation has all too often been carried on without a clear appreciation of just how the benefits are to be collected, or how the costs are to be imposed upon Canadians.

The same calculations for Western Canada show gross benefits from immigration of professionals over the period 1953-70 to be in the neighbourhood of one billion dollars.[10] Lack of information on the provincial origins of emigrants from Canada[11] makes the computation of net benefits to Western Canada impossible, but if the proportions are similar to those for Canada as a whole, the West obtained net benefits in the order of six hundred million dollars from international migration of professionals.

On a provincial basis, British Columbia and Alberta have obtained the greatest gross benefit from immigration, with approximate human capital values of five hundred million and three hundred million dollars respectively, with Manitoba benefitting by one hundred and thirty million dollars, and Saskatchewan by one hundred million.

From the data available,[12] it appears that the overall transfer of human capital via interprovincial migration to and from the West is relatively small, although the redistributive effects are likely to be considerable. Alberta and British Columbia have both gained significant numbers of migrants from other provinces, while Saskatchewan has had a significant net outflow and Manitoba a somewhat smaller net loss (Table III).

Even assuming the human capital values can be measured accurately, however, there remains the question of how the benefits accrue to an area receiving net inflows of that capital. In addition, it is important to investigate *to whom* the benefits accrue, who is made better off when "the West" or "Alberta" receives these benefits, who is made worse off when emigration of skilled and educated individuals takes place from Saskatchewan or Manitoba.

Approaching the latter question first, there are several alternative ways of looking at the set of individuals receiving benefits in "Western Canada." We might mean, for instance, the group of all residents of Manitoba, Saskatchewan, Alberta, and British Columbia at the *beginning* of a time period under consideration; or we might deal with the welfare of those individuals in the area at the *end* of that time span; or we might look at the well-being of individuals present at the beginning of the period and remaining there at the end, to identify three possibilities. (The welfare of a region is assumed to be some aggregation of the welfares of its residents. There are, of course, many problems both theoretical and practical in obtaining that aggregate.)

In the first case, we would have to measure the effects on the welfare of that set of individuals after migration had taken place whether or not those individuals had emigrated in the meantime. If we assume that emigrants from Western Canada only move in expectation of greater utility than they would have obtained had they remained in their original location, then that portion of the original set of residents will be better off after migration has occurred. Similarly, we assume that immigration to the West took place in expectation of higher real incomes, so that that segment of the population at the end of the time period can be considered to be better off. As a consequence, we are left with only one group of individuals who are potentially made better or worse off by immigration or emigration: those present at the beginning of the time period and remaining at the end of it. If they are made better off, then we are entitled to conclude that the change benefitted "the West," since some individuals identified with the region are better off, and no one is made worse off. This application of the Pareto Criterion would probably meet with general agreement, but it would certainly be rare to find a change which would make *no* one worse off. We have simplified here by dealing with three *groups* of individuals so that we neglect gains and losses within the groups themselves. If they are made worse off, then we will have to decide whether or not their losses should be balanced off against the gains to those individuals who were formerly residents, those who have just become residents, or both.

The choice between these alternatives can only be made on the basis of a value judgement, although it seems likely that it is either the welfare of initial residents or of remaining residents which will be judged of greatest concern. If it is the former, then the welfare of "the West" extends far beyond its geographical boundaries; if it is the latter, then it is confined to a specific area of Canada.

With these problems of definition in mind, what sort of transmission mechanism is at work generating benefits (or costs) as a result of migration? Will the dollar measures of embodied human capital accurately measure benefits to Canada from immigration, or to Western Canada from interprovincial migration, for example? Analysis of taxation and government expenditures provide us with the key to these questions.

It is assumed that government services are provided for the residents of each province out of provincial tax revenues. That is, consumption of private goods must be reduced in order to free the resources necessary for the provision of public goods. One of the services provided by the government is assumed to be education, and it is assumed that individuals are taxed in proportion to their incomes, which in turn will generally reflect their educational costs. If we now add to this economic system through immigration an individual who possesses some education or training, and who adds to the production of goods and services in proportion to that education, he will be taxed not as a function of the social services (including education) he receives, but at a considerably higher level. Other individuals in the system will as a result have to forego a smaller amount of private consumption combined with the same quantity of public goods, and hence will be better off by the amount of "excess" tax revenue collected. If taxes are collected so that over his working life each individual exactly pays for the cost of his education (in terms of resources expended on that education), then an immigrant at the very beginning of his working life will generate benefits precisely equal to the value of human capital he embodies, and the figures mentioned earlier for Canada and Western Canada will in fact be received by residents of those areas.

Using a parallel argument, it can be shown that emigrants impose a cost upon those remaining behind in the region as a direct function of their education level and the number of years of production lost by the economy as a result of their departure.

In fact, then, it may be appropriate to measure the economic benefits from immigration, and the economic costs of emigration, by adding up human capital values. This should not be taken to imply, of course, that we can necessarily represent accurately the total of all costs and benefits in this fashion. There may well be non-economic "externalities" both positive and negative which are generated by inflows and outflows, and which should be taken into account in making policy decisions. The presence of other persons of similar (or different!) tastes, ethnic and cultural backgrounds, and so on might contribute to an individual's welfare, or subtract from it, for instance, and it is unlikely that these effects are valued in the market. And a major issue has of course been sidestepped: how is the within-group aggregation of benefits and costs to be performed? What if the arrival of an immigrant worker displaces somehow a worker currently employed, or results in his obtaining a lower salary than would otherwise have been the case? The distributional questions must be left to the political process for solution; the best the economist can do here is to point out the trade-offs which are involved in coming to a conclusion.

One further economic effect of migration, one which does not appear to have been given much attention within this particular context, is the resultant change in the level of aggregate demand (and ultimately income) within an area. Articles by Mishan and Needleman[13] in

Britain, and Vanderkamp[14] in Canada have pointed out that immigration will tend to increase the level of demand in a region, and that there will be a "multiplier effect" on demand, income, and employment so that the final increase in these variables will be several times as great as the initial effect of the immigrant's consumption.

Vanderkamp's study, which is unfortunately limited to areas with net outmigration between the 1951 and 1961 *Census of Canada* reports (consisting of twenty-nine counties in the Maritimes), estimates that for every five unemployed workers leaving that region, two currently employed individuals lose their jobs. The rationale behind these findings is relatively simple:

> When the unemployed leave a labour surplus area they take their expenditures with them, which then through multiplier effects creates an increase in unemployment. . . .
>
> Thus outmigration produces somewhat of a ratchet effect for the labour surplus region. Out-migration which may take place in response to unemployment conditions, adds to unemployment at the same time as it subtracts from it.[15]

The process is a stable one, since in net terms the out-migration tends to reduce unemployment levels, but the results do indicate that improving the potential for labour force mobility must be approached with caution, and that those who advocate it as a solution to all of the problems of regional disparities must recognize the difficulties involved. The above argument is particularly significant in that it deals with the migration of the unemployed; it would seem plausible that if it is employed workers who are emigrating, and if their jobs are not immediately occupied by previously unemployed workers, then the effects may be even larger than those indicated by Vanderkamp.

Looking at the multiplier effects of immigration, it seems reasonable to conclude that the increased employment generates demand which in turn stimulates the demand for labour in the region. In a sense, then, we are faced with a situation where the rich get richer, and the poor, poorer; a region which has job opportunities attractive to immigrants tends to generate still more employment potential, leading to another round of immigration. Again, the process is stable, but in the interim it provides what could well be (depending upon the education and skill characteristics of the migrants) of considerable benefit to current residents.

A Brief Comment on Policy

This paper has attempted to develop a simple model of migration movements for Canada and to take a look at the primary ways in which regions gain or lose from population inflows and outflows. The previous discussion has several policy implications, and it is interesting to consider migration and manpower policy in the light of our findings.

It has been pointed out that a policy aimed at moving unemployed workers to employment opportunities will not provide an immediate once-and-for-all solution to regional surplus labour problems. The outflow will ultimately generate, through the multiplier process, further unemployment in the source region, and more job opportunities in the area receiving the flow. A policy of "bringing jobs to the workers," rather than moving workers to the jobs, begins to look somewhat more plausible. It might even be desirable to establish and support some form of "hothouse industry" in a region rather than to pay the costs (in both resources and social loss) of moving surplus labour to more efficient locations.

Further, the real costs of education and training embodied in emigrants from a region are borne by those remaining behind, so that unless some form of inter-regional compensation is set up to "pay" for the immigration of human capital, or unless a means is found to check the outflows, we shall continue to see the wealthy regions expand, and the poorer regions contract. The economist, in his concern for efficiency, generally lauds efforts to enhance the geographical mobility of labour; given the distributional effects, perhaps more attention should be paid to development efforts aimed at *reducing* interprovincial migration, not by setting up barriers to mobility, but by generating employment opportunities which induce workers to remain.

The discussion is particularly relevant for Western Canada, where British Columbia and Alberta have experienced heavy inflows, a large proportion of which came from Manitoba and Saskatchewan. *Table III* shows interprovincial migration flows for Western Canada, and points up the fact that British Columbia had net gains from all other Western provinces; Alberta gained from all but British Columbia; Manitoba had net gains only from Saskatchewan; and Saskatchewan suffered net losses to each of the other three. The result has been relatively large subsidization of Alberta and British Columbia growth and development by Saskatchewan and Manitoba, a trend which seems likely to continue unless steps are taken to generate employment opportunities in those provinces.

Expressing the effects in dollar terms is rather hazardous, since precise information on the composition of the interprovincial flows is unavailable. On the (rather questionable) assumption that interprovincial flows are roughly similar to international flows, Saskatchewan suffered a net loss of human capital exceeding forty million dollars for the period 1956-61, and Manitoba, a loss of approximately fifteen million.

Alberta gained by some twenty-eight million dollars, British Columbia by thirty million dollars. Remembering that these figures include only the human capital values, we can conclude that the interprovincial wealth transfers which have taken place in Western Canada have been significant.

Table III - INTERPROVINCIAL MIGRATION FLOWS FOR WESTERN CANADA, 1956-61*

From	To					
	Man.	Sask.	Alta.	B. C.	West.	All C.
Manitoba	0	3538	4988	5079	13,605	24,579
Saskatchewan	4889	0	12,617	7182	24,688	29,647
Alberta	2326	4050	0	11,598	17,974	25,568
British Columbia	2167	2523	9299	0	13,989	23,746
Western Canada	9382	10,111	26,904	23,859	0	
Canada, Total	18,013	13,526	36,955	36,013		0

*Source: DBS, *Census of Canada, 1961*, Bulletin 4.1-10, Tables J.4 and J.1.

Whatever the dollar values which emerge from the analysis may be, one must be careful to avoid the automatic conclusion that "population growth is good; population decline is bad." The gains from higher immigration and lower emigration must be carefully weighed against the losses in efficiency and the external diseconomies likely to accompany "growth" as it has traditionally been measured.

Conclusion

This paper has attempted to develop a number of conceptual tools useful in the analysis of migration and its effects, and has shown how those tools can be applied to the recent experience of Western Canada. It was shown, first, that migration responds to economic incentives in the form of job opportunities and income differentials. Second, it was argued that there are potentially large benefits and costs associated with immigration and emigration, respectively, and that manpower policy aimed at improving the working of the labour market should take those benefits and costs into account.

Footnotes

1
That this view is still a pervasive one is evidenced by an article, "Immigration and Emigration" by L. H. Officer, in L. H. Officer and L. B. Smith, eds., *Canadian Economic Problems and Policies* (Toronto: McGraw-Hill, 1970), pp. 142-156, which starts from the premise that: "Canada is an underpopulated country." (p. 143).

2
SOR/62-36, *Canada Gazette Part II*, Vol. 96, No.1 (January 18, 1962), and P.C. 1967-1616, August 16, 1967. See *Office Consolidation of the Immigration Act* (Ottawa: Queen's Printer, 1968), pp. 37-62. The revision merely put into writing the types of policies which were informally being pursued in any event, so that the shifts in the composition and timing of flows has not been particularly great as a result.

3
See the information release from the Office of the Minister of Manpower and Immigration (mimeo), September 12, 1967. The Section "Background to the New Immigration Regulations," notes that: "The main objectives of these new regulations are to achieve universality and objectivity in the selection process." (p. 1).

4
Parliament, House of Commons, *Official Report of Debates* (Ottawa: Queen's Printer), May 1, 1947, pp. 2644-2647.

5
See D. C. Corbett, *Canada's Immigration Policy* (Toronto: University of Toronto Press, 1957) for a discussion of policy and policy determinants during the early 1950's.

6
Ibid., p. 3.

7
T. A. Courchene, "Interprovincial Migration and Economic Adjustment," *The Canadian Journal of Economics*, III, No. 4 (November, 1970), pp. 550-576.

8
Seldon, "Some Aspects of Canadian Immigration Policy," Appendix Table A-7 and A-8.

9
See for example, H. G. Grubel and A. D. Scott, "The International Flow of Human Capital," *American Economic Review*, LVI (Proceedings, May, 1966), pp. 268-274, and more recent work by the same authors.

10
Source: Data on immigration from *Immigration Statistics*, various years, issued by the Department of Citizenship and Immigration and the Department of Manpower and Immigration (Queen's Printer). Human and capital values from L. Parai, *Immigration and Emigration of Professional and Skilled Manpower During the Post-War period*, Economic Council of Canada Special Study No. 1 (Ottawa: Queen's Printer, 1965), Table 31, p. 80.

11
Emigration data in general is difficult to obtain. U. S. figures on immigration from Canada give some indication of the size of the flows, but differences in recording criteria and the problems involved in recording flows of returning residents make any precise figures on emigration rather questionable.

12
DBS, *Census of Canada*, 1961, Bulletin 4.1-10, Tables J.4 and J.1 provide figures on interprovincial flows for the period 1956-61.

13
E. J. Mishan and L. Needleman, "Immigration: Some Economic Effects," *Lloyds Bank Review* (January, 1968), pp. 33-46. E. J. Mishan and L. Needleman, "Immigration: Long-Run Economic Effects," *Lloyds Bank Review* (January, 1968), pp. 15-25.

14
J. Vanderkamp, "The Effect of Out-Migration on Regional Employment," *The Canadian Journal of Economics*, III, No. 4 (November, 1970), pp. 541-549.

15
Ibid., p. 541.

Local Histories as Source Materials for Western Canadian Studies

Hugh A. Dempsey

The publication of local histories has gained great popularity in Western Canada during the past decade. Prior to that time a few specialized studies or the efforts of particularly progressive communities have resulted in the production of such works. However, the celebration of golden, silver, and diamond jubilees in Western communities and, more important, the celebration of Canada's Centennial in 1967, have created a greater awareness of the importance of local histories.

My definition of a local history would compare with that of Bowsfield, who described it as "a work dealing with an area less than that covered by a provincial history."[1] In actual fact, most local histories deal with municipalities and small towns, while in a few cases larger cities may commission professional writers to prepare histories for special anniversaries.

There is no intention in this paper to deal with the writing of local history. This has already been discussed at length by D. D. Parker in *Local History, How to Gather it, Write it, Publish it;*[2] in Hartwell Bowsfield's *Writing Local History;*[3] and my own *How to Prepare a Local History.*[4] Rather, the intention here is to look at the publications which have been created as a result of local history projects and to provide some idea of the importance of these in the larger fields of Canadian history. While one local history in isolation has little relevance to the general Canadian scene, a collection of forty or fifty such histories provides an important source of primary information on a segment of Western Canadian studies.

Many local histories may contain page after page of names, quarter sections, marriages, births, and deaths, but hidden among the mass of local trivia, one may turn up primary references which are pure gold. A local history in one place might say: "Ben Trayer, Senior, with his family consisting of his wife, Ben Junior, Jack, Lella, and Elsie, came to Alberta in the spring of 1905 from Souris, Man. His oldest daughter, Haddie, married Robert Dawson the year before and they had settled just north of George Wells' home."[5] However, a few pages farther on, one might get completely away from the local scene, when a pioneer re-collected:

> The tribe of the Sioux that got the best of Custer was camped in the vicinity of Fort Walsh. I saw the American mules, horses, guns and scalps, for they had killed 312 men, the whole of Custer's command. I had the pleasure of being one of the escort of police to hand Sitting Bull over to the American soldiers . . . Sitting Bull was very sedate as he sat on his cayuse, his legs almost touching the ground, surrounded by squaws and warriors . . . all dressed in their war paint. Nevertheless, they moved along very quietly and peaceable.
>
> When we reached the contingent of 400 American soldiers, who were to meet us at the line, papers were exchanged, the signs of courtesy advanced and accepted. The Americans swung in between us, and the Indians bunched like sheep into a compact body. They wailed and cried, for the poor Indian felt he had made his last stand. The last I saw of Sitting Bull, he was stretched as high as he could get, roaring at the top of his voice, prevailing on his people to go quietly along and give no trouble.[6]

The majority of local histories have been prepared by amateurs. Many of the histories are from rural areas or from small towns which lack anyone with the knowledge or skill to handle a scholarly research project. Often these projects have been undertaken by women's committees with no one empowered to edit the final work. Indeed, with the cliques and factions so often present in rural communities (as well as urban ones), it probably would be worth the life and reputation of anyone to tamper with another's work. The result often is a local history filled with inaccuracies, needless repetition, and marginal material which should never have appeared in print. Yet the historian must accept the local history for what it is - the effort of a group of untrained persons who have succeeded in publishing a history of their community. If these people had not undertaken the project, it would never have been done. There are few professional historians willing to accept such a task. One cannot condemn the poor or marginal material which may exist in local histories, but rather, be grateful for the valuable sources of primary information which these histories sometimes contain.

Local histories usually contain four types of information. One is the historical narrative that has been written by a member of the local committee and deals with events which occurred before agricultural settlement. In most cases, this information has been drawn from published sources and is of questionable historical value.

A second type is the narrative dealing with one segment of the local story, such as the history of a school, church, club, or family which has been drawn from published and unpublished sources. These must be approached with caution, but one can usually quickly discover whether or not the information is accurate.

The other two types are the ones which are of most interest to the historian. One is the narrative or reminiscences of a person who actually participated in the events he is describing; the other is the documentary source - the letters, diaries, or minute books which exist in the community and are appearing in print for the first time.

A good example of the latter is the Julia Short diary in *Leaves from the Medicine Tree*.[7] This eleven-year-old girl was on a ranch near High River at the outbreak of the Riel Rebellion. Here are some of the entries which in printed form can be found only in this local history.

> March 31st. Mr. Spalding says that the Indians are uprising and a whole settlement have been killed. They are afraid there will be uprising down here too.
>
> April 1st. Got 3 eggs. Set the goose today. Papa heard that the Government is going to give rifles and ammunition to every man who wanted them.
>
> April 7th. Got 3 eggs. Papa went around to tell people that there was to be a meeting at Buck Smith's so as to build a block house. But most of them did not want to build one so they threw that aside. They sent a man up to Calgary for arms though.
>
> April 9th. Planted potatoes today. The man that went to Calgary for arms came back today and he says that they cannot get arms unless 10 out of every forty volunteer to fight between here and Medicine Hat if needed. Heard that 2,000 Fenians have crossed over into Canada between Montreal and Toronto. Four eggs.
>
> April 10th. Ten men volunteered to fight between here and Medicine Hat and they formed a Home Guard but they have to be sworn in yet. Got my watch. Charlie is one of the Home Guard. They take turns watching out on the Ridge for signs of Indians coming and have material to light a warning fire. We girls are supposed to stay close to home but we have a place in the woods to hide in case of emergency. Each night the horses are left with harness on, except the bridles, and the wagon hauled up close to the house, our telescope bags packed with valuables and necessaries in case we have to start for Calgary in a hurry.

Local histories may vary greatly in their content and subject matter. Some offer practically no primary source material, and what they do have can be discarded as mere localisms. Others can be rich sources for the historian whose interest goes far beyond that particular region.

In quality, these histories are uneven and within the cover of a single volume there may be the efforts of several authors which vary greatly in accuracy and detail. In one the general level of writing and documentation may be good, while in another the author may not bother to provide initials or Christian names because everybody knows "Old Man Jones." In spite of these obvious deficiencies, each local history has an opportunity to make a contribution to the larger field of history, and only careful examination will reveal whether or not it has succeeded.

Western Canada is in the unique position of still having a few living members of the first generation and many of the second generation pioneers of our agricultural communities. They often can provide valuable information about immigration, pioneer life, politics, social life, and the problems in establishing a new community. But these details are preserved only in memory and, if historians cannot gather and record them, they must rely on people in the communities who, experienced or not, will gather what they can as best they know how.

As editor of the *Alberta Historical Review,* my duty has been to read and review many local histories which have been published. In the past few years, literally dozens of these histories have been examined and one cannot help but be impressed by the accumulation of information within their covers. The best way of illustrating this is to offer a few examples of the type of information which has turned up among the mass of trivia.

For example, local histories provide some fascinating details on the origin of the settlers and their reasons for coming to Western Canada. While government reports provide statistics on immigration and countries of origin, they cannot give the whole story. Local histories, on the other hand, tell about world adventurers, gold seekers, sailors, and ordinary persons who chose to come to the Prairies.

May Sloan wrote in the regional history of Majestic-Farrell Lake that "at this time, a great deal of literature was being freely distributed, encouraging settlers to come to western Canada. Uncle Will had made a trip up here and he wrote to Dad, telling him of this great new country with its many opportunities. So, in the spring of 1902, Dad and Mother prepared to emigrate."[8] In the same book, Mrs. Glenn Thompson observed, "We came to Canada from Colorado in 1914 on the 'Trainload of Settlers' brought in by the C.P.R. to settle on their ready-made irrigation farms at Gem, where we farmed until 1917."[9]

Ben Griffiths recorded in *Shadows of the Neutrals* that he came to Western Canada because of a labour strike in England in 1905. "I hung around for two weeks and then went to see the immigration officer and he advised me to go to Canada."[10] In the same book, a Mr. Sibley (they do not give his first name) commented, "I had read about Alberta in

Government Literature I used to send to Ottawa for, and knew much about building sod and log shacks, that I could put into practise."[11] Wallace McComish had another reason for coming. He said that he "came west in 1903 on a Harvest Excursion to Deloraine, Manitoba."[12]

One of the best accounts of westward immigration is contained in *Pioneer Days in Bardo, Alberta*. This book is superior to the average local history, probably because it was published in 1944, at a time when many original settlers still were actively engaged in farming. The authors, Ragna Steen and Magda Henrickson, were part of the Norwegian community which made up the Bardo settlement. They commented as follows:

> It was in 1892 that Nels Jevning and Martin Finseth, two neighbors farming near Crookston, Minnesota, first dreamed of going to Canada. A Canadian immigration agent had recently opened an office in Crookston. The literature distributed gave glowing accounts of the productivity of the Canadian soil. Displays of grasses and grains, and even letters from settlers already there, seemed to establish the fact that here indeed was a vast area of exceedingly productive soil awaiting development. Railways had begun to penetrate the wilderness. Free homesteads in all of this immense territory were offered to any prospective settlers.

> The Jevning, Finseth and Anderson families, who had been living in the Red River Valley since they arrived there from Norway in 1876, were intrigued by the prospects of free land. Business reverses, sickness and lack of land for their sons and daughters were among the reasons which caused them and many of their neighbors to be more or less dissatisfied with this district around Crookston where they had been among the first settlers. They had often talked of moving to the Pacific Coast or to the Sunny South. But the cost of establishing themselves in any other place in the United States was too great.

> Then when Canada beckoned, several Norwegian families became interested. Other settlers opposed the idea of going to Canada. Remarks as follows were often heard: "We are too far north now; why go further north? It is cold enough here." "We won't leave good old Uncle Sam to live under a petticoat government." "We fought the tyranny of England once. We will not join her now."

> Undeterred by such protests, Martin Finseth started negotiating with the Canadian Government agent and finally obtained the promise that several representative farmers of the district would be given free transportation if they wished to inspect the country he represented. The result of these negotiations was that in the spring of 1893 Nels Jevning, Martin Fin-

seth, Andrew Malmberg, and John Wallerbeck went to inspect the Canadian Northwest.[13]

This study goes on to describe the success of the advance party and how a large group of Norwegians from Minnesota came to the Bardo community.

Interestingly enough, an examination of local histories has revealed extremely little information on politics. One would almost think that farmers were not interested in politics - something that we know is not true. In telling the stories of their communities, emphasis has been given to the trials and tribulations of establishing a homestead, social activities, sports, and family records. It may be that politics was an emotional subject and that the farmer, after seeing his views on such issues as tariffs and railway rates either supported or defeated, promptly lost interest and returned to his world of farming. In recollecting events of his lifetime in later years, such activities would not loom so large unless he had been a political activist. Another reason for a scarcity of political recollections could result from the fact that many histories have been prepared by women who were not politically oriented and would not actively have attempted to gather such information for their books. Even the one direct reference to Social Credit found among a sampling of twelve local histories was more social than political in its content.

> In 1935 a Social Credit group was formed and operated until several farmers moved to the cities or other parts. This group sponsored a few dances and other entertainment. The ladies who brought cake to these dances were admitted free of charge. The meetings were held at the different homes ... After the business was attended to, we would have lunch. We took a large freezer of home made ice-cream. Then the afternoon was finished off with a ball game with the children.[14]

There have been a few exceptional writers who have dealt with the political aspects of pioneer life. They probably had a personal interest in the subject or were particularly keen observers. For example, John Martin, the author of a number of local histories, wrote of the political activities at Gleichen during a federal campaign. He stated:

> I recall the hard feeling among the men over politics while I was in school in 1896 and almost every day we would witness some sort of a fight. The Conservatives and Liberals started sparring one day in front of the Palace Hotel, when Doc Rose, a strong Liberal, was reading from Frank Oliver's Edmonton Bulletin. Jack Clark called it a Liberal rag and the row was on but it wasn't serious enough to warrant calling the N.W.M.P. sergeant

Jack Marshall. The Liberals composed a song for the kids to sing about the two candidates and even they got into brawls over the election issue, especially while the song was being sung.

The Conservative kids would fight but were in the minority and got the worst of it. I can recall part of the ballad ran as follows:

Oliver rides on a white horse,

Cochrane on a mule,

Oliver is a gentleman

Cochrane is a fool.

Oliver was elected to the Federal house as an Independent backed by the Liberal party.[15]

The author also mentioned some of the political activities which took place out on their homestead near Rosebud. During the 1898 election he went with his dad to the polling booth about twenty miles away. There they found that the Conservatives were being directed to see the "sparrow in the barn." This "sparrow" proved to be Angus Sparrow, a local Conservative who was providing free liquor to anyone who promised to vote their way. "Dad had more than he could carry," recalled the author, "and I had to drive the team home while he lay in the bottom of the wagon box."[16]

In this vein, it should be pointed out that most local histories are relatively devoid of humour. It seems as though the authors have feared offending local families by discussing some of the well-known pranks and incidents of the areas. One exception was the *Big Valley Story*, which told of "questionable young ladies" who visited the town regularly each weekend until 1921. Then, according to the author,

> in order no doubt to get things on an orderly and business like basis, a "Madame" arrived in Big Valley and had a very nice home constructed about a mile north on the east side of the C.N.R. In due time she brought in her "filles de joie" and opened for business. Everything flourished for some time, but apparently there must have been a number of suspicious wives around at that time because they formed a sort of Vigilante committee and in the small hours of the morning in midwinter they had someone put the torch to this house and in one fell swoop exterminated the first and only business of its kind in Big Valley. It has never been replaced.[17]

Another area somewhere between tall tales and folklore is that of the "wild west" stories which sometimes appear in family histories. One example dealt with a man who was involved in a shooting incident at

Stettler. Afterwards, according to the author, "he went to Medicine Hat and one night a bunch of cowboys got him down and spurred him pretty nearly to death and then finished him off by shooting him."[18] Another account dealt with the life of Valentine Neis, who had wandered across the United States for several years before coming to Western Canada. During his adventures he was captured by Indians in Arizona, knew the Jesse James gang, and saw Wild Bill shot to death in a card game.[19] Another man, Orville Smith, seemed to miss his biggest adventures. He was on his way with supplies for General Custer at the Little Big Horn in 1876, then missed Chief Joseph's refugee Nez Percés by fifteen miles a year later. He was at the turbulent Sounding Lake Treaty with Big Bear's followers and was rescued from hostile Sarcees by Chief Crowfoot. He also was in partnership with the man who was supposed to have found the Lost Lemon Mine - a mine, incidentally, which is still lost.[20]

Another man, relating his family's adventures, told a story which had broad social implications. "Father made three trips back to Havre [Montana], picking up some Chinamen at Medicine Hat and smuggling them across the border. He would get one hundred dollars each for getting them across. On one trip he had to hide the Chinamen in the water in a creek to keep the Mounted Police from catching them. There were no customs along the border in those days and the Mounted Police patrolled it. He then bought horses and trailed them back, as horses were cheap in Montana."[21] He concluded by observing that his father was a Polish count in exile.

Another indication of frontier discrimination was recorded in *Memories of Verdant Valley* in discussions of the First World War:

> At last the Armistice was signed . . . That night a gang of young men got together in Drumheller and started out to celebrate. They first called on a German blacksmith in Drumheller, put him on the radiator of a car and drove him around town . . . Next they drove out to Mr. Arnold's. He was in bed and did not know the war had ended. The men threw stones at his windows. They opened his door and yelled, "We've got you now you German son-of-a-bitch." Arnold grabbed his rifle and loaded it. He fired a shot through the roof and said, "If anyone comes any nearer, I'll shoot."
>
> Tip Blane didn't pay any attention. He kept on towards Arnold and was shot through the heart . . .[22]

The author described the man's flight from his home and his arrest. "When his trial came up there wasn't anyone there to testify against him. Not one of the men appeared. He told what had happened and was acquitted." Adding to the significance of the account is a letter of appeal from a local resident which is reprinted in full.

The use of extensive quotations from local histories in this paper has been deliberate for it may be possible from these selections to see that such publications can be a source of useful history and colourful folklore. While it is true that the average local history is devoid of humour and adventure, a body of them examined as a group can provide some fertile sources for many areas of historical study. Generally speaking, the more recent the publication, the less significant its contents. One reason for this is that the more recent publications contain tales related by the children of those who actually participated in the events. The stories have become a part of family tradition and often are more folklore than fact. This is not always true, though, for recent local histories may contain old diaries or letters which take the reader back to the primary source.

Local histories do not make good casual reading and usually lack indexes or other finding aids, but they cannot be ignored as a source of history. They offer a challenge to the historian, for the information does not come easily. One may search for days to discover a piece of pertinent information but, like the reading of early newspapers or a voluminous collection of private papers, it sometimes takes great effort to reap a rich reward. Seldom does one see the local history cited as reference source, and seldom does a scholar try to tap this source in a specialized library. The information is there, and it should be used, for it is a legitimate and fruitful source of Canadian history.

Footnotes

1
Hartwell, Bowsfield, "Writing Local History," *Alberta Historical Review*, vol. 17, no. 3 (1969), p. 10.

2
D. D. Parker, *Local History, How to Gather it, Write it, Publish it* (New York: Social Science Research Council, 1944).

3
Bowsfield, *op. cit.*

4
Hugh A. Dempsey, *How to Prepare a Local History* (Calgary: Glenbow-Alberta Institute, 1969).

5
Edith J. Lawrence Clark, ed., *Trails of Tail Creek Country* (Stettler, 1967), p. 321.

6
"Ed. Barnett" in Clark, *op. cit.*, p. 70.

7
Leaves From the Medicine Tree, by High River Pioneers' and Old Timers' Association (High River, 1960), pp. 79-80.

8
Harvest of Memories, by Majestic-Farrell Lake Women's Institute (Craigmyle, 1968), p. 261.

9
Ibid., p. 275.

10
Shadows of the Neutrals, by Old-Timer's Centennial Book Committee (Coronation, 1967), p. 77.

11
Ibid., p. 145.

12
Ibid., p. 153.

13
Ragna Steen and Magda Hendrickson, *Pioneer Days in Bardo, Alberta*, The Historical Society of Beaver Hills Lake, Tofield, Alberta (1944), pp. 15-66.

14
Harvest of Memories, *op. cit.*, p. 220.

15
John Martin, "Prairie Reminiscences," *Alberta Historical Review*, vol. 10, no. 2 (1962), p. 8.

16
Ibid., p. 8.

17
Mrs. Gordon Fowler, *The Big Valley Story* (Big Valley, 1964), p. 43.

18
Clark, *op. cit.*, p. 410.

19
Ibid., pp. 317-18.

20
Shadows of the Neutrals, pp. 98-101.

21
Ibid., p. 71.

22
Memories of Verdant Valley, Cassell Hill, Livingston, Rainbow, Drumheller East Farmers' Union of Alberta (1966), pp. 105-07.

British Visitors' Perceptions of the West, 1885-1914

Lewis H. Thomas

Many narratives were written by British travellers in Western Canada before 1885, and include such popular and frequently reprinted works as those of Milton and Cheadle, Lieutenant W. F. Butler, and the Earl of Southesk. But notable changes in the character and extent of this literature occurred in the following thirty years. Prior to 1885 the visitors were usually members of the aristocracy whose interests centred on hunting and adventure. This type of visitor was also represented in the later period, but he was now vastly outnumbered by travellers belonging to the British middle class. Whereas in the sixties and seventies it required a large financial outlay and the employment of native-born guides to penetrate the Western wilderness, after 1885 the middle-class visitor could complete a journey out and home using relatively fast and cheap steamships and the facilities of a transcontinental railway. The result was a proliferation of published works which is surprising in number and diversity.

During this period, there was scarcely a year in which a new travel book on Canada did not appear in the lists of British publishers. An exact count is difficult to make, but it is certain that there were more than seventy-five titles, while in 1911 alone there were eight, or more different works. This does not include the numerous articles that appeared in periodicals during the period. Among the authors were British businessmen, men and women concerned with opportunities for British migrants, newspaper reporters, politicians, at least one distinguished economist (J. A. Hobson), the famous author Rudyard Kipling, and the poet Rupert Brooke. At the very end of the period there was the enthusiastic user of the newest mode of transportation, T. W. Wilby, who in a fit of optimism and endurance traversed the country from Halifax to Vancouver in an automobile, to the immense astonishment of those Canadians whom he encountered en route.

What were the conditions in the United Kingdom which explain this sustained interest in Canada? In the first place the influx of cheap foreign wheat had a profound impact on British agriculture; farmers found it difficult to remain on their land thus reducing the need for agricultural labourers and increasing the number of city workers in the low-income brackets. So far as industrial workers were concerned, there was no improvement in real wages between 1895 and 1913, and for part of the period there was an actual decline. Beneath the glitter of Edwardian prosperity there were vast numbers of poor, ill-housed, undernourished, and unhealthy city workers. Prosperity was more unevenly shared than ever before, and it has been said that class divisions were never so acutely felt as by the Edwardians. The middle class was numerically so small that, in the judgment of one historian, it "turns out to be largely a matter of aspiration, imitation and snobbery." One third of the population was trying to maintain a lifestyle that only one seventeenth had sufficient income to provide.[1] Elizabeth Lewthwaite, who visited Western Canada at the turn of the century, lamented the fate in Britain of "that vast army of gentlewomen, daughters of professional men, impoverished landed gentry and others" who were left "to drift as best they can."[2] Another third of the British people were living on incomes too low to maintain working efficiency.

These conditions account for the rise of new trade union organizations, of socialism, of social reform movements, as well as the hesitant beginnings of government intervention to curb the rapaciousness and insensitivity of capitalist private enterprise. Another solution for economic distress in Britain was the encouragement of emigration to areas overseas where opportunities for individuals to make a new start in life looked promising.

No doubt the majority of British emigrants in this period moved on their own initiative, but there was a proliferation of philanthropic organizations designed to assist the emigration of the more timid and insecure low-income British workers. As in the earlier part of the nineteenth century, the United States continued to attract emigrants, but the rising tide of imperialist sentiment in the period with which this paper is concerned resulted in a very significant increase in migration to the self-governing colonies, notably Canada, Australia, and South Africa. In the first decade of the twentieth century one and a half million Britons went abroad, and 56 percent of them (double the proportion of the previous decade) settled in lands within the Empire. After 1910 the flow increased to a quarter of a million annually, and again the proportion going to countries within the Empire increased.

Of the self-governing colonies, Canada had the earliest and best opportunities to attract British immigrants. It was only a short sea voyage away; it had the prestige of a federal union of transcontinental dimensions; it had great and diversified underdeveloped natural resources; and after 1885 its varied regions could be investigated by the railway traveller. Offsetting these advantages, there was the fact that in the minds of many Britons Canada was regarded as a land with a harsh climate, and a lonely and dangerous wilderness. A. S. Hurd, writing in 1902, states:

> Canada is the one colony which has been continually misunderstood in England. Just as the English people were awakening to its real character and were beginning to take an interest in its future, Mr. Rudyard Kipling checked the movement with a phrase. Canada is "My Lady of the Snows" in the imagination of Englishmen ... In the minds of nine out of ten persons in the Old Country Canada stands for the Siberia of the British Empire.[3]

The style of life in Western Canada was believed to be crude and uncivilized, and successful settlement problematical. The travellers of the period set themselves the task of assessing the validity of these stereotypes. As might be expected, they devoted a great deal of attention to describing the physical features of the country, the climate, the character of economic activity, the experiences of British settlers, the cosmopolitan stream of immigration, Canadian society and manners, and the interaction of Canadian, American and British institutions and influences.

Reactions to the physical features of Western Canada, then as now, are highly subjective - hence they are the least uniform of the impressions which one receives from the observations of these travellers. To Kipling "the tedium of it was eternal."[4] To some, during the drought years of the 1880's and 1890's large stretches were depressing, arousing suspicions of Macoun's optimistic estimates of its fertility.[5] But somewhat later another observer wrote:

> The ordinary English conception of prairie vegetation is utterly erroneous. It would be quite correct to describe it as, for the most part, a rich natural pasture, variegated here and there with thickets of dwarf shrubs, and frequently turned to a carpet of gorgeous colouration by the profusion of wild flowers, which bloom in endless succession from the advent of summer to the fall of the year. The prairie is almost destitute of trees; no tangled bush confronts the settler ...[6]

An Englishwoman who remained some time on the Prairie wrote as follows:

> From the first moment I found the prairie entirely attractive - its stillness, its serenity, together with its strong and eager pulse of life ... It could raise one's mood to the power of wings and the seventh heaven, and hurl one down to those tiresome regions where one has to move with fixed determination ... but it never bored.[7]

Since most of the travellers in this period went to the West by
C.P.R., there are fewer accounts of the country traversed by the Grand
Trunk Pacific and the Canadian Northern, whose transcontinental lines
were not open for traffic until late in 1914 and 1915. In *The Land of
Open Doors*, J. B. Bickersteth, a lay worker for the Anglican church in
northern Alberta in the neighbourhood of the Grand Trunk line, describes the bush country north of Edmonton which made homesteading
there different from that on the open plains:

> ...I soon caught sight of a tent [he wrote] and not far off two
> men, apparently father and son, hard at work "clearing" their
> land. The younger was cutting down trees, undergrowth, and
> every obstruction, and the elder was gathering it together into
> high piles ready for burning; the green logs would have to dry
> out for months before they would burn, and the stumps would
> either be left to rot, which takes some years, or else would be
> pulled out with block and tackle and oxen; it means hard work
> before bush is converted into prairie. The homesteader earns
> his farm many times over before it is his.

Travel in such districts, he frequently notes, was arduous: "The trails
which wind through the bush never have a chance of drying up as they
would in open country, and after really wet weather . . . they are little
better than one long mud hole." Yet this type of country could also im-
press the eye, as another visitor using the partly-completed Grand
Trunk line noted, as he stood on the bank of the McLeod River:

> Stretching away from my feet in gentle undulations was an
> endless ocean of forest. It was trees, trees, trees on every side,
> with their sombre, majestic tone of dark green . . . Winding to
> and fro through the sea of colour like a ribbon was the placid
> blue water of the McLeod River on its ways to the slopes of the
> divide.[8]

Most of the writers confess a general inability to find words to do
justice to the impressions which the mountains conveyed to them. But
Rupert Brooke was uninhibited. He wrote of "the homeless grandeur of
the Rockies and the Selkirks." "This is one of the chief differences," he
continued, "between the effect of the Rockies and that of the Alps.
There, you are always in sight of the civilization which has nestled for
ages at the feet of those high places . . . These unmemoried heights
are inhuman - or rather, irrelevant to humanity. No recorded Hannibal
has struggled across them, their shadow lies on no remembered
literature. . ."[9] Perhaps by his time the epic of railway exploration and
C.P.R. mountain construction was beginning to be forgotten, whereas
earlier British travellers were eloquent in their testimonies to the won-

ders wrought by the surveyors, the engineers, and the navvies - the Hannibals of the Canadian West. But Brooke found the Canadian scene generally "wind swept and empty":

> A European can find nothing to satisfy the hunger of his heart. The air is too thin to breathe. He requires haunted woods, and the friendly presence of ghosts . . . So, I imagine, a Canadian would feel our woods and fields heavy with the past and the invisible and suffer claustrophobia in an English countryside beneath the dreadful pressure of immortals.

The tough-minded soldier, Major General Sir Francis de Winton, found in the mountains "the silence of God, and that silence fills you with a solemn awe as one seems to hear, far, far away in the avenues of the ages, the Voice which created and commanded the world to be made."[10] But there were other reactions. ". . . the Rockies are not to be compared with anything," wrote another traveller in 1911. "They are individual, apart, strenuous, with the teeth of ferocity in them. They are not beautiful, nor sublime - not any of the other easy adjectives that slip from the lips. They are gaunt, foreboding, things of drear strength."[11]

But most of the travellers who crossed the continental divide confined themselves to particulars, like Wilby in his *A Motor Tour Through Canada*, published in 1914. "A new-comer might claim all the sensation and honour of discovery," he wrote. "Threading forest paths, past whirling pools and the icy blue waters of silent lakes and of rivers that rushed through canyons and ravines, . . . now climbing towards snow-capped peaks, we pursued a road that followed the line of least resistance and took us more often north and south than westward." There were "perilous divides and the sites of abandoned mines." "Again and again placid vistas, beautiful in their domesticity, were succeeded by all that was wild and rugged and stamped for ever as Nature's undisputed own."

A number of writers claimed to see the effects of this geography on the character of Western Canadians. British Columbians, one observed, were "less angular, their skins are clearer, their bearing is more leisurely, their voices brighter and pleasanter, their expression kindlier, their manner softer."[12] "When the Rockies are reached and passed," E. W. Elkington noted in *Canada, The Land of Hope*, in 1910, "a new country, a new climate and a new people are met . . . anyhow they are quite different from the people of the Eastern provinces; they are British Columbians and not Canadians, and do not think much of those who come from the other side of the mountains."

In general Western towns and cities, understandably, aroused much less enthusiasm in the minds of the visitors than the physical features of the land. The exceptions were Winnipeg and Victoria, the former for the rapidity and scale of its growth and vigour, the latter for its beauty and its English character. In 1885 Professor Tanner wrote about Winnipeg that:

> Youthful she certainly is, but she is more complete in the comforts and conveniences she offers as a place of residence, than many of our old English cities. She has certainly all the advantages arising from having adopted many of the most recent improvements associated with town life. For instance nowhere in England is the telephone so completely used for superseding the necessity for messengers.[13]

Tanner justified these and similar comments, he said, "chiefly to correct the many erroneous ideas which are so commonly entertained in England, that the Canadians have habits of life rather more consistent with those of the proverbial backwood's men, than with the usual comforts of British life. No greater mistake can possibly be made, for the homes of very many of our Canadian families are replete with conveniences of which we have in England only a limited knowledge." James Lumsden, a Scottish journalist, saw the city in different terms in 1902, in his *Through Canada in Harvest Time:*

> If I wish to flatter the people of Winnipeg, I should compare their city to the capital of Peter the Great. It certainly does not deserve the comparison, but Winnipeg forcibly reminded me of a Russian town. The length and breadth of the streets and the huge size of the buildings were suggestive of modern Russian cities, but what possibly gave realism to the resemblance was the number of moujiks and Finns wandering about the street.

Every visitor noted the civic pride of Winnipeggers. Here is one:

> Every man in Winnipeg believes in Winnipeg. He is proud of Winnipeg. He believes the Almighty must have overlooked the neighborhood or it would have been chosen as the Garden of Eden. He will quit business to sit down and talk to you by the hour about Winnipeg.[14]

Of course civic pride was not confined to Winnipeg. As Rupert Brooke noted, "It is imperative to praise Edmonton in Edmonton, but it is sudden death to praise it in Calgary."

Calgary aroused various reactions. Lumsden was astounded by his first-in-a-lifetime clear night view of the Milky Way galaxy "with a brilliance and definition never beheld through the more humid skies of the British Isles." The basis of Calgary's prosperity and encouraging future prospects was attributed by the engineer, J. W. C. Haldane, in 1898, to its role as a trade centre for the ranching country, its good local building stone, its position on transcontinental and branch railway lines, as an administrative centre for the N. W. M. P. and the Indian reserves, and as the locale of various mercantile and manufacturing operations.[15] A number of observers remarked on the strength of English influences in Calgary, even near the end of our period. "In Calgary," J. F. Fraser wrote in 1911, in *Canada As It Is*, "you strike a new stratum of Canadian, distinct, unique. These men are hardly of the traditional bronco-breaking, cow-punching sort. They are Englishmen of the county class, younger sons who have taken to horse-rearing and cow-breeding on the foothills of the Rockies. You cannot start ranching with nothing but faith and muscle, as you can wheat-growing . . . Ranching means money. Accordingly, the rancher is a different class from the farmer." Some of those attracted to the district were remittance men. "The remittance men," a correspondent of the London *Standard* wrote in 1905, "form a notable element in Albertan society, and Calgary is their headquarters. They abound in the lounges and bars in the hotels, clad in riding breeches and Norfolk jackets . . ."[16] Although English immigrants, J. F. Fraser noted, had lost their English mannerisms, "Calgary is English - the truest, most sterling lover of the old land between Toronto and Victoria." How curious a background for today's outpost of the American Empire! But then perhaps Calgary and Victoria have never been Canadian cities in tone and social characteristics.

The travellers had few kind words for the smaller towns and villages in the West. One such, in the mountains, was chiefly notable for the number of prostitutes and the liquor of all kinds at twenty-five cents a glass. "We saw plenty to assure us that, in those days, Donald was not a highly moral place," one visitor noted.[17] Fraser disparaged the smaller Prairie towns for another reason - their sameness, "as though turned out to the same pattern in the same machine, as lacking in individuality as factory-made furniture, with no ambition to be pretty, but serviceable, workable, dollar-earning." Western architecture earned some justifiably hard knocks: Bickersteth, writing of Edmonton in 1913, noted:

> Most of its brick buildings are at present extremely ugly. We are told that the art and especially the architecture of a particular age is the expression of its ideals. I must say I think that even Western ideals should not be judged by Western architecture.

Of Calgary, in 1910, Elkington wrote, ". . . like all Western towns in

Canada there is the half-finished, hastily-put-together appearance that gives an Englishman gooseflesh down the middle of his back."

Vancouver, it was almost universally agreed, had a great future. A visitor in 1894 saw it as the Glasgow of the Northwest - "beyond the reach of permanent misfortune. It needs no prophet to foretell the future of a city which is at once the terminus of the biggest railway in the world and the head of navigation for the trunk lines of steamships from Asia and Australia. The newest of new cities, unforgetful of an old-world ideal . . . There has been no Pacific Coast rowdyism, no revolvering, no instance or need of lynch law."[18]

There was also almost complete unanimity on the qualities of Victoria. "Everything about you is so suggestive of rustic England that it comes on you like a sudden shock to see a yellow-faced Chinaman shaking a foot-rug out of a bedroom window. By degrees you realize that Victoria is one of the most bewildering spots on the globe. It is a combination of old-fashioned English civilization and of wild, virgin wilderness."[19] Elkington summed up Victoria society in the following terms:

> It has its aristocracy and the ways of England are the ways of Victoria, and the language is the same. Here it is a case of "no Canadian need apply," as a set-off to the Eastern cities, where it is better for an Englishman, if he be in search of work, to disguise his language, forget his country, his grammar, and the proper pronounciation of all two-syllable words.

Almost all the British visitors deplored the presence of Asiatics in British Columbia, although they were ready to admit that they were hard-working, honest, law-abiding, cleaner than the white worker, and an essential element in the labour force ever since the period of railway construction. The ambivalent attitude of the British Columbians to this group was generally noticed. Lumsden reported that at a dinner reception "a grave Canadian . . . who was a large employer of labour, whispered in my ear as a secret that could not be proclaimed from the housetops, 'the Chinese are hated not for their vices but for their virtues'."

Descriptions of farming in the West abound in these books. For those travellers who sought or were offered the opportunity, every type of farming activity was examined in detail - wheat and mixed farming on the open plains, ranching in the foothills, market gardening and fruit growing in British Columbia. Homesteading attracted particular attention because of the publicity which had been given to this form of land acquisition by the Canadian Government and the C.P.R. in the United Kingdom. Throughout the whole period the homesteading experience could be observed - in Manitoba in the 1880's; in the most fertile parts of Saskatchewan and Alberta in the 1890's; and in the semi-arid south country and in the northern bush after the turn of the century. It was noted that some of the most successful British settlers were, however, not homesteaders, but those who purchased an acreage of good or improved land near a railway line from the railway company or from a Canadian farmer on the move; their time payments were frequently no greater than the rents paid on farm land in England, and, with the crops of a few good years, the debt was quickly paid off.

The reader of any of these many accounts would, however, never be left with the impression that success was easy in the Canadian West. The representative of the Charity Organization Society wrote in 1893:

> Every family, however commonplace, has a history to tell of hard battles against homesickness, the strangeness of surroundings, and the discomforts, small and great inseparable from a first year in Canada.[20]

The British immigrant, every visitor noted, must be prepared to bring some capital with him, and accept a rough and frugal life on the land at the start. "To speak broadly," the London *Times* correspondent wrote in 1894, "the young Englishman of the better classes sent out to the North-West to be a farmer is not a success . . . The public school life of the young Englishman develops qualities which make him a good soldier or sailor, but not a good farmer. No greater mistake can be made by English parents than to think that North-Western life may prove corrective for tendencies to dissipation. The very opposite result flows naturally from the absence of social restraint." On the other hand, "In the North-West Mounted Police young Englishmen have done well. The military discipline and the life on horseback in the open air draw out their better qualities."[21] The observations of the Irish politician and reformer, Michael Davitt, were common:

> In my inquiries about the relative success of various classes of colonists, I found that in almost every instance where a man brought a pair of willing hands and some knowledge of land labour with him he succeeded, even without a penny capital to start with.[22]

It was noted that while many Englishmen tried homesteading, a large number gave up before securing title to the land. These were usually town labourers or younger sons who were completely unsuited to life on the land. Since the Englishman is nothing if not articulate, the complaints of this class aroused widespread hostility. Keir Hardie, the leader of the British Labour Party, was one of many observers of this phenomenon. "I was not long in the country," he stated, "before I ran up against a fact which surprised and startled me. The English emigrant is not popular in Canada. This remark applies in a special degree to the Londoner ... Scotsmen, Welshmen, Irishmen, and Scandinavians are the favourites, pretty much in the order given. The reason is ... the Englishman's inveterate habit of grumbling, and his unwillingness to adapt himself to new conditions."[23] A Liverpool immigrant remarked, "I had to come to Canada to learn that the English, Irish, and Scotch were representatives of three, and not one nation."[24] One wonders what sort of Liverpudlian it was who had to come to Canada to discover the Celts! While admitting the faults of their fellow-countrymen, some observers, including Basil Stewart in *The Land of the Maple Leaf*, felt that Canadians contributed to the discord: "He seldom makes allowances. His rampant materialism reminds him all day and every day that 'he is not in business for his health' ... He is not always tolerant, not always patient, and not always fair."

Two of several women visitors were naturally concerned with the position of English women in the West. "One sees in England," Mrs. Cran wrote in 1910, in her *A Woman in Canada*, "a surplus of women working hard ... working at a ridiculous wage with no hope of ultimate independence, no hope of marriage or motherhood, no hope of anything but moment's pence for the moment's meal." What kept them away from the West, she concluded, was "a hardship to be faced which makes women justly shrink from the country. First from one prairie wife and then from another I heard a cry about the hardships of birth on the homesteads. Myself a trained maternity nurse as well as a mother, I know what lack of skilled attention must mean at the hour of travail."

The more class-conscious English women visitors lamented the absence of opportunity for the single male immigrants to marry middle-class English spinsters, with the result that they often married beneath them.[25] "If ignorant women of our lower orders go out and marry - as they will - farmers, who are often men of decent breeding, their children will go down, not up, in the scale of progress," Mrs. Cran commented. Emigration was not always an escape from the disabilities which women suffered in Britain. "To say that the conditions of life for educated gentlewomen in Canada were not a daily round of toil and monotony, for the most part, would be to obscure and pervert truth," Mrs. Pullen-Bury reported in 1912, in her book *From Halifax to Vancouver*. The life of the girl wage earner in the towns was often hard, she noted: "Wages may be higher on the American continent, but rent is ruinous and living distinctly dearer than in European countries." On the other hand, a number of visitors reported that English school mistresses were highly valued and did well in the West.

Coming from a land where natural wealth was available on a less lavish scale than in Canada, the British visitors were struck by the wastefulness which was associated with the use of these resources. One shares their revulsion at the dense volumes of smoke in British Columbia valleys and the fires deliberately started by prospectors in their search for ore-bearing rock. The mining of the prairie soil was also lamented, and more than one traveller noted that the farmers seemed to care nothing for fertilization. "He boasts about his bounteous crops, ignoring the circumstance that he himself does not stir a hand to assist in their propagation ... If he wishes to increase his aggregate production he does not attempt to study the soil to consummate this end, but merely ropes in a further area of virgin prairie for cultivation."[26] A number of the visitors preached the virtues of mixed farming instead of exclusive concentration on wheat growing, and recommended cultivation methods to conserve soil moisture. The despoliation of sport fishing lakes and streams caused critical comment as it would frustrate the increasing need for recreational resources: "the great waterways, once destroyed, can never be replaced," one visitor asserted in 1911.[27]

The materialism of Western life is a constant theme in the observations of the travellers. The following observation by the same visitor is typical:

> The many opportunities which the Golden West afford, have a tendency to monopolize the energies of the inhabitants to the exclusion of other interests of civilized life. In the eager desire to grow rich the aesthetic side generally suffers. Even in the great cities the commercial spirit dominates everything.

Boosterism dominated the minds and energies of the Westerner in the prewar years and astonished the English visitors.

> I travelled from Edmonton to Calgary in company of a citizen of Edmonton and a citizen of Calgary [wrote Rupert Brooke]. Hour after hour they disputed. Land in Calgary had risen from five dollars to three hundred; but in Edmonton from three to five hundred. Edmonton had grown from thirty persons to forty thousand in twenty years; but Calgary from twenty to thirty thousand in twelve ... "Where - as a respite - [they asked] did I come from?" I had to tell them, not with shame, that my own town of Grantchester, having numbered three hundred at the time of Julius Caesar's landing, had risen rapidly to nearly four hundred by Domesday Book, but was now declined to three-fifty. They seemed perplexed and angry.

The visitors seem for the most part to be entirely unconscious of

English middle-class materialism. But a number of the travellers found the "one tune - money-making" quite understandable. "No man ever came to Winnipeg because he was rich," J. F. Fraser wrote. "The men who came were the poor, the driven, the restless under social conditions on the other side of the world, the men who were strong and willing to dare, who saw riches round them, but beyond them, and who went West to strive, to battle, to conquer, to gain riches for themselves." In similar vein, Kipling remarked in 1907:

> ... The Elementary and High Schools of the Prairie Provinces came as a surprise. It was in my mind that the British immigrant must surely find, in his new sphere, some disadvantage to set against a better livelihood and a brighter climate. As the only thing I could think of, I pictured him with impaired opportunities for the mental training of his children ... [but] those governments have established a system of popular education that is free, universal, unsectarian, and so sound and attractive that it scarcely needs to be compulsory.[28]

A few years earlier Lumsden had noted that "wherever we went, we were struck with the size and number of school buildings ... Far from complaining of the school tax, it is a subject of honest pride."

H. R. Whates, writing in 1906, found "the absence of distractions which militate against religion in old civilizations - which have made the Canadian population essentially religious in temperament":

> The church or chapel on the prairie, in the forest clearing, in the mining settlements, in the bush lands in the far North and North-West are, and for generations must be, the chief, indeed the only centers of social life. These, and these alone, afford relaxation for lives of arduous toil. They are the only outlet for activities - mental, moral and artistic - which lift men above the level of mere labourers burrowing, as Kingsley once wrote like vermin in the earth's hide.

It appears that the pioneer was less concerned with doctrine than with the fellowship and sociability which was provided by church organization. Bickersteth, viewing conditions from the standpoint of a devout Anglican churchman, found a "rather depressing broadmindedness" as typical of Western religious life. He naturally deplored the union church idea, which was beginning to find expression in the West.

Many of the travellers noted the egalitarianism of Western Canadian society, particularly in the early years and in the rural areas. "There is more of the spirit of liberty, equality, and fraternity among the people of Western Canada than in any other democracy of the Old or New World," one of them told the Royal Colonial Institute.[29] "Men seemed to be taken much more on their merits, and less on their wealth or the nature of their employment. Of civility we found no lack, of servility hardly a trace," wrote another.[30] But Miss Sykes, an English author, came to a different conclusion regarding class distinctions in the larger towns: "England," she wrote, "acknowledged these distinctions, and Canada pretended to ignore them."[31] Despite the obvious evidence of class bias in many of the writers' comments on socio-economic conditions in the West, most of them were glad to see that this aspect of English society had not been transplanted to the new land.

The assimilation of American and continental European immigrants emerges as a theme in many of the travel narratives after 1900. It was generally noted that these settlers were dedicated and effective farmers who justified the welcome extended to them by the Dominion authorities. But the visitors were divided in their estimates of the social and political effects of this migration; some saw evidence of their rapid adoption of the value structure of English-speaking Canadian society and citizenship; others saw omens of weakening ties between Canada and the United Kingdom and of the Americanization of the country. The presence of large numbers of Eastern European immigrants was usually not deplored because of their idiosyncrasies, but because they were enjoying opportunities denied to the poor in England whom the British Government should assist by a policy of state-aided emigration.

The controversial policies of Joseph Chamberlain, and the discussion of Imperial defence and trade relations which were important issues in British politics in the early years of the century, were very much in the minds of some of the travellers and are reflected in their interest in Canadian public opinion in both the East and the West. They were unanimous in detecting a vigorous national feeling. ". . . Canada is a nation to be approached as an equal and not as an inferior," A. M. Low wrote in 1899.[32] "In feeling, as in industry and government, Canada has become one of the nations of mankind," Lumsden observed. "There is a very strong feeling of Canadian nationality, which is growing every year," Bickersteth noted. J. A. Hobson's comments in 1906, in *Canada Today*, were similar:

> This faith in Canada is visibly unifying the diverse section, races, and religions and is taking shape in a "nationalism" which, at present mainly economic, is certain to have important political bearings when Canada has leisure to think out her political career.

It was noted that there was a strong tone of anti-Americanism in this nationalism, although the paradox of a willingness to accept American immigrants, American trade unionism, and American capital impressed the observers. Of affection for Britain there was little, but regard for the Empire and for the monarchy was very much in evidence. "Canada has a vision of her destiny," J. F. Fraser wrote in 1911. "It is not to be a mere Colony of Britain; it is not to be swallowed by the United States; ... It is to be a real integral part of the British Empire ... and with the ambition that one day she will be the predominant partner in the nations of the Empire. That is the vision which touches the Canadian imagination."

One finds in no single travel account of this thirty-year period the full range of the Western Canadian frontier experience. Inevitably, each visitor had his own special practical and intellectual interests: opportunities for journeys off the beaten track differed; the range and number of interpersonal associations were unequal; the capacity for objectivity and the gift of insight varied. There is no de Tocqueville among them. But taken together they provide the historian with substantial, and in some respects unique, data on the formative period of the development of the Canadian West.

J. A. Hobson defended the utility of a visitor's observations in the following terms:

> ... apology is unwarranted, at any rate in cases where the impressionism that belongs to such work is executed with honesty and care ... A visitor to a country which like Canada, in spite of its size, is extremely compact, strung on to two railroad lines running east and west with few offshoots, can really get a substantially complete bird's-eye view of the main features of its external development ... So, too, of the broader aspects of the character of its people - their interests and aspirations (industrial, political, recreative), what they talk about, how they occupy their leisure, what they read ... Of course he will miss all the finer texture of the spirit and life of the people, will learn very little of their domestic life or the subtler psychology that underlies their social and religious institutions ... But the large points of similarity and difference, distinctive of the present place and prospects of such a country as Canada in the progress of the world, will stand out more plainly to an observant newcomer than to a native who sits too near and whose intelligence and feeling are too closely involved in the details of the life in which he lives.

Lumsden quoted the Scottish proverb, "fuils and bairns should never see half-dune things," and, generally speaking, the visitors were prepared to make allowances for what they regarded as imperfections in Western Canadian life. The chief impression which their accounts convey is of a future-oriented society, exhibiting a mood of self-confidence; work obsessed; nationalistic; puritan in tone. Insofar as these are the components of a revolution, we can view the prewar years as the first revolutionary period of Canadian history, with

Western Canada supplying the most dynamic element in the rapid transformation of Canadian society.

Footnotes

1
Marghanita Laski, "Domestic Life," in S. Nowell-Smith, ed., *Edwardian England 1901-1914* (London, 1964), p. 142.

2
E. Lewthwaite, "Women's Work in Western Canada," *Fortnightly Review* (October, 1900), p. 709.

3
A. S. Hurd, "The Foreign Invasion of Canada," *Fortnightly Review* (December, 1902), p. 1055.

4
Rudyard Kipling, *Letters of Travel (1892-1913)* (London, 1920), p. 26.

5
S. Cumberland, *The Queen's Highway from Ocean to Ocean* (London, 1887), p. 176.

6
J. Lumsden, *Through Canada in Harvest Time: A Study of Life and Labour in the Golden West* (London, 1903), p. 117.

7
G. Binnie-Clark, *A Summer on the Canadian Prairie* (Toronto and London, 1910), p. 135.

8
F. A. Talbot, *The New Garden of Canada* (London, etc., 1912), pp. 14-15.

9
C. Hassall, *The Prose of Rupert Brooke* (London, 1956), p. 54.

10
Major General Sir Francis DeWinton, "Canada and the Great North-West," *Journal of the Manchester Geographical Society*, Vol. 8 (1892), p. 94.

11
J. F. Fraser, *Canada As It Is* (London, 1911), p. 182.

12
H. R. Whates, *Canada, the New Nation: A Book for the Settler, the Emigrant and the Politician* (London, 1906), pp. 173-174.

13
H. Tanner, *The Canadian North-West and the Advantages It Offers for Emigration Purposes* (London, 1885), p. 24.

14
Fraser, *op. cit.*, p. 103.

15
J. W. C. Haldane, *Thirty Eight Hundred Miles Across Canada* (London, 1900).

16
Whates, *op. cit.*, p. 159.

17

E. Roper, *By Track and Trail: A Journey Through Canada* (London, 1891), p. 142.

18

D. Sladen, *On the Cars and Off: Being the Journal of a Pilgrimage Along the Queen's Highway from the East, from Halifax in Nova Scotia to Victoria in Vancouver's Island* (London, 1895), pp. 366, 368.

19

C. Hanbury-Williams, "Vancouver to Victoria," *Blackwood's Magazine* (March, 1903), pp. 376-377.

20

Charity Organization Society, Emigration Sub-Committee, *Report, 1893* (London, 1893), p. 5.

21

Manitoba and the Canadian North-West. A Reprint of Two Letters from the Times of January 30th and 31st, 1894 (London, 1894), pp. 14-15.

22

M. Davitt, "Impressions of the Canadian North-West," *The Nineteenth Century* (April, 1892), pp. 632-633.

23

Quoted in C. Watney, "Why the Englishman is Despised in Canada," *National Review* (November, 1907), p. 439.

24

Quoted in Binnie-Clark, *op. cit.*, p. 158.

25

E. Lewthwaite, *op. cit.*, pp. 709-719.

26

F. A. Talbot, *Making Good in Canada* (London, 1912), p. 206.

27

J. Adams, *Ten Thousand Miles Through Canada. The Natural Resources, Commercial Industries, Fish and Game, Sports and Pastimes of the Great Dominion* (London, 2nd ed., 1912), p. 245.

28

A. E. Copping, *The Golden Land. True Story and Experiences of British Settlers in Canada* (Toronto and London, 1911), pp. 251-252.

29

E. B. Osborn, "The Future of Western Canada," *Proceedings of the Royal Colonial Institute*, Vol. 32 (1905-6), p. 60.

30

J. Dendy, "A Holiday in the Far West," *Journal of the Manchester Geographical Society*, Vol. 23 (1907), p. 2.

31

E. C. Sykes, *A Home Help in Canada* (London, 1912), p. 127.

32

A. M. Low, "Some Light on the Canadian Enigma," *The Forum* (June, 1899), p. 490.

Romance and Realism in Western Canadian Fiction

Eli Mandel

I

Sometimes it appears as if literary and cultural history find their organizing principles not in causality but in synchronicity. Like a shooting star, the burning flare of coincidence lights up for a brief moment a whole intellectual landscape, an eerie incandescence before all collapses again into the prosaic darkness of unresolved events. Thus, while it is staggering to hear an American president proclaim the week of the moon-landing the greatest week since creation, it is even more dislocating to encounter a new Canadian anthology entitled *Creation*. One scarcely wants to suggest an occult connection between the first moon-landing and the appearance of the new anthology, let alone between Genesis itself and the Canadian publishing industry. But such is the temper of the times; the possibilities do arise. Norman Mailer, one suspects, would not find the possilibity of moon madness among Canadians an unlikely consequence of the technology that put three men on the moon. Improbable, no doubt. But what is suspect as sociology may very well be the appropriate language of cultural criticism.

Posing as Mailer's usual madcap journalism, his *Of a Fire of the Moon*, for example, puts to us a most difficult critical puzzle, that of the relationship between a cultural symbol and its literal realization. What happens to lunacy after lunar landings? Can the frontiers of literature ever become actual places? To take another example: in a remarkable essay, Leo Marx considers the possibility that literary landscape can help us plan the future of actual landscape, even to the extent of clarifying the principles of urban and rural planning commissions - a point of view which at first glance seems little short of madness.[1] One tries, hopelessly, to imagine a city built to the imagination of Irving Layton. Of course, Marx points to the difficulties: the problem of connecting different kinds of discourse; the differences between speech controlled by image patterns and speech controlled by pragmatic or practical ends, between metaphoric structures and logical statement.

I am not fond of distinctions between discursive and affective language. Far more satisfactory as critical guides, it seems to me, are Mailer's moon metaphors and moon men, positing as they do the great complex structures of culture and science opposed and interacting in ways we cannot yet even begin to understand. But whether we begin with Marx or Mailer, at least we remind ourselves of the difficulties in attempting to speak of something called realism or romance in the fiction of the Canadian West. *Creation* may be an unfortunate title, yet it does imply a tension between fiction and fact, symbol and actuality. Talking with Margaret Laurence, a conversation recorded in *Creation*, Robert Kroetsch remarks, "In a sense, we haven't got an identity until somebody tells our story. The fiction makes us real."[2] It is important to understand the implications of that comment, particularly as it applies to the fiction of Western Canada, because, like many of his contemporaries, Kroetsch has obviously reversed the usual order of things. Whatever we might mean by realism, itself a problem in literary terminology, with regard to one of its senses - the priority of circumstance to symbol - we often assume the primacy of historical and social event over the derived quality of portrayed existence. For a writer like Kroetsch, the life is in the symbol.

There is thus a problem. Contemporary Canadian writers turn to legends, mythology, and folklore that carry few of our supposed historical and social values or experiences. Michael Ondaatje's *The Collected Works of Billy the Kid* perhaps could be dismissed as an anachronism were it not that it belongs with Leonard Cohen's *Beautiful Losers*, Sheila Watson's *The Double Hook*, and Robert Kroetsch's *The Studhorse Man*, all of which are part of a contemporary primitivism, a world of romance that sorts oddly with our seasonally-adjusted social order. Of course, by no means all contemporary primitivism ignores Canadian material. Margaret Atwood discovers the wilderness behind the eyes of Susanna Moodie; Al Purdy seeks both the comic and tragic affinities of Indian, Eskimo, and contemporary Canadian life; John Newlove sees in Pawnee stories the identity of a land and its people. But whether in the form of a reincarnated Susanna Moodie at the University of Alberta in 1969 or the Dorsets living again in Ameliasburg, Ontario, the same question remains. Its proper dimensions seem to me best outlined in the work of Sheila Watson and Robert Kroetsch, for reasons I hope will be clear after I look briefly at the context within which their work takes its shape.

II

One of the magical words in literary criticism is "identity." I say "magical" because it is a word that enables a critic to maintain two contradictory notions: the notion of the writer's uniqueness and at the same time, of his representativeness. Mere forked writing animal, he lives imaginatively, and yet his work acquires social dimensions. He is only himself, largely ignorant of society and history, and yet there is in his writing a sort of metaphysical or ontological force that enables him to identify a people. So we have the common enough resort in our criticism to a notion of "the Canadian imagination."

Consider the difficulties. A casual use of the definite article elevates Canadian artists to the position of Canada's unacknowledged constitutional historians; at the same time, an unexamined ideology - nationalism - slips in, one hesitates to say for reasons of propaganda, but at least as a consequence of assuming that cultural and political aspects of Canadian life are identical and unitary.

The same problems exist in discussing regional writing and culture. To speak, for example, of something central to the imagination of Western Canada scarcely makes any sense in the light both of the variety of Western Canadian fiction and the virtual impossibility of deciding what it means to speak of the "West" itself. There is no single kind or genre of Western fiction in Canada: there are regional novels, rural novels, ethnic novels, pastorals, urban novels. And these, in turn, reflect a bewildering variety of concerns and themes: the encounter with the land; the impact of mechanization and urbanization on rural life; the curious rootlessness of the Prairie population; the conflict of generations and of varied cultural traditions. Any cultural history of Western Canada simply must begin with this problem of pluralism.

Of course, nothing I have said in any way denies the importance and value of critical and historical attempts to sort out and order these disparate materials and perhaps even to account for both the richness and variety of the literature, particularly the fiction of the West. Certainly, as social realists, we would find ourselves in such an attempt in sympathy with, say, Edward McCourt or Henry Kreisel, both of whom resort to the kind of environmentalism that sees the land itself as the determining feature of a portrayed existence. At the same time, the possibility remains that a peculiar achievement of the fiction of Western Canada is not social realism. To say this is at once to move out of some of the difficult and contradictory notions implied by the terms used, for it is no longer the historical and social, or even the geographical West, so much as the literary one, that concerns us. Equally, a value judgment is implied, a preference for one kind of writing over another. That is not necessarily wicked, even if it prefers its archetypes nude and asks for literary intelligence in its writers.

It is instructive here to think about the role of folklore in our literature. Early incongruities, like Sangster's attempt to populate the St. Lawrence with fairy creatures out of some watery version of Romantic or Victorian poetry, we dismiss as exceptions, despite not only the evidence of most Confederation poetry, but also of more immediate examples such as Reaney's importing of Spenserian motifs in his eclogues for Stratford, Layton's panoply of gods and satyrs, or Margaret Laurence's blending of Lear and the Old Testament. Literary nationalism consistently ignores the necessarily unfavourable balance of payments in literature. And whatever explanations we seek, whether Edward McCourt's view that domestic order in the West prevented the development of a regional folklore, or the more usual version of the repressive effect of frontier puritanism and materialism that E. K. Brown advances, it seems we are to find our folklore outside of our own boundaries and that we must discover once more that literary and physical frontiers do not coincide. The oddly strained effect of Indian and northern imagery in Canadian writing, as if Trinity College graduates were to wear war paint, seems to me part of the same story.

But accepting that a large part of our folklore is imported, it remains that we have to be clear about the nature of a folkloristic tradition. We assume there is something we can call an American imagination that takes the form of a frontier myth or story possessing, for Americans, a powerful allegorical force. From Melville to Mailer, the same story has been able to draw within its field all currents of American life. A contemporary version is the film *Little Big Man* which not only suggests by a process of ironic inversion analogies between General Custer and General Westmoreland, the Cheyenne and the Vietnamese, but works out as well the motifs of initiation through bloodletting and acquiring identity through role-playing. Analogies and comparisons with Huck Finn are virtually inescapable. And yet it is impossible to ignore the incongruities in the film. The great American myth, as it happens, is played out in Alberta by a Canadian Indian of the Squamish tribe and a Jewish boy from Brooklyn. There are, after all, some limits to the willing suspension of disbelief.

I mean to be literal-minded here, since I take it that Arthur Penn must have been perfectly conscious of the sound of Dustin Hoffman's voice just as he is conscious of the film techniques of alienation which he employs so adroitly. His imagination, I suppose, could best be described as literary. His films consist of a superb counterpointing of images from the rich repertoire of cinematic allusion that he possesses; *Bonny and Clyde*, for example, presents itself not as realism but as a film about American films of the 1930's in which a gangster mythology took visible shape. Fantasies, whether of the city outlaw and his beloved Model A or of the Western outlaw and his beloved horse, remain fantasy, not reality. The American frontier myth is myth.

In literature as in film there is an inward looking quality (an assimilative, identifying force) that denies the disparities, perplexities, and contradictions of social life and historical development. This I take to be the meaning of Frederick Philip Grove's remarks in his note to the fourth edition of *A Search for America:*

> Imaginative literature is not primarily concerned with facts; it is concerned with truth . . . In its highest flights, imaginative literature, which is one and indivisible, places within a single fact the history of the universe from its inception as well as the history of its future to the moment of its final extinction.[3]

Now that may be bad history and worse sociology, but it is first-rate criticism. It suggests that the writer's own sense of creativity and inventiveness (making it new) pulls him away from what Grove calls "fact" toward something else. That "something else" is often taken to be the realm of the subjective, the writer's dreams or feelings or imaginings or what not. But Grove indicates his meaning: paradoxically a rewriting of the traditional story. For a writer like Grove, then, the imaginative process is not a mirroring of experience, still less a dream process. It is, in the act of writing, the creation of a self or an identity. In less grandiose terms, we might want to say "an interpretation of experience," though that scarcely carries the burden of meaning Grove puts upon a word like "truth." His West is not so much discovered as created.

The point is worth pursuing a little further both because of Grove's importance as a writer of Western Canadian novels and because in the paradoxes of his life and work he so brilliantly poses the paradoxes criticism itself must face. He concerned himself with truth, yet if we are to believe Douglas Spettigue, whose study of Grove is one of the few genuinely startling pieces of detective work in Canadian scholarship, Grove must have been an extraordinary liar, and his celebrated autobiography, *In Search of Myself,* false in all its details. Spettigue seems to believe that in trying to conceal certain events in his life in America, Grove altered times and details in his story. This may be so. What is equally apparent is that the outline of the story is fantasy rather than manipulated fact. But why would Grove indulge himself - if that is the appropriate term - in so *profound* a fiction, even were there facts to be concealed? Somewhere Morley Callaghan remarks that Grove was capable of believing the strangest dreams. Believing the strangest dreams, in search of himself, one could say Grove's life was created by his own fiction, his novels that - it seems now - literally wrote him into existence. "The fiction makes us real," says the younger novelist, Robert Kroetsch. And so it is. The writer's task becomes an increasingly sensitive articulation of his literary tradition - not to write up the experience of the country but to articulate the forms of its fiction. So Western Canadian fiction may be seen to involve a double process, and, to judge from comments like Grove's and Kroetsch's, one that is conscious as well: on the one hand, it involves finding forms appropriate to new sets of experience or, more exactly, the placing of new experience in its metaphorical context; on the other, it involves integrating or unifying literary experience itself, finding out, in other words, whether existing literary tradition, in all its richness and variety, connects with the "literary" materials at hand - folklore, legend, tall tale, whatever has filtered down in its curious ways from older lore which is itself part of the tradition that now seeks to connect with it.

From this point of view, more interesting than Grove's sociology of Prairie life in his use of the pastoral contrast of city and country. Similarly, it is not the highly praised depiction of Prairie boyhood that is important in W. O. Mitchell's *Who Has Seen the Wind* so much as the Wordsworthian pastoral of innocence and experience. It becomes more interesting to locate and define motifs of Scandinavian saga and figures of romance in Martha Ostenso's novels than to praise her boldness and so-called realism for daring to write surely one of the more modest nude scenes in twentieth-century literature. Farm machinery in Robert Stead's *Grain* undoubtedly depicts farm machinery, the fact of mechanization in a rural world, but just as surely images of machines are structural principles in storytelling, the purest form of which we find, in Canadian writing at least, in Archibald Lampman's "City of the End of Things." Nor is it, then, surprising that as we turn from writers of the generation of Grove, Ostenso, and Stead, to our more immediate contemporaries - Margaret Laurence, Adele Wiseman, Henry Kreisel, John Marlyn - we discover that symbolic patterning becomes more explicit, as in Henry Kreisel's use of wasteland imagery in *The Betrayal*, Margaret Laurence's use of the biblical story of Hagar in *The Stone Angel*, Adele Wiseman's retelling of the tale of Abraham and Isaac in *The Sacrifice*.

To argue that Western Canadian fiction develops an increasing awareness of its own forms ought to come as no surprise. This, after all, is the sort of argument given currency in Northrop Frye's influential criticism, and it has served in the essays of Warren Tallman and James Reaney and in Douglas Jones' *Butterfly on Rock* as the groundwork for a thematic and cultural history of Canada. An essay on the West in fiction should in fact read simply as an elaborated footnote to such criticism. But at the risk of repetition, it is worth noticing the extent to which our cultural historians, like many of our social philosophers, remain environmentalists. Our understanding of ourselves and our country would be more than impoverished were it not for the deeply felt and serious essays of George Grant and it is no matter for easy dismissal that he sees, particularly in *Technology and Empire*, the land writing itself into the Canadian imagination as surely as W. L. Morton sees the north imprinting itself on us in his own account of our character, *The Canadian Identity*. The sense that there is in this environmentalism a Protestant eschatology, to which Saint Sammy's Jeremiads might serve as appropriate choral accompaniment, does not diminish the force of the argument. Of course, regional literature, say Western Canadian fiction, is especially susceptible to an environmental approach, possibly because we tend to equate regions with particular space. But the land tells us little about genuine folkloristic elements; the western as outlaw story, the rogue figure of tall tales, ballads telling of domestic and border violence and terror. And it leaves unanswered the most peculiar question of all: in what sense could we say a fiction, particularly a fiction of America or Greece or Judea, makes us real, defines our identity?

I don't know whether questions of that sort can be answered but the reasons for asking them become apparent the moment one looks at novels like Sheila Watson's *The Double Hook* and Robert Kroetsch's *The Studhorse Man*. The former gives us the western story as parody; the latter turns the form of tall tale, odyssey, and rogue's story into metaphors of book and dream. Both, it seems to me, seek to locate Western Canadian fiction within a coherent, developing tradition and therefore to expand rather than contract its dimensions and possibilities, and though both are relatively brief, it is not unreasonable to see them as encyclopaedic in range.

III

Concise and intense, *The Double Hook* relies on more than flashing phrase and oracular remark for its effects. Elaborately structured and closely integrated, like some highly-charged atomic accelerator, it radiates microcosmic suggestions of fundamental energies. So lapidary a form, of course, raises questions about the place of artifice, contrivance, and self-consciousness in literature. Yet literacy could scarcely be said to disqualify a writer, though since it appears to be a matter of degree, it might very well determine style and form. Certainly, those works which we might want to describe as "artificial" now appear not as sports but as definitions in Canadian writing. *The Double Hook* belongs with, say, the poems of James Reaney, Jay Macpherson's *The Boatman*, A. M. Klein's *The Second Scroll* (and just possibly one should add Atwood's *Journals of Susanna Moodie*), writing distinguished by its capacity to assimilate varied materials, to comment on and construct - or at least rewrite - a literary tradition. Obviously, to isolate any element of a work so carefully wrought is to do violence to it, but at the risk of distortion, it seems necessary, in the context of this discussion, to look at the element of parody in the novel.

In a perceptive introduction to the New Canadian Library edition, John Grube comments on Mrs. Watson's use of parody: her parody of folk wisdom, of the "quaintness" (as he puts it) of the ethnic novel, of the "illusions" of regionalism and of the setting and action of the western or cowboy story. In each instance, Grube tells us, the novelist attempts through parody to break out of imposed limitations - limitations of regionalism, ethnicity, and popular art - in order to arrive at a universal form. No doubt Mrs. Watson does intend to explode the limitations of provincialism and parochialism. A rough and wicked humour, not unlike that in a mediaeval morality play, cuts deliberately across the high poetic lines, the buzzing energy of the novel. I pause only to notice how the laments of a wailing widow punctuate the revelatory moments of the story: dear god, why must there be so much violence; dear god, the bacon's not done; dear god, another child in this world. The earthy incongruities offer their own comment on both homely tale and high wisdom. Thus, at the concluding nativity scene, a vision of the child like something out of Breughel:

> Dear God, said the Widow, it's a feeble cry. Quick. Quick, she called and clambered down from the box as Ara pulled the horses to a stop before the door.
>
> We don't want any trouble, Angel said as she jumped down from the seat.
>
> The Window's hand was on the knob.
>
> If there's trouble, Mrs. Prosper, she said, it won't be of my making. Dear God, she said, the latch needs oil.[4]

Yet it seems to me inadequate to view parody simply as a reductive force. Parody indeed "explodes" a form, but it may also elevate (a famous example is Pope's *Rape of the Lock*); it may be used to isolate formal elements, and, if it is so used, enable an author to work out sharply and clearly the design of the work.

Through the exaggerations and distortions of parody, then, Mrs. Watson writes an ethnic, regional western, deliberately exploiting the conventionality of the forms she has chosen to work with. The resulting work is angular, diagrammatic (though not in any way rough-hewn), for it establishes what otherwise remain obscure, possible connections between conventional forms. Those connections, I believe, are its heart, the source of its incredible energy.

From the form of the ethnic novel, Mrs. Watson takes the sense of folk wisdom, as in gnomic sayings and earth-philosophizing, and the sense of community essential to her sacramental theme of sacrifice, communion, redemption. (It is not entirely an aside to note that this ethnic pattern has its Yiddish and Judaic parallel in Adele Wiseman's *The Sacrifice* and in a grotesquely inverted parody of a parody, Mordecai Richler's *Cocksure*.) From regional novels, Mrs. Watson takes the sense of place as mythic home, and for her plot line, one event, the killing of the mother. As in, say, Martha Ostenso's *Wild Geese*, or in Grove's Prairie novels and especially in *Our Daily Bread*, the suffocating closeness of family, and the murderous oppression it involves, define one extreme of regionalism, so an idyllic childhood world precariously close to the threat of adulthood - as in W. O. Mitchell's or E. A. McCourt's novels - defines the other extreme. Thematically, regionalism tends to define identity as place and community, both located within an individual and yet outside in the communal culture. If character is defined as both peculiar and representative, then we see how it is that in regional writing characterization tends toward grotesque types and caricature.

But of the three forms that provide structural principles for Mrs. Watson's novel, the western is at once more compelling and puzzling than the other two. It is clear, of course, that, as the most familiar of the three, the western allows for the most extensive play; additionally, recalling films, it both opens up technical possibilities and connects immediate visual imagery with older romance forms, a point to which I shall return. One could, I suppose, object that the cowboy story sorts badly with Western Canadian history, if not our setting. Bankers and clergy rode our plains, and the Mounted Policeman, never quite large enough for myth, played the role that elsewhere was the outlaw's. My own knowledge of Canadian westerns is limited to some early writing of Edward McCourt and to Wallace Stegner's *Wolf Willow*, although, of course, only part of Stegner's work devotes itself to western material proper, a section on the Fort McLeod incident, and one on the legendary winter of 1906 and a cattle-herding story. Leslie Fiedler argues that there are not only westerns, but southerns, easterns, and northerns as well; it begins to appear that, whenever Canadian novels are neither idyllic nor pastoral, they should be something like Fiedler's version of a northern. And no less an historian than W. L. Morton argues that the contrast of pastoral and northern is a principle of Canadian life, though he seems to take this clear literary principle as a fact of geography and national character. Yet the point is not that Mrs. Watson is bound by any interpretations of this precarious society and its past. If history calls for a northern mode, apparently something else insists on a western. For Mrs. Watson, one suspects, that "something else" is literary design: desert setting, dry land, stereotyped characters, community, town, outsider, the pattern of a good-bad, black-white contrast, all connected with notions of law and outlaw, justice and revenge, murder and hanging. It should be apparent now that with the design of the western, the formal pattern of her novel is complete: home and community become as elemental as place itself, while out of elemental design is born the terrifying poem that is at one and the same time the voice of a god and the voice of an animal howling in the night:

I have set his feet on soft ground
I have set his feet on the sloping shoulders of the world. (p. 134)

The western tale unifies the novel because it enables Mrs. Watson to take the forms in which our imagination expresses itself - regional novel, ethnic story, the cycle of generation - and shows us the connections between them and a larger imaginative world that extends to Shakespeare and the Bible. The forms with which we perceive ourselves in our own society (or the metaphorical form of our society) then may be seen as part of a larger pattern that is the pattern of Western culture itself, at least its romance pattern of questing knight and mysterious grail. That story, we have been told more than once, links together images of a stranger riding out of desert country, a people in bondage in Egypt, a wandering in the wilderness, a return to a promised land; it connects images of dry land and water with the mysteries of aloneness, community, justice, and mercy.

It is, surely, difficult to contemplate the fierce images of *The Double Hook* - the old lady fishing, the blazing furnace of valley and house, messengers in the dry land - without recalling something of the iconography of *The Wasteland, The Tempest*, and the Bible. Nor is it difficult to anticipate objections: that either this interpretation of the novel is mechanical or the novel itself is a machine; that where literature presents itself as myth rather than experience, its contrivance fails to create that authentic human world we ask of even our most learned writers. One answer, of course, is that *The Double Hook* need fear nothing from the limitations of this commentator. It would be unforgiveable to identify the work with an interpretation in order to dismiss it. By the same token, it would be a misrepresentation of the novel to ignore its deliberately diagrammatic quality. More important than one's taste in matters of iconography is an understanding that allusiveness - the use of convention and parallel story in what T. S. Eliot, commenting on Joyce's *Ulysses*, called the mythic method - seeks those metaphors that put local story and fable into the context of the literature of a whole culture. To speak of the result as artifice is not a value judgment so much as a description.

Still, a more accessible version of the mythic method is that in which myth presents itself as experience, not literature. In lurid tales of rogue and fool, for example, we feel we can discern a recognizable world, for no matter how oddly tilted it might be, it is after all distorted only to the extent that the hero of the tall tale proves to be himself eccentric, one of the town's oddities: the Old Ben, beer-parlour ranconteur extraordinary; Saint Sammy, wild man of the Prairies, counting underwear labels in his piano-box house; Jake, the hired man, whose sense of history is defined purely by his mastery of contradiction; all are rogue-fool figures, part of a tradition in Canadian writing that goes back at least to Sam Slick, Yankee pedlar and ring-tailed roarer, and includes such varied fool-innocents as Earle Birney's Turvey, Mordecai Richler's Duddy Kravitz, and as the latest honourable addition, Hazard Lepage, or perhaps more accurately, the narrator of Lepage's story in Robert Kroetsch's *The Studhorse Man*.

Like his forebears, Lepage is a questing knight, a displaced Ulysses seeking not only his Penelope but a mare for his great stallion, Poseidon. Yet to present the story as myth does not do it justice. For experience, an intensely realized world, plays an extraordinary part in this novel, and it is the role of experience that I want to look at. Certainly the story is grounded in place: coulee, gulch, boneyard, Edmonton's 109th street and its Woodwards, river, bridge, farmyard, and schoolhouse, all presented with that particularity and lucidity characteristic of more than one Prairie novel, Mitchell's *Who Has Seen the Wind*, for example. And even the wild wandering events, grotesque and off-centre as if viewed through a flawed glass, seem at least possible, if not probable: a Ukrainian wedding remembered as through a glass dimly; a Doukhobour-like school-burning; a night in a museum; a beer-parlour horse-trading session; a brawl in a boneyard; a discovery of a use for mare's urine. Familiar, yet so distorted in the novel that one looks again at the familiar, doubting its validity. For, remarkably, this Alberta and all its people, including it seems the reader, turn into a book and a dream. To suggest the energy - ferocious, bawdy, hilarious - involved in that transformation could very well exceed any normal critical capacity and certainly the decorum of this article. But Kroetsch's method, at least, can be indicated.

On the one hand, experience turns into a book, rather as everything turns into clothes in *Sartor Resartus*. Almost compulsively the narrator insists on turning events into lists, genealogies, catalogues, histories, and more often than not for him the lists gravitate, as his world does, toward a subsuming metaphoric vision, the radical metaphor implied in the title of the book, man as stud horse. Horse, itself, as we shall see, is as much art as life. On the other hand, as we begin to comprehend the complex narrative structure and understand who tells the story and from what vantage point, experience dissolves into dream.

Book metaphors appear even in the hero's name, Lepage, at once "the page written upon" and a glue label. The label-man, now labelled, is also horse-man (studhorse man), fabulous creature out of a mythic past. More pervasively, the book metaphor makes itself felt as we encounter catalogues and genealogies: genealogies of horses; genealogies of men. It is as if generation itself, that *axis mundi* on which, as the narrator redundantly remarks, wise men tell us the world itself turns, had been transformed into a catalogue. To take one example: *The General Stud Book* rests on the bookshelves beside Hazard's desk in the great house where he lives with his horses and his seven beds. The desk and its contents are presented to us with the sharpness and presence of experienced life. So we hear of

> currycomb, a broken hamestrap, a spoon wired to a stick for dropping poisoned wheat into the holes of offending gophers, saltpetre, gentian root, a scattering of copper rivets, black antimony, a schoolboy's ruler, three mousetraps in a matchbox, two chisels for trimming hoofs, Cornucrescine (for making horn grow), ginger, horse liniment and liniment for his back, Elliman's Royal Embrocation, blue vitriol, an electuary, nux vomica, saddle soap in a Spode (a simple blue and white) saucer. Spanish fly. . . .[5]

A list surely worthy of that famous one Huck gives us as he catalogues his findings in the house of the dead, this one is immediately followed by the genealogy of horses from the book of studs that, we are told, is Hazard's poetry and philosophy, his history of man and his theology. And as we read with Hazard of the horse world, we can wonder which is real, the desk or the book, and whether one dissolves into the other:

> The old book opened of itself to the list of brood mares, and Hazard read defiantly the words he could so easily quote: ALCIDES MARE, *Bred by Mr. Bland, in 1764, her dam by Crab, out of Snap's dam.* Hazard, let me explain, was no loafing, snivelling schoolmarm of a man: those words were pain to him. Those beautiful words. He read on: BLANK MARE, *Foaled in 1755, her dam, Dizzy, by Driver* . . . Don't you see why he read, why he ached, why he had to read? Let me go on, for I, too, on sleepless nights, on lonely afternoons, have sought out that dark volume: *Dizzy, by Driver - Smiling Tom - Miss Hipp, by Oyster-foot - Merlin - Commoner - D. of Somerset's Coppin Mare.* Not that Hazard wept as I have. Hazard cursed. 'God damn the damned,' he said . . . He must have put a stained finger to the

old print. He cursed and read on, caught in and dreading
that beautiful dead mad century: A-LA-GREQUE ... *got by
Regulus - her   damn   by   Allworthy - grandam   by   Bolton
Starling - great   grandam,   Dairy   Maid,   by   Bloody   But-
tocks* ... (pp. 10-11).

The ceremony of naming continues with other catalogues: of the
Lepage family, of the Proudfoots (Martha, Thatcher, Toreador, Ten-
nyson, and Titmarsh Proudfoot), of the hockey players of Canada, the
food and drink at a Ukrainian wedding, the diseases of the horse. It is as
if the novel itself, certainly the narrator of the novel, is driven by the
desperate need to classify everything, as in a book, and to see it all
arranged finally as a taxonomy of the horse, for its cry is, in the
narrator's own words, "The exquisitely piercing mortal cry, the cry half
horse, half man, the horse-man cry of pain or delight or eternal
celebration at what is and what must be." (p. 163)

But if the moving principle of the novel is the horse - Poseidon, giver
of life, *mer*, mare, mother, father - the horse of Kroetsch's fictional
world must be described in images not of Prairie life but of Chinese art:

> It strikes me that I have been remiss in describing, not this per-
> verse human caricature of the essential animal, but that animal
> itself. Let me make amends, my dear reader; and I can best
> describe Poseidon by referring you to the superlative grace and
> beauty of Chinese art.
>
> I hardly now where to suggest you begin. Those old Chinese
> artists: they drew their horses true to life, true to the rhythm of
> life. They dreamed their horses and made the horse too. They
> had their living dream of horses ... Ah, where to begin? Why is
> the truth never where it should be? Is the truth of the man in
> the man or in his biography? Is the truth of the beast in the flesh
> and confusion or in the few skilfully arranged lines ... But
> study for one day that one horse - Han Kang's bold creation,
> Shining Light of the Night .... Our pitiful world: we pack a
> corpse off in copper and steel that it might for an extra year
> bewilder the dust. And yet one horse for the spirit's night and
> we would be immortal. ... (pp. 130-131)

But if the horse (and horse-man) can best be realized in images of art
and book that resolve "the flesh and confusion" in a "few skilfully
arranged lines," both art and book themselves dissolve into dream. The
one who tells this story of horses, we discover, sits naked in a bathtub
in a mental institution, viewing the world through a clever arrange-
ment of mirrors that enables him to see where the action of the novel
once took place, though its past is now his present. Possessed by
Hazard's dream, as Hazard was possessed by Poseidon, the narrator

looks at mirror images of mirror images. What follows though is worse, the suggestion that the dream includes ourselves: ". . . we are all, so to speak, one; each of us is, possibly, everyone else . . . ." (p. 115)

We have been dreamed by our fiction. A preposterous claim, surely. Those clumsy tales. Those distortions. The exaggeration. The falsification of history. How little to the point about the labour movement of the thirties, about Jewish immigrant families in Hirsch or Hoffer, Saskatchewan, about narrow cities in their pride and greed and oil. Only, say, Sinclair Ross's *As For Me and My House* to tell of how (in Grove's phrase) the wilderness uses up human material. Only Robert Stead's *Grain*, a creaking vehicle for the realities of farm life. We expected the land itself would speak, as Grove dreamed it might, but it has not been so. Not the land, but art. Not experience, but vision.

It is perhaps too easy to put the differences between Watson's work and Kroetsch's as the differences between myth as literature and myth as experience. It is equally easy to say one is a closed structure that simply diagrams a literary pattern and the other an open structure that seeks to turn experience itself into representative pattern. These distinctions may serve critical or literary purposes of evaluation but say little to the point about the nature of dream, romance, and identity. My own sense is that the literature of Western Canada has its own coherence, not in relation to place, society, or history, but to its own developing forms. And with Kroetsch's novel, the fiction of the West looks back not only to the forms from which it grew but to the literature that it has brought into existence. Paradoxically, a Western Canadian myth becomes possible in the contemporary world as the writer assimilates the techniques, patterns, and vision of Faulkner, Barth, Borges, and Nabokov, and presents to us as our own identity a fiction dreamed by writers of America, Europe, and South America. Nor is that all: the fiction that dreams us proves in the end to have been a madman's dream. For the horse lives on with the discovery of a use for pregnant mare's urine, a dream of art become technology. Now, and I use the narrator's words, "Scurrilous, barbarous, stinking man would soon be able, in the sterility of his own lust, to screw himself into oblivion." (p. 167) The future of Western Canada seems even more tenuous than a passing dream.

IV

I doubt it possible to improve on the theme, as a conclusion to this paper, of the disappearing West. And these last remarks simply elaborate that. I began by suggesting how little could be said about difficult critical questions and how little we know about cultural history. It should be clear now that nothing said in this paper in any way relieves our ignorance. Claims to the contrary notwithstanding, it seems to me eminently sensible to remain sceptical about what has been added to our knowledge of the Canadian West by discussions or literary depictions of regional cultures. Like cultural nationalism, the fictional West contributes little, if anything, to discussion in this country of educational policy, constitutional arrangements, or political theory, and it proves nothing at all about the quality of provincial government or even Prairie life.

To say, then, as Robert Kroetsch says, that we have no identity until someone tells our story, that fiction makes us real, is not paradoxical but tautological. The statement surely means identity is fictional; it exists only in stories, in dreams, in fantasy. About this, we may say one of two things: fantasy plays no historical or social role *or* its role is much stranger than anything we yet know. There are those - writers like George Steiner, Susan Sontag, George Grant - who remind us from a variety of perspectives and convictions that there are questions to be asked of the spiritual enterprise that is Western culture.

Not to be implicated in history, of course, implies an incredible intellectual hubris. But to claim historical and social validity for the worlds of fiction may have even wider and more disturbing implications. What are the consequences of claiming a defining presence where there is none, an identity where (to use the term as George Grant uses it) there is only technique? And why, after all, should a wind-blown, dust-driven, rootless place, its people eager for the limitless power of productivity, be proclaimed that world, favoured among all others, where a long lost - if ever held - wholeness finally reveals itself?

Footnotes

1
Leo Marx, "Pastoral Ideals and City Troubles," *The Quality of Man's Environment* (Washington, D.C., 1968), pp. 121-144.

2
Creation, ed. Robert Kroetsch (Toronto, 1970), p. 63.

3
"Author's Note to the Fourth Edition," *A Search for America* (Toronto, 1971).

4
Sheila Watson, *The Double Hook* (Toronto, 1966), p. 130. All other references are to this edition.

5
Robert Kroetsch, *The Studhorse Man* (Toronto, 1969), p. 10. All other references are to this edition.